ACCOUNTING AND FINANCIAL ANALYSIS IN THE HOSPITALITY INDUSTRY

ACCOUNTING AND FINANCIAL ANALYSIS IN THE HOSPITALITY INDUSTRY

Jonathan A. Hales
Northern Arizona University

Prentice Hall

Boston   Columbus   Indianapolis   New York   San Francisco   Upper Saddle River
Amsterdam   Cape Town   Dubai   London   Madrid   Milan   Munich   Paris   Montréal   Toronto
Delhi   Mexico City   São Paulo   Sydney   Hong Kong   Seoul   Singapore   Taipei   Tokyo

Editor in Chief: Vernon R. Anthony
Acquisitions Editor: William Lawrensen
Editorial Assistant: Lara Dimmick
Director of Marketing: David Gesell
Senior Marketing Manager: Leigh Ann Sims
Senior Marketing Coordinator: Alicia Wozniak
Marketing Assistant: Les Roberts
Project Manager: Holly Shufeldt
Cover Art Director: Jayne Conte
Cover Designer: Margaret Kenselaar
Cover Photo: Fotolia
Manager, Cover Visual Research & Permissions: Karen Sanatar
Cover Art: iStockphoto
Full-Service Project Management and Composition: Integra Software Services
Text and Cover Printer/ Binder: Courier

Credits and acknowledgments borrowed from other sources and reproduced, with permission, in this textbook appear on appropriate page within text.

Library of Congress Cataloging-in-Publication Data

Cataloging-in-Publication Data for this title can be obtained from the Library of Congress.

This book is not for sale or distribution in the U.S.A. or Canada

1058420

10 9 8 7 6 5 4 3 2 1

Prentice Hall
is an imprint of

www.pearsonhighered.com

ISBN 10: 0-13-245866-7
ISBN 13: 978-0-13-245866-5

To my family—Judy, Laura, and David, my parents Lynn and Eleanor Hales, and Ben Bearden

CONTENTS

Part 4   Other Financial Information

Chapter 11   Corporate Annual Reports   252

Chapter 12   Personal Financial Literacy   268

FOREWORD

Accounting and Financial Analysis in the Hospitality Industry by Dr. Jonathan A. Hales is the first text in the new Pearson series *Hospitality Management Essentials*. Dr. Hales served as a controller, resident manager, and general manager for the Marriott Corporation in nine different hotels for 25 years, prior to moving into higher education in 1995. Not only does Dr. Hales know exactly what students and entry-level managers need to be aware of when it comes to managerial accounting, he also has the educational expertise to convey this knowledge in a very applied and easy-to-understand format. He teaches this subject every day and has incorporated the comments of many of his colleagues around the country in the text.

The Pearson series *Hospitality Management Essentials* is designed to cover all aspects of the management of hospitality enterprises from an *applied perspective.* Each book in the series provides an introduction to a separate managerial function such as human resources or accounting; a distinct management segment in the hospitality industry such as club management, resort management, or casino management; or looks at other topic areas closely related to hospitality management, such as information technology, ethics, or services management.

The books in the series are written for students in two- and four-year hospitality management programs, as well as for entry- and mid-level managers in the hospitality industry. They present readers with three essential features they are looking for in textbooks nowadays: they are *affordable,* they are of *high quality,* and they are *applied,* and their approach to hospitality management issues appeals to students and instructors alike. The authors in the series are selected because of their classroom and industry expertise and experience and their ability to make complex materials easy to understand. As with Dr. Hales, they all enjoy sharing those experiences with the aspiring hospitality managers of the twenty-first century.

Students and educators alike will find affordability, relevance, and high quality in this and all other texts in the series. As we say in the hospitality industry: welcome and enjoy!

Hubert B. Van Hoof, Ph.D.
Series Editor

PREFACE

This textbook is written for college students in two- and four-year programs. The objective is to provide hospitality students with a solid foundation of accounting concepts and methods of financial analysis that he or she will need to possess to be successful in their hospitality industry careers. This book can also be used by any hospitality manager who has operations responsibilities in a hotel, restaurant, or any other business. It is not a textbook for accounting majors as it does not contain the details, procedures, processes, and requirements to prepare financial information to meet established accounting and reporting guidelines.

Most hospitality accounting textbooks provide too much accounting information that is very complicated and difficult for college students to understand. More importantly, hospitality managers responsible for operating Rooms Departments or Food and Beverage Departments will never use that kind of accounting information in their daily operations. However, accountants and financial managers do need to understand and use this detailed information to prepare management reports and financial statements to conform to established standards and requirements. Hospitality operations managers just need to understand the accounting basics and be able to use them in performing and evaluating their job responsibilities.

Hospitality students need to have a fundamental understanding of using numbers in order to operate their departments and analyze management reports and financial statements. This textbook focuses on the following important goals in teaching hospitality accounting:

1. Presenting students with a solid foundation of fundamental accounting concepts and methods of financial analysis.
2. Teaching students to understand numbers and to enable them to use numbers in performing their managerial responsibilities more effectively.
3. Assisting students in understanding that using financial analysis to evaluate business operations involves basic arithmetic and fundamental formulas and need not be complicated and overwhelming.
4. Teaching students to understand that numbers resulting from operations are used as a management tool and as measures of financial performance.
5. Enabling students to apply accounting concepts and methods of financial analysis in managing their departments and understanding and evaluating financial statements.

I wrote this book based on how I have taught Hospitality Managerial Accounting at Northern Arizona University the last ten years. The examples, exercises, and materials included in the book are based on what hospitality students need to know about accounting and financial analysis to be successful. Directors of Finance for several major hotel companies have reviewed a major portion of this book's content. Their input was instrumental in enabling this textbook to be current and consistent with the actual accounting processes and procedures used in today's hospitality industry. I appreciate their willingness to share detailed information about their management reports, financial statements, and operational procedures, as well as their expectations of what graduating seniors should know and understand about accounting concepts and financial analysis to be successful managers.

The fact that most students are intimidated by and afraid of working with numbers greatly influenced the way the contents are presented. Often, students just get by in accounting classes, are relieved that they have passed, and are happy that it is over, rather than use the class as an opportunity to learn important information about accounting and financial analysis that will help them in their careers. This textbook seeks to reduce students' fears and anxieties by focusing on the fundamentals of using numbers to operate a business. The objective is not to teach them to prepare financial reports or make them understand the complexities of the accounting discipline, but to enable them to understand and use management reports and financial statements to help them operate their departments.

CHAPTER DESCRIPTION

Chapters 1 and 2 are written to provide an introduction to accounting and to provide a solid foundation of accounting concepts and methods of financial analysis. The focus is on the fundamentals of using numbers as a management tool and to measure financial performance in hospitality operations.

Chapter 3 explains organization charts for hotels and for the accounting Department and how they establish accountability and responsibility for operating results and financial performance. This is intended to help hospitality students understand how accounting department operations fit into hotel operations and how they can help hospitality managers operate their departments.

Chapters 4 and 5 explain the three main financial statements used in financial analysis. **Chapter 4** discusses the importance of Consolidated and Department P&L Statements in successfully understanding and managing hospitality operations and the financial results that they produce. **Chapter 5** discusses the important aspects of Balance Sheets and the Statement of Cash Flows in operating a hospitality business. These chapters also discuss how the three statements interrelate by organizing and presenting the financial results of a business.

Chapters 6–8 discuss the hotel management reports that are used as management tools and as measures of financial performance. **Chapter 6** provides examples of daily revenue and labor reports that hospitality managers review daily and weekly. **Chapter 7** focuses on revenue management and discusses its importance in maximizing total hotel revenues and profits. Variation analysis and comparative reports are presented in **Chapter 8**. It also discusses how they are used to measure and understand financial performance. The purpose of these three chapters is to introduce students to the actual use, application, and analysis of financial statements and management reports in the operations of departments within a hotel or restaurant. The focus is to present accounting and financial information that students will need to know and be able to use in managing their departments on a daily and weekly basis.

Chapters 9 and 10 emphasize the importance of budgeting and forecasting as management tools and as ways to measure financial performance. The different types of budgets and how to prepare annual operating budgets are discussed in **Chapter 9**. Forecasting revenues and scheduling wages are two important responsibilities of hospitality managers and **Chapter 10** provides detailed exercises to practice forecasting revenues and scheduling wages. These chapters focus on the importance of a manager's ability to review current operations and to prepare weekly forecasts that update the budget and reflect current market conditions.

Chapters 11 and 12 are intended to provide students with additional knowledge to broaden their financial skills and understanding. **Chapter 11** introduces Corporate Annual Reports and familiarizes students with their content and use. **Chapter 12** focuses on personal financial literacy and is intended to encourage students to apply fundamental financial skills to the management of their personal finances. This includes fundamental financial concepts such as budgeting and planning for today, tomorrow, and for retirement.

The **Glossary** includes over 160 key terms and summarizes the key terms presented in each chapter that students should understand and be able to use in their hospitality careers.

As students read this text and progress through a hospitality managerial accounting course, it is my hope and intent that they will be able to not only learn fundamental accounting concepts but also confidently use them as management tools and to measure the financial performance of their departments. By focusing on accounting fundamentals and building on accounting concepts, students' fears and anxieties of accounting will hopefully be replaced with a solid and useful understanding of accounting that they will be able to use and apply in their hospitality careers.

The textbook is organized in such a way that the fundamentals of accounting concepts and financial analysis are clearly presented. The content is written in a user-friendly manner, avoiding complicated terminology, detailed rules and procedures, and endless spreadsheets. Definitions come from operations or Webster's Dictionary rather than from accounting manuals and complex accounting codes and rules with requirement after requirement.

At the end of each chapter are the following sections:

- Hospitality Manager Takeaways, which highlight how students will apply the material as a hospitality manager.
- Key Terms that are essential for students to understand in working with numbers and that relate to the accounting concepts presented in the chapter.
- Review Questions that reinforce an understanding of the chapter material.
- Practice Exercises that give students the opportunity to use formulas, analyze numbers, and apply the chapter content to examples and problems.

FEATURES OF THE BOOK

The book includes the latest information provided in the 10th Revised Edition of the *Uniform System of Accounts for the Lodging Industry*, published in 2006 by the American Hotel and Lodging Educational Institute. Further, it incorporates the recent changes in format and terminology recommended in the 10th Revised Edition. Students will find the most current lodging accounting information available in this textbook.

Practice exercises are included at the end of each chapter that will provide students the opportunity to work out problems and answer questions that will help them apply and understand the material presented in the chapter. These are basic exercises with the objective of creating a strong foundation of the fundamentals of accounting concepts and financial analysis.

Each chapter has a picture of a hotel, restaurant, or other hospitality operation and a description of that property. Specific questions about material presented in the chapter are asked and applied to the property pictured. This is intended to provide students an opportunity to visualize an actual property and think about how that property would use the accounting concepts and material presented in the chapter. Web sites for these hospitality properties are provided so that students can refer to them and see what that property looks like and consider the accounting processes that support the operation of the property.

As this book was being written, the recession of 2009 was unfolding. The United States and the world had slipped into the deepest recession since the great depression of the 1930s. This provided the opportunity in several chapters to discuss and analyze the impact of such important economic changes on the daily operations and financial performance of businesses in virtually all industries. Dramatic changes in trends and financial history, large and continuous decreases in RevPAR, pressures on profits and cash flows, and significant changes in customer behaviors and market segments have forced hospitality managers to adjust to new trends, patterns, and customer expectations in providing expected products and services to their customers. All of these have also emphasized the importance of understanding and being able to use numbers in operating a hospitality operation or a business in any industry.

SUPPLEMENTS

There is an Instructor's Manual that will provide answers to Chapter Review Questions, Practice Exercises, and the discussion points relating to the hospitality property featured in each chapter. It also includes examples of midterm exams, final exams, and projects. It does not have accompanying PowerPoint slides or Excel programs as I believe that students can best learn accounting fundamentals by doing the actual calculations for the practice exercises. If they have this strong foundation, they will generally be able to understand and work with the systems that companies use in their daily operations.

ABOUT THE AUTHOR

Dr. Jonathan A. Hales spent 25 years with Marriott International, with the first half of that time in the accounting department as Assistant Controller and Controller and the second half in operations as Resident Manager and General Manager. This included working in nine different full-service hotels, including resorts, convention hotels, airport hotels, and corporate hotels ranging from 300 to 800 rooms. This presented him the opportunity to work in different market environments with different management teams in different positions in Washington, DC, New Orleans, Scottsdale, Philadelphia, St. Louis, Palm Springs, Houston, Miami, and Tampa. These many years of working with accounting concepts, management reports, and financial statements have provided Dr. Hales a strong background in how numbers are used to successfully operate a business.

Dr. Hales has been a professor at Northern Arizona University since 1995, teaching a range of classes, including those on front office operations, resort management, hospitality managerial accounting, hospitality finance, and revenue management, and senior seminars. He has completed faculty internships with Four Seasons, Hyatt, Marriott, and Omni Hotels and Darden Restaurants. He has also attended senior management meetings or orientations at Hilton Hotels, White Lodging, and Pappas Restaurants. Keeping up with what companies are doing in the hospitality industry has always been a priority for him.

Dr. Hales' academic background includes a bachelor's degree in Economics and Certificate in International Relations from the University of Utah, graduate business study at the University of Virginia, MBA in Finance from Arizona State University, and a master's and doctorate in Education Leadership from Northern Arizona University.

ACKNOWLEDGMENTS

I would like to acknowledge several hospitality industry leaders who graciously took their time to review specific chapters and make suggestions that greatly improved the material in this textbook. As a result of their contributions, this accounting textbook is current and real and teaches the accounting concepts that hospitality companies expect their managers to know, understand, and apply in operating their departments.

Mark Koehler, Area Director of Finance for Four Seasons Hotels and Resorts in Scottsdale, Arizona, reviewed the entire text and contributed many examples that clearly explain key accounting concepts and their importance in the successful operation of a hospitality department. Mark has been a guest speaker in many of our HRM classes since 2001 and has provided students valuable insight into the actual operations of resort and luxury hotels. His perspectives have made this a more useful textbook for college students.

Tom Forburger, Senior Director of Finance for the J. W. Marriott Desert Ridge Resort and Spa in Phoenix, Arizona, also reviewed the manuscript and provided valuable insight regarding the use of financial statements and what is expected of operating managers in their ability to work with management reports and financial statements. His comments and suggestions helped make the text more consistent with and relevant to the accounting reports and financial analysis that are used on a daily basis in the hospitality industry. Many other industry managers also provided helpful comments regarding the content of the book. They include financial and operations managers with Hyatt, Radisson, White Lodging, and Host Hotels and Resorts on the hotel side, and Pappas Restaurants and Red Lobster Restaurants on the restaurant side. I would like to thank the people at Northern Arizona University who helped make this textbook a reality. Kathleen Krahn took the time to help organize the photographs and make suggestions to convert material to the necessary electronic media. Marc Chopin, Dean of the W. A. Franke College of Business, and Rich Howey, Interim Executive Director of the School of Hotel and Restaurant Management, also provided support and direction that helped make this book a reality.

At Pearson Prentice Hall, Andrea Edwards was of great value to me in reviewing the manuscript, organizing all the necessary components, and guiding me through the initial manuscript submission process. She kept the process on track and I appreciate very much her assistance and support. Bill Lawrensen provided many answers and directions that helped bring this book to publication.

Finally, I would like to thank Bert Van Hoof, Director of the School of Hospitality Management at Penn State University, for inviting me to author a textbook in the hospitality series that he developed. Bert was a colleague at Northern Arizona University before accepting the Director position at Penn State and encouraged me early on to write and publish an accounting textbook.

Reviewers of the Book

Daniel Bernstein
Seton Hill University

Evelyn Green
The University of Southern Mississippi

Sheila Scott-Halsell
Oklahoma State University

Amy Hart
Columbus State Community College

Dr. Robert A. McMullin
Professor of Hotel Restaurant and Tourism Management

Paul Wiener
Northern Arizona University

ACCOUNTING AND FINANCIAL ANALYSIS IN THE HOSPITALITY INDUSTRY

CHAPTER

1

Introduction to Numbers, Accounting, and Financial Analysis

LEARNING OBJECTIVES

- To understand the three most common measures of a company's success.

- To understand how important effectively using accounting and finance is to the career of any hospitality manager.

- To learn about and describe the three fundamental financial statements.

- To become familiar with fundamental revenue accounting concepts.

- To understand fundamental profit accounting concepts.

- To learn the revenue and profit formulas.

CHAPTER OUTLINE

INTRODUCTION

Accounting concepts and methods of financial analysis generally sound intimidating and complicated. Visions of certified public accountants (CPAs), financial advisors, tax laws, attorneys, giant textbooks, spreadsheets, paperwork nightmares, and migraine headaches often accompany any mention of accounting and finance. And this is often the case. However, entry-level hospitality managers need to be able to understand and use accounting concepts and methods of **financial analysis** in conducting the daily operations of their departments.

Numbers are also used in measuring a company's performance in meeting its goals and objectives. Typically, the three most commonly used measurements of business success are as follows:

- Customer satisfaction
- Employee satisfaction
- Profitability and cash flow

Performance is measured and defined against these goals with numbers.

This chapter introduces fundamental accounting concepts and explains how numbers are used to apply these accounting concepts to daily operations. It likewise introduces fundamental methods of financial analysis and explains how numbers are used to perform financial analysis. The objective is to *first* understand these fundamental concepts, *second* to be comfortable working with them, and *third* to be able to apply them to hotel and restaurant operations. Subsequent chapters deal with these concepts in more detail.

NUMBERS: THE LIFEBLOOD OF BUSINESS

Numbers—understanding them and working with them—form the foundation of both accounting concepts and methods of financial analysis. Numbers provide descriptions and measurements that relate to the operations of a business. Let's define a few terms.

Definitions and Formulas

ACCOUNTING CONCEPT: Accounting is the bookkeeping methods involved in making a financial record of business transactions and in the preparation of statements concerning the assets, liabilities, and operating results of a business. A concept is a general understanding, especially one derived from a particular instance or occurrence. These definitions are from Webster's dictionary and not from an accounting book. We combine the two definitions and the resulting definition of accounting concepts is as follows: "*a general understanding of the book-keeping methods and financial transactions of a business.*"

FINANCIAL ANALYSIS: Finance is the management of monetary affairs. Analysis is the separation of an intellectual or substantial whole into its parts for individual study. These definitions are also from Webster's dictionary. We combine the two definitions and the definition of financial analysis thus becomes "*the separation of the management of monetary affairs of a business into parts for individual study.*"

Fundamental arithmetic is all that is required to use and apply numbers to understand business operations. Four of the most important formulas in financial analysis require only multiplication, division, and subtraction:

$$\text{Revenue} = \text{Average Rate} \times \text{Volume}$$

$$\text{Profit} = \text{Revenues} - \text{Expenses}$$

$$\text{Retention or Flow-through} = \frac{\text{Change in Profit Dollars}}{\text{Change in Revenue Dollars}}$$

$$\text{RevPAR} = \frac{\text{Total Room Revenue}}{\text{Total Available Rooms}}$$

or

$$= \text{Average Room Rate} \times \text{Occupancy Percentage}$$

Although these formulas can be applied to many market segments, departments, and volume levels and can become rather detailed, the fact remains that they are each calculated with arithmetic and not calculus, trigonometry, or college algebra.

Customers, Associates, and Profitability

There is a common theme in today's business world about how to measure the success of a company or business. It involves satisfied customers, satisfied employees, and satisfactory profitability and cash flows. As an example, we can look at one of the largest and most successful companies in the world to examine these concepts.

By two important measures—market capitalization and recognition—General Electric (GE) is a company we can learn from. For many years, GE was the largest company in the world in terms of market capitalization. The formula for **market capitalization** is the stock price times the number of shares of outstanding stock. To be the largest capitalized company in the world means that more individuals and institutions are investing in GE than in any other company. Quite an accomplishment! GE is regularly in the top ten of the most admired companies in the world and was also the Most Admired Company in the world from 1997 to 2001, according to *Fortune* magazine.

Former CEO Jack Welch, in discussing the GE management philosophy in *Jack Welch and the GE Way*, by Robert Slater (1999), says,

> We always say that if you had three measurements to live by, they'd be employee satisfaction, customer satisfaction, and cash flow. If you've got cash in the till at the end, the rest is all going to work, because if you've got high customer satisfaction, you're going to get a share. If you've got high employee satisfaction you're going to get productivity. And if you've got cash, you know it's all working. (p. 90)

This statement highlights the relationship or balance between three essential elements of a successful business: *customers*, *employees*, and *profitability*. These three measurements are interrelated and problems with one will lead to problems with the others. Numbers are involved in measuring the organization's success in each one of these areas.

Customer satisfaction can be measured by percentage of market share, percentage of revenue growth, or the successful introduction of new products and services. All these measurements use numbers. For example, market share can increase from 7% to 8%. This tells us that customers are buying more of our products and our sales have now increased from 7% to 8% of the total market. If a company's market share is growing, it means that customers prefer to buy its products rather than the products of competitors because of quality, value, or both. That is obviously a good thing. If our market share is declining, that means customers are not buying as many of our products and services and that is a bad thing. Numbers tell us to what degree our business is improving our declining.

Another way to measure customer satisfaction is through customer satisfaction surveys. This process provides direct customer feedback based on questions asked in a survey. A typical question is, "Are you willing to return?" The hotel will have a historical score that shows the performance of the previous year and will set a new goal to aim at in the next year of operations. Each time the current score is reported—generally monthly—it is compared with the previous year's actual score to see if the hotel is improving. It is also compared to the current year's goal to see if the goal will be missed, met, or exceeded.

Employee satisfaction is measured in the same way. Each hotel will have its score from the previous year for the questions asked as well as a goal for the year. The current score on the survey is compared to these benchmark scores and then evaluations are made to see if there has been progress toward reaching the goal. For example, the most recent employee satisfaction score of 85% favorable would be compared to previous year's 83% and this year's goal of 84%. The 85% current score is a 2-point improvement over the previous year's and is 1 point above this year's goal. In this example, the actual score of 85% beat both last year's actual and this year's goal. Numbers define the relationship between the scores and determine if performance is declining, stagnant, or improving.

Profit or *Profitability* is the third measure. Is a company making or losing money? The equation for profitability is revenues minus expenses. For example, $1,000,000 in revenues minus $750,000 in expenses would result in a $250,000 profit. In addition to being expressed in dollars, profit can also be expressed in terms of percentages. The equation for profit percentage is profit dollars divided by revenue dollars. In the above example, the profit percentage is 25% ($250,000 profit divided by $1,000,000 in revenues).

Each of these numbers or measures tells us something about the operations of the business. The $250,000 in profit dollars tells us that we have that much money in the bank after recording all the revenues and paying all the expenses. It is a tangible amount. In other words, there is a $250,000 balance in the cash account of the business. The 25% profit percentage tells us the amount of every revenue dollar that is left over as profit. It is a relationship measure. In other words, 25 cents out of every sales dollar represents profits and 75 cents out of every sales dollar represents expenses. Add the two together and you get $1 or 100%.

Positive cash flow, like profitability, is essential to the success of any business. Positive cash flow ensures that the ongoing operations of a business are generating sufficient sales and efficiently collecting the sales amount to have enough cash in their cash account to pay all bills and financial obligations. It is not enough to show a profit to be successful. A business should be able to pay all its operating expenses consistently and on time.

The bestselling book *Built to Last, Successful Habits of Visionary Companies*, by James E. Collins and Jerry I. Porras (1994), talks about the role of profits in some of the most well respected companies in the world. Consider this comment.

> Profitability is a necessary condition for existence and a means to more important ends, but it is not the end in itself for many of the visionary companies. Profit is like oxygen, food, water, and blood for the body; they are not the point of life, but without them, there is no life. (p. 55)

The authors point out that the visionary companies focus on other elements of their business that reflect their core values, not profits. This focus can be on new product development, customers, employees, or stretch goals. Because they do this so well, products and services are well received in the marketplace and sufficient profits result.

These discussions of customer satisfaction, employee satisfaction, and profitability and cash flow illustrate the role that numbers play in measuring or defining results and achievements. Numbers assign a tangible value to performance and results. Instead of saying "revenues are up," numbers enable us to say, for example, "revenues are up $100,000 or 8.5%." This is more specific and helps a business identify and compare its performance from month-to-month or year-to-year. These concepts will be discussed in more detail in later chapters.

CAREER SUCCESS MODEL

Certain skills and abilities are required for any manager to have a successful business career. Stephen R. Covey talks about three of these in his book *The 7 Habits of Highly Effective People* (1989). Covey defines skill as "how to do," knowledge as "what to do," and attitude as "want to do" (p. 47). The use of these three abilities determines how successful a manager can be.

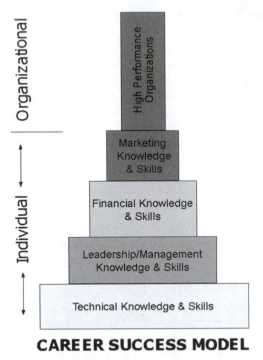

CAREER SUCCESS MODEL

FIGURE 1.1   Career Success Model.

The Career Success Model (Figure 1.1) identifies four individual skills and one organizational skill that are very helpful in enabling managers grow and advance with a company. It is very important that managers continue to grow and learn and this includes new areas that will broaden their knowledge and skills.

Technical Skills

These are the day-to-day operational knowledge and skills required to get the job done. Entry-level managers in the hospitality industry will start out, for example, as Assistant Desk Managers, Assistant Housekeeping Managers, Assistant Restaurant Managers, and so forth. The job title defines what they are expected to know and be able to do to perform all the tasks and responsibilities in operating their department. So they spend the first year learning and doing. Their focus should be on learning all the technical and operational aspects of their job. This includes knowing and being able to perform the job responsibilities of all the employees that report to them. Assistant Desk Managers will be checking guests in and out, managing room inventories, handling group business, staffing the concierge level, running fronts for the bellman, and so on. Assistant Restaurant Managers will be seating customers, bussing tables, expediting food orders, and so on. Understanding these technical aspects of a department's operations is essential to its success and to establishing a solid foundation for a manager's personal career growth.

Management/Leadership Skills

The first promotion provides a manager with the opportunity to manage a wide range of employees in getting the job done. The knowledge and skills needed include that of working with other managers as well as hourly employees. This step involves the progression from managing (we manage things) to leading (we lead people) (Covey). A manager is now paid to get other people to do the job. This includes the typical management responsibilities of planning, organizing, and controlling but has now progressed to the leadership responsibilities of motivating, challenging, engaging, supporting, and recognizing employees. The real leader should possess the ability to teach and inspire the people he or she works with to do the best job that they are capable of.

Leaders also have the responsibility of allocating company resources. This includes allocating time, money, labor, and ideas to the most productive or profitable areas. They do this by listening to employees and customers and then prioritizing projects or job responsibilities, and then supporting them with sufficient resources.

Effective leaders take the time to organize their work and make sure that they are spending as much of their time as possible operating in Covey's Quadrant 2—important but not urgent. Refer to Covey's Time Management Matrix, which demonstrates that every activity we do during the day can be put in one of four quadrants:

1. urgent and important
2. not urgent and important
3. urgent and not important
4. not urgent and not important

Most managers operate in Quadrant 1, urgent and important, which can best be defined as putting out fires and going from one situation to another. By shifting to Quadrant 2, not urgent but important, a manager has more time to plan, prioritize, and organize the work to be done. Quadrant 2 is proactive and Quadrant 1 is reactive (Covey, 1989, p. 151).

What does this have to do with accounting and finance? Everything! Specifically, the more knowledgeable and comfortable managers are working with numbers and completing the accounting and financial analysis part of their job, the more time they will have to spend with their customers and employees—their top priorities! Being efficient with numbers enables a manager to operate in Quadrant 2 and have more time to be with their employees and guests.

Unfortunately, the careers of many managers slow down or stop at this point. They do not have the interest, knowledge, or ability to learn the next skills that will help them to do a better and more complete job, and advance to taking on more and wider levels of responsibility. It is not enough to have just technical skills and management/leadership skills to advance to higher positions within a company. These positions require managers to have the knowledge and ability to understand and use accounting concepts and apply financial analysis and marketing concepts in the daily operations of their company.

Financial Skills

Financial knowledge and skills begin with understanding numbers, having the ability to communicate or teach what the numbers mean, and finally having the ability to apply what is learned from numbers to improve the operations of the business. Specifically, it is the ability to interpret and discuss the information contained in all types of management reports and financial statements with all levels of management. A manager must be comfortable talking about the financial aspects of his or her department with the hotel's Director of Finance and the General Manager. Explaining revenues and expenses, comparing actual results to budgets and forecasts, and making adjustments to improve operations are all important financial skills for any manager to possess.

The rest of this textbook will be devoted to developing an understanding of accounting concepts and methods of financial analysis. At this point, it is important to understand that any manager must have a fundamental understanding of accounting and finance to grow and advance with a company. They do not have to be CPAs or Directors of Finance. But they must be able to understand and intelligently discuss their department operations and financial performance with senior management.

Marketing Skills

The next step in the Career Success Model is developing Sales and Marketing knowledge and skills, which begins by understanding customers and their expectations. What does a hotel or restaurant do to develop and maintain a competitive advantage over its competitors? Why does a customer choose to stay in a particular hotel or eat in a particular restaurant? The Marketing Department is responsible for identifying customer preferences, expectations, buying patterns, and behavior patterns. These customer descriptions are then classified into different market segments. A hotel or restaurant chooses the market segments where it wants to be and can successfully compete.

Examples of major hotel market segments are transient, group, and contract. The transient market segment includes concierge customers at the higher end of room rates; progressively lower market rate segments of regular, corporate, and special corporate; and finally the discount segment. The discount market segment can further be separated into government and military, AARP, travel industry, and special promotions like weekend or super saver rates. Examples of the major restaurant market segments are fine dining, casual dining, and fast food.

Each of these market segments is defined by specific customer expectations and behavior patterns. For a manager to continue to advance, he or she must understand the marketing of the hotel or restaurant. What are the strengths and competitive advantages of a **property**? What are the expectations and preferences of customers? A manager must be able to discuss the customers with the Director of Sales or Marketing and understand the marketing plan and positioning of the hotel or restaurant.

High Performance Organizations

When a manager is knowledgeable and comfortable with these four individual skills—technical, management/leadership, financial, and marketing—he or she has the potential to be a part of a "high performance organization." A manager with strong individual skills and knowledge and with a positive attitude can then create or be a part of an organization that not only meets but also exceeds the expectations and goals it has set. This should be an important career goal.

The ultimate goal of any department within a hotel or restaurant is to achieve outstanding performance and results. This requires a team effort by all involved in the operation. The greater the degree of knowledge and skill in these four areas, the greater the contribution a manager can make to the performance of his team or department. Only when a manager can translate excellence of individual performance into excellence of team performance, can he or she truly excel and achieve excellence.

The Career Success Model outlines the knowledge, skills, and abilities that are required to be successful in business and to advance to senior management positions.

The goal of this textbook is to provide students with the accounting and financial knowledge, skills, and abilities that are required to be successful in the careers that they choose.

FINANCIAL STATEMENTS

It is important for any business manager to be aware of and understand the financial statements that are used in evaluating the performance of a business. These financial statements are applied in many different ways in describing and evaluating the operations and financial strength of a business. Each of these financial statements or reports measures a specific aspect of the operations of a business. They are introduced here and explained in more detail in a later chapter.

The Profit and Loss Statement

The **Profit and Loss Statement (P&L)** measures the operating success and profitability of a business. It is also known as the Income Statement. This is the main financial report that describes and measures the profitability of the daily operations of a business. Key characteristics of the P&L are as follows:

1. It covers a specific time period, for example monthly, quarterly, or annually.
2. It reports the actual financial results for a business in terms of revenues, expenses, and profits for the specific time period.
3. It evaluates the actual performance with respect to other measures such as budget, forecast, and previous (e.g., last year's or month's) performance.

EXHIBIT 1.1
CONSOLIDATED P&L STATEMENT

The ABC Company
December 31, 2008

	Current Period				Year to Date	
Actual	Budget	Last Year		Actual	Budget	Last Year

Rooms Sales
Restaurant Sales
Catering Sales
Total Sales

Rooms Profit
Restaurant Profit
Catering Profit
Total Dept Profits

G&A Expense
R&M Expense
Utilities
Sales and Marketing
Total Expense Center

House Profit or Gross Operating Profit
Fixed Expenses
Net House Profit or Adjusted Gross Operating Profit

4. It includes a summary or consolidated P&L Statement and supporting department P&L Statements.
    A. Consolidated P&L Statements *summarize* revenues, expenses, and profits, by department.
    B. Department P&L Statements report *in detail* revenues, expenses, and profits, by department.
5. A new P&L Statement is generated each month or each accounting period and records current month information and year-to-date (YTD) information.
6. Managers are expected to analyze or critique their monthly P&Ls to explain both positive and negative variations from budgets, forecasts, or previous year's performance.

The P&L is the most important financial statement for a manager to understand and work with on a daily basis. This is because managers work with and can affect revenues or can control most of the costs and expenses. Their daily activities in operating the business produce the numbers reported on the P&L.

Consequently, a manager who knows and understands the P&L will provide accurate and timely information that is used in preparing the P&L and that gives it credibility. It will be an accurate report that measures the financial profitability of a business. A manager who does not understand the P&L might omit important information, provide the wrong information, or miss deadlines, thus preventing information that should be reported from being included in the proper timeframe.

This textbook dedicates most of its content to explaining the P&L and discussing how it is used as a management tool and to measure financial performance. It is also important to understand how the information on the P&L relates to the other key financial statements or reports. Exhibit 1.1 is an example of a consolidated P&L for a full service hotel.

The Balance Sheet

The **balance sheet** measures the value or worth of a business. It is also known as the Asset and Liability Statement (A&L). This is the main financial report that measures what a company is worth at a specific point in time. Key characteristics of the Balance Sheet are as follows:

1. It measures the value or worth of a company at a specific point in time. For example, the Balance Sheet at the end of the year, December 31, 2008, is a snapshot of the balances in the accounts at that specific point in time that identifies what a company owns (assets), what it owes (liabilities), and how it is owned (owner equity).
2. The fundamental account equation describes the A&L.

$$\text{Assets} = \text{Liabilities} + \text{Owner Equity}$$

3. It is made up of accounts organized by asset, liability, or owner equity.
4. These accounts are divided into current accounts (under 1 year obligations), also referred to as working capital, and long-term accounts (over 1 year obligations), which are referred to as capitalization.
5. Each account has a beginning balance, monthly activity, and an ending balance.
6. Unlike the P&L, managers are not expected to provide critiques of monthly balance sheet activity. This is done by the accounting department.
7. Each month Accounting Managers balance or reconcile the accounts on the balance sheet.

It is important for managers to understand the balance sheet because of two reasons. First, they use the current assets and liability accounts (working capital) in the daily operations of their business. **Working capital** is the amount of money utilized in the daily operations of a business. Second, it shows how the company is capitalized with long-term debt or owner equity, or both. **Capitalization** is the source and methods of raising money to invest in and start a business. Managers are expected to efficiently use the assets of a business to operate it profitably. Exhibit 1.2 is an example of a Balance Sheet.

EXHIBIT 1.2
BALANCE SHEET

The ABC Company
December 31, 2008

Assets	*Liabilities*
Cash	Accounts Payable
Accounts Receivable	Taxes Payable
Inventory	Wages Payable
Total Current Assets	Total Current Liabilities
Property	Bank Loan
Plant	Equipment Loan
Equipment	Line of Credit
Total Long-Term Assets	Total Long-Term Liabilities
TOTAL ASSETS	TOTAL LIABILITIES
	Owner Equity
	Paid In Capital
	Common Stock
	Retained Earnings
	TOTAL OWNER EQUITY

The Statement of Cash Flows

The **Statement of Cash Flows** measures the liquidity and the flow of cash of a business. Specifically, it is the activity of the cash account of a business. Sales are recorded as cash inflows through point of sale systems (cash registers), and expenses are recorded as cash outflows through accounts payable or electronic transfers. It is important for a manager to know how much cash is available in the company's cash account to pay expenses and plan for future operating obligations. If a business does not have sufficient cash in its cash bank account, it will not be able to pay expenses. It is an important responsibility of any manager to understand the business's working capital accounts and to be able to use them efficiently and effectively.

The increases and decreases in account balances of balance sheet accounts also affect cash flow. Referred to as the "Source and Use of Funds Statement," this report describes how cash flows in and out of the different accounts in the Balance Sheet. It also reflects the cash strength or liquidity of a business. **Liquidity** is the ability of a business to pay its short-term obligations and the amount it has in current assets, specifically cash and cash equivalents.

It is important for every manager to understand that a business can be profitable from month to month and still go out of business. This is because these businesses are not effectively managing their cash. They simply do not have enough money in their cash account to pay their expenses on a daily or weekly basis; therefore, they go out of business even though they show profits on their P&L and have a fairly good balance sheet. If you cannot pay your expenses, you cannot stay in business. Therefore, understanding the basics of liquidity and cash flow is critical to the success of both managers and a business.

Key characteristics of the Statement of Cash Flows are as follows

1. It involves the cash account of the Balance Sheet.
2. It has beginning and ending balances.
3. It shows how money is used in the daily operations of the business.
4. It measures liquidity.
5. It is a fundamental component of working capital.
6. It reflects the increases and decreases in Balance Sheet accounts.

There are three classifications of cash flow activities.

1. Operating activities that involve the daily operations of a business that produce sales.
2. Financing activities that involve raising and spending cash. This is also referred to as capitalization.
3. Investing activities that involve investing cash in other financial options (see Exhibit 1.3).

EXHIBIT 1.3
STATEMENT OF CASH FLOW

	ABC Company December 31, 2008		
		2007	2008
Net Income from Operations			
Plus Sources of Funds			
Decreases in Assets			
Increases in Liabilities			
Increases in Owner Equity			
Minus Uses of Funds			
Increases in Assets			
Decreases in Liabilities			
Decreases in Owner Equity			
Total Sources and Uses of Funds from Operations			
Total Sources and Uses of Funds from Investments			
Total Sources and Uses of Funds from Financing			
TOTAL SOURCES AND USES OF FUNDS			

The Statement of Stockholders Equity

There is one other financial statement that may be required depending on how the business is organized. That is the Statement of Owners' Equity. Typical forms of ownership are corporations, S corporations, limited liability corporations (LLCs), and partnerships. This statement provides details of the structure of owner equity, including the type of corporation, number of shares authorized and issued, changes in the owners'/members' accounts during the year, and end of year amounts or values.

The 10th revised edition of the *Uniform System of Accounts for the Lodging Industry* provides four different formats for the Statement of Owners' Equity. They are as follows:

1. Statement of Stockholders' Equity, which is organized by common stock, preferred stock, or treasury stock. It comprises the account balances at the beginning of the year; activities during the year such as net **income**, gains or losses, and dividends declared; and the account balances at the end of the year.
2. Statement of Partners' Equity, which is organized by general partners or limited partners. It comprises the account balances at the beginning of the year; income, contributions, and withdrawals; and the account balances at the end of the year.
3. Statement of Members' Equity that lists the members of the business. It comprises the account balances at the beginning of the year; income, contributions, and withdrawals; and the account balances at the end of the year.
4. Statement of Owners' Equity that lists the owners of the business. It comprises the account balances at the beginning of the year; income, contributions, and withdrawals; and the account balances at the end of the year.

Depending on the structure and organization of the business, one of the above statements will be prepared each year to show the changes in owner equity accounts and the account balances at the beginning and ending of the year.

J. W. Marriott Desert Ridge Resort and Spa Phoenix, Arizona

This is a view of the resort water park and golf course. This 950-room convention/resort hotel includes 240,000 square feet of meeting space, 10 restaurants and lounge outlets, a 28,000 square foot spa with 41 treatment rooms and two 18-hole golf courses. The resort includes 22 departments, over 1,000 employees, and 104 managers. There are nine members of the Executive Committee/Leadership Team. Annual revenues are over $100 million. Consider the complexity of managing the many departments in this resort, with the additional amenities and services required of a four diamond resort. Consider the financial responsibilities of the department managers in maximizing revenues and controlling expenses to ensure that expected profitability and cash flows are met. Because of the seasonality of resorts, additional emphasis is placed on managing the resorts' many departments in high and low seasons.

J. W. Marriott Desert Ridge Aerial View—Horizontal. Photo Courtesy of J. W. Marriott Desert Ridge Resort and Spa, Phoenix, Arizona.

Go to the Web site at www.jwdesertridge.com and view the many areas and features of this resort. Answer the following questions:

1. What do you think is the largest market segment for this resort—group or transient? Explain why you chose the market segment that you did.
2. Which department do you think generates more revenue, the rooms department or the food and beverage department? Explain why.
3. Arrange the following departments according to the size of their profits: restaurants, banquets, golf, spa, rooms, and beverages. What would be your reason for picking the most profitable and the least profitable?

REVENUES: THE BEGINNING OF FINANCIAL PERFORMANCE

One of the fundamental business concepts is that a company is in business to make money. The company produces products or services and exchanges them with customers for an agreed-upon price. The assumption is that the business will be in operation for many years, continually offering not only the existing products and services but new ones as well. This process generates **revenues** or sales, which are the monetary amount that customers pay to purchase a product or service and involves the following actions:

- The company receives money from customers for products or services.
- Mode of payment can include cash, credit cards, debit cards, electronic transfers, personal checks, traveler's checks, or company checks.
- The sales transaction is recorded through a **point-of-sale (POS)** system, which is the equipment and system that records the customer transaction.

POS systems were previously know as cash registers and are now referred to as computer terminals and systems. This completes the sales transaction.
- The method of payment is balanced to the amount of product purchased or type of service experienced.

Revenues are the first step of financial analysis because they start the cash flow process of a company. Revenues result in cash increasing, or flowing into the company's cash account. The next step is paying all expenses associated with producing the products or services the company offers. Paying expenses results in cash decreasing, or flowing out of a cash bank account, through accounts payable, payroll disbursements, or other disbursements. Any remaining amount is **profit**—the amount of revenue left over after all appropriate expenses have been paid.

Revenues are also reported in the monthly, quarterly, or annual P&Ls. The P&L is the financial report that lists revenues, expenses, and profits in a logical and orderly format. Chapter 4 discusses the P&L in more detail.

In the chapter introduction, we discussed two important formulas. We will now discuss a third important formula. Each involves revenue. The first formula calculates revenue (*Rate × Volume = Revenue*). The second formula calculates profit (*Revenue − Expenses = Profit*). The third formula measures revenue performance, which is called RevPAR. RevPAR can be calculated in two ways. The formulas are *Total Room Revenues/Total Available Rooms* or *Average Room Rate × Occupancy Percentage*. Let's learn more about these important formulas.

Formulas

$$Revenues = Rate \times Volume$$

All revenues for a business are the result of the number of customers buying a product or service. This is combined with how much they pay for that product or service to calculate revenues or sales. For example,

$$Room\ Revenues = Rooms\ Sold \times Room\ Rates$$

$$Restaurant\ Revenues = Customers\ Served \times Menu\ Prices$$

$$Golf\ Revenues = Player\ Rounds \times Greens\ Fees$$

$$Spa\ Revenues = Treatments \times Treatment\ Prices$$

$$Gift\ Shop = Merchandise\ Sold \times Price$$

Volume is defined as the number of units sold, served, received, or bought by customers during a specific time frame. Rooms sold are generally recorded daily. Restaurant customers are generally recorded by meal period—breakfast, lunch, and dinner. **Rate** is the dollar amount paid by a customer to a business to receive a product or service. Each one of these transactions has a rate or price associated with it. This is called a rate structure, price list, or menu. For example, rooms sold might be divided into the transient market segment and the group market segment. Each would have a room rate associated with it. Transient rate = $99 and Group rate = $85. Golf would have a daily price list per player. Greens fees = $50 with cart, $36 without cart, and twilight special rate is $25. Restaurants have menus listing the items available and their price. Customers in a restaurant choose what they want to eat and how much they are willing to pay for it.

To calculate any of the three revenue variables, we just need to know two variables and apply the appropriate formula. Following is an example for rooms revenue:

$$\text{Rate} \times \text{Volume} = \text{Room Revenue, or } \$99 \times 150 \text{ Rooms Sold}$$
$$= \$14{,}850 \text{ Room Revenue}$$

$$\frac{\text{Room Revenue}}{\text{Volume}} = \frac{\text{Room Rate, or } \$14{,}850 \text{ Room Revenue}}{150 \text{ Rooms Sold}} = \$99 \text{ Average Rate}$$

$$\frac{\text{Revenue}}{\text{Room Rate}} = \frac{\text{Volume, or } \$14{,}850 \text{ Room Revenue}}{\$99} = 150 \text{ Customers}$$

Following is an example for restaurant revenue:

$$\text{Rate} \times \text{Volume} = \text{Restaurant Revenue, or } \$8.00 \text{ Average Check} \times 75 \text{ Customers}$$
$$= \$600 \text{ Restaurant Revenue}$$

$$\frac{\text{Restaurant Revenue}}{\text{Volume}} = \frac{\text{Rate, or } \$600}{75} = \$8.00 \text{ Average Check}$$

$$\frac{\text{Restaurant Revenue}}{\text{Rate}} = \frac{\text{Volume, or } \$600}{\$8.00} = 75 \text{ Customers}$$

The POS records all of this information and produces two types of financial reports. First, it reports financial performance in daily revenue reports.

Second, it provides management with reports that are used as management tools to operate the business. A hospitality manager will be expected to understand these reports and use them to analyze rates, price lists, or menu prices, along with the number of customers served. These managers are expected to understand their daily operations, identify how successful or profitable they are, and determine how to solve problems and improve operations.

When analyzing revenues, it is important to identify where increases or decreases are coming from and what caused any such changes. Are there increases in the number of guests or in the amount they are spending/paying? In identifying causes, any of the following might apply:

Did lower rates or prices produce higher volumes?

Did an advertising campaign produce higher volumes?

Did new competition lower volumes?

Did a rate increase result in lower volumes?

$$\text{Profit} = \text{Revenues} - \text{Expenses}$$

All profits for a department, restaurant, or hotel can be calculated with this formula. Although this formula appears quite basic, it is broken down into many different categories that reflect different market segments for sales and specific types of costs or expenses. For example, the Rooms Department profit is calculated by adding Transient, Group, and Contract revenues to identify Total Room Revenue. Then, all direct expenses are deducted from Total Revenue to calculate Total Room Profit. The formula is as follows:

Total Room Revenue	$500,000
Minus	
Wage Expense	$ 60,000
Benefit Expense	$ 21,000
Direct Operating Expenses	$ 44,000
Equals Total Room Profit	$375,000

$$\text{RevPAR (Revenue per Available Room)} = \frac{\text{Total Room Revenues}}{\text{Total Hotel Rooms}} \quad \text{or}$$

$$\text{Room Rate} \times \text{Occupancy Percentage}$$

The most important measurement used to evaluate room revenues is RevPAR or revenue per available room. The reason RevPAR is so important is that it considers both rate and volume in identifying the amount of revenues generated by a hotel. It is only used to evaluate room revenue and is expressed as a dollar rate. For example, RevPAR is $88.43. There are two formulas that can be used to calculate RevPAR. The first formula is the most accurate but the second formula will also be very close and it is acceptable to use either one.

$$\text{RevPAR} = \frac{\text{Total Room Revenue}}{\text{Total Rooms Available}} \quad \text{or}$$

$$\text{Average Room Rate} \times \text{Occupancy Percentage}$$

Let's calculate RevPAR using the information from our previous revenue example. Room revenue was $14,850 with an average rate of $99 with 150 rooms occupied. We need to include the total number of rooms in our hotel to calculate the occupancy percentage. If we have a 200-room hotel, we can calculate our occupancy percentage by dividing rooms sold by total rooms, or $150/200 = 75\%$ occupancy. Now we can calculate the RevPAR as

$$\frac{\$14,850 \, \text{Room Revenue}}{200 \, \text{Total Rooms}} = \$74.25 \, \text{RevPAR}, \quad \text{or}$$

$$\$99 \, \text{Average Room Rate} \times 75\% \, \text{Occupancy} = \$74.25 \, \text{RevPAR}$$

RevPAR is the first and most important measure used to evaluate financial performance of hotels because it is an indication of how well management is able to increase average rate and also achieve higher volume and occupancy to maximize room revenue. If only one of these measurements is used, it will not be able to tell if a hotel is maximizing room revenues.

For example, if we use occupancy as the main measurement of maximizing room revenue, operating a hotel with 99% occupancy but with a $25 average rate, it is probably not maximizing room revenue. The hotel is probably selling its rooms too cheap. Likewise, if a hotel has a $175 average rate but is running only 15% occupancy, it also is probably not maximizing room revenue. It is probably pricing its rooms too high. If we use occupancy as the most important measure, the hotel in the first example is doing excellent and the second hotel is doing terribly. If we use average rate as the most important measure, the hotel in the first example is doing terribly and the second hotel is doing excellent. *RevPAR combines rate and occupancy to more effectively measure management's performance in maximizing revenue.* It shows how well management is able to achieve a high occupancy percentage as well as attain a high average room rate and effectively use both to maximize total room revenues.

$$\text{Retention or Flow-through} = \frac{\text{Change in Profit Dollars}}{\text{Change in Revenue Dollars}}$$

Retention is a very valuable financial measure and management tool because it identifies the change in profit with the change in revenue. It shows how effectively managers control variable expenses given changes in business volumes. Retention is a percentage and retention goals are established for each operating department.

Market Segments

RevPAR shows how well the hotel is managing average room rate and rooms sold in an effort to maximize total room revenue. To provide more specific information on room revenue maximization, the hotel separates its customers into **market segments**. Market segments define the customer in terms of expectations, preferences, buying patterns, behavior patterns, and why the customer is traveling. Each market segment has distinctive characteristics. Three of the main market segments used in hotel operations are illustrated herein:

Weekday/Weekend—Most weekday travel is business and most weekend travel is pleasure.

Business/Pleasure—People traveling on business generally have their expenses paid for by their employer. People traveling for pleasure are generally with family or friends and pay their own expenses.

Transient, Group, and Contract—These three primary room market segments identify who is traveling and why they are traveling.

CONTRACT   The contract market segment includes a fixed number of rooms sold per night at a fixed room rate for a specific company. The company is charged for this number of rooms each night whether they are occupied or not. The best example of contract rooms is airline crew rooms. For example, American or Delta airlines would contract with a hotel for 25 rooms per night at a room rate of $40. This is for weekday and weekend rooms, year round. Hotels agree to a substantially lower room rate because this business will provide a base amount of business each day of the year. Unless a hotel is selling out with 100% occupancy, a $40 contract room sold will generate some additional room revenue and is much better than an empty room that will generate no incremental revenue.

GROUP   Groups are guests associated with a specific company or organization who occupy two or more rooms, stay more than one night, and generally have meetings and meal functions. They generally get a discounted rate because they provide a larger volume of room nights at one time. A hotel will specify what qualifies as a group rate. For example, three or more rooms for one night, or two or more rooms for two nights or more. The larger the number of rooms for the group, generally the lower the room rate. Groups can be business or pleasure, and generally involve additional catering and meeting room rental revenue. Some group market segment examples are as follows:

Corporate Group	Sports and Government Group
Association Group	Other Group

TRANSIENT   The transient market segment refers to individual business or pleasure travelers. They can be further segmented by the room rate they are willing to pay. Following is an example of a transient room rate structure that defines specific market segments and identifies room rates from highest to lowest.

Concierge	$249 room rate
Regular or rack rate	$225
Corporate	$199
Special corporate	$190–$125 depending on the number of rooms
Discount	
AARP	$175
Government	$150 (should be the same as the per diem rate)
Travel industry	$125
Weekend super saver	$99

The Customer

A final thought on revenues. The actual event of checking a customer in or out of a hotel, serving a meal in a restaurant, providing a treatment at a spa, or assigning a tee time at the golf course involves employees talking with the guests and providing them with the products or services they are requesting. How this transaction takes place is extremely important to the success of a business. Next! Checking In? Name? These are hardly gracious or friendly greetings. A friendly greeting, eye contact, personal customer recognition, and a smile all go a long way in making the customer feel good about the amount they are paying and the service they are receiving. While it is important to accurately record the transaction with the customer for the accounting records, it is equally important to do it in a friendly and efficient manner. The point of sale system will generally take care of all the financial information, leaving the employee more time to talk with the customer and maximize the customer's experience. The end result—the customer wants to come back!

This goes back to our three measurements of a successful business—satisfied customers, satisfied employees, and sufficient cash flow or profitability. While this textbook focuses on accounting and financial transactions and reports, it is always important to remember that employees and guests are the ones that make the whole cycle work.

PROFIT: THE ULTIMATE MEASURE OF FINANCIAL PERFORMANCE

Just as revenues provide the starting point for measuring financial performance, profits provide the end result of all the effort and activities in operating a business. This section will discuss the different aspects of profit. We will review once again the general formula for profits: *Revenue minus expenses equal profits.*

Calculating profits is a simple process, but it gets more detailed when you apply it to the different departments involved in operating a large business such as a hotel. Profits are what are left over after recording all revenues and paying all expenses associated with generating those revenues. Just as there are different types of revenues, so are there different types of expenses and different levels of profits. The types of profits will be discussed next.

A hotel has four important levels of profits, each at a different stage in the operation of a hotel. They are as follows:

Department Profit identifies and measures the profitability of a specific department. Examples are Rooms Department profit or Restaurant Department profit.

Total Department Profits is the total profits of all profit departments.

House Profit or Gross Operating Profit is generally the profit line from which management bonuses are calculated. That is because management can control or affect all of the accounts included in the House Profit line. It measures the effectiveness of management in maximizing revenues and minimizing expenses.

Net House Profit or Adjusted Gross Operating Profit generally measures the financial success of the hotel. All direct and indirect costs, fixed and variable costs, and overhead costs have been paid and this profit amount is available to be distributed between owners, management companies, and any other entities that have a vested interest in the business either before or after the appropriate taxes have been paid.

The 10th revised edition of the *Uniform System of Accounts for the Lodging Industry* uses profit and income in describing different types of profit. These will be discussed in more detail in Chapter 4.

Department Profit

Department operations are the foundation to operating any business. Each department separates the business into different and distinct operations and the revenues and expenses involved in operating those departments are shown on the department P&L. These departments are called revenue centers or profit centers. The largest profit departments in a hotel are rooms, restaurants, beverage, and banquets. The basic profit formula, revenues minus expenses, can be applied but with more detail:

Rooms Department

> Transient, Group, and Contract Revenues
> Less Expenses
>> Wages
>> Benefits
>> Direct Operating Expenses
> Equals Rooms Department Profit

Restaurant Department

> Breakfast, Lunch, and Dinner Revenues
> Less Expenses
>> Cost of Sales
>> Wages
>> Benefits
>> Direct Operating Expenses
> Equals Restaurant Department Profit

All the department profits are added up to get Total Hotel Department Profit.

House Profit or Gross Operating Profit

These two profit terms are interchangeable and reflect basically the same profit measurements. While Marriott identifies these profits as "House Profit," Four Seasons and Hyatt prefer to call them "Gross Operating Profit." They are the next level of profitability after Total Department Profits.

After Total Department Profits have been calculated, there are other indirect expenses involved in operating a hotel that must also be paid as part of daily operations. These departments are called expense centers or support costs because they generate no revenue, but incur expenses in support of those departments that do generate revenues. Examples of expense centers are general and administrative (G&A), repairs and maintenance (R&M), utilities or heat, light, and power (HLP), and sales and marketing (S&M). These departments have total department expenses instead of total department revenues and department profits.

An example of department statements for expense centers is

> Expenses
>> Wages
>> Benefits
>> Direct Operating Expenses
> Total Department Expense

All the expense centers are added up to get Total Expense Center costs and this Total Expense Center cost is subtracted from Total Department Profits to produce House Profit or Gross Operating Profit. Our equation for house profit or gross operating profit becomes

House Profit or
Gross Operating Profit = Total Department Profit − Total Expense Center Costs, or
= Total Department Profit − Support Costs

House Profit/Gross Operating Profit is used primarily as a measurement of management's ability to maximize revenues, control expenses, and maximize profits. The hotel management team is organized to have influence and control over all the revenues and expenses recognized at the house profit level. Therefore, it is the profit level that is generally used to calculate management bonuses.

Net House Profit or Adjusted Gross Operating Profit

There are still expenses associated with operating a hotel that have not been recognized and recorded at the house profit level. These expenses are generally referred to as fixed expenses or overhead expenses. What distinguishes these types of expenses is that they are fixed and have no relationship to the business levels of the hotel. The hotel could be closed, or running a low or a high occupancy level, and regardless, these expenses will be the same and will have to be paid. Because management has no control of or say over these expenses, they are not included in bonus calculations. Examples of these fixed expenses are bank loans, mortgage payments, insurance costs, licenses, permits, and fees.

The equation for Net House Profit or Adjusted Gross Operating Profit is

Net House Profit = House Profit or Gross Operating Profit − Fixed Expenses

Net House Profit or Adjusted Gross Operating Profit is a true or accurate measure of the overall profitability of the hotel. It is the total profit generated by the hotel or the money that goes to the bank. All direct and indirect costs and fixed or variable costs have been recognized and paid. Think of this profit as the profits that are available to be split among the owner, the management company, the franchisee, or any other entity that has an operating stake in the hotel.

Profit Before and After Tax

The final expense to be recognized and paid is any taxes associated with operating the hotel. It is important to determine who will pay these taxes. It could be the owner or the management company. This will have an impact on Net House Profit/Adjusted Gross Operating Profit depending on how the payment of taxes is defined. Generally, Profit Before Taxes are the same as Net House Profit/Adjusted Gross Operating Profit. After all applicable taxes are paid, the true bottom line profit or Profit After Taxes is determined. We will not spend much time discussing this profit level as a hospitality manager has very little involvement with this profit level.

Summary

The use of accounting concepts and methods of financial analysis begins with using numbers to measure financial performance. Numbers are a language that provides specific and detailed information that explains and measures company operations. Numbers evaluate operational performance, determine value, measure liquidity, and provide management with a detailed tool to manage their business.

Hospitality managers need to develop business financial literacy, which is the ability to understand numbers and to be comfortable working with numbers and using them for analyzing business operations. Numbers are a means to an end; in other words they help to measure and evaluate business operations. In order to realize career advancement, it is equally important that a hospitality manager is able to understand and use numbers in business operations *and* to discuss and explain his or her operations in financial terms with senior management, including the General Manager and the Director of Finance of their hotel.

There are three financial statements that are used in evaluating a company or business. The first and most important is the P&L Statement (also called the Income Statement), which measures financial performance over a period of time. Second is the Balance Sheet (also called the Asset and Liabilities Statement), which measures the net worth of a company or business at a specific time. Third is the Statement of Cash Flow, which measures the liquidity and cash balances of a company or business over a period of time.

Four important formulas for hospitality managers to know and use are the formulas for revenue, profit, RevPAR, and retention. They also need to understand the main profit levels of a hotel—Total Department Profits, House Profit or Gross Operating Profit, and Net House Profit or Adjusted Gross Operating Profit.

Hospitality Manager Takeaways

1. Hospitality accounting is about using numbers and fundamental arithmetic in evaluating and improving operating performance. It is all about fundamentals!
2. The Profit and Loss Statement (P&L) is the most important financial statement that a hospitality manager needs to completely understand and be able to use in operating his or her department.
3. Understanding and using numbers (accounting and finance) effectively is essential to the career advancement of every hospitality manager.
4. Numbers contained in financial statements are used to measure financial performance and to provide managers with a valuable management tool.
5. Accounting and financial management is all about maximizing revenues, minimizing expenses, and maximizing profits, using numbers to measure and improve financial performance.

Key Terms

Accounting concepts: the bookkeeping methods and financial transactions used in daily business operations.
Balance Sheet: measures the value or net worth of a business.

Capitalization: the source and methods of raising money to invest in and start a business.
Financial analysis: the separation of a business's management of monetary affairs into parts for individual study.

Income: a term interchangeable with *profit* and *earnings.*

Liquidity: the amount of cash or cash equivalents that a business has to cover its daily operating expenses.

Market capitalization: a measure of the value of a company that includes the number of outstanding shares held by individual and institutional investors times the current stock price of the company.

Market segment: customer groups defined by expectations, preferences, buying patterns, and behavior patterns.

Point-of-sale (POS): the equipment that records the customer transaction, including identifying the method of payment and reporting the type of transaction.

Profit: the amount of revenues left over after all appropriate expenses have been paid

Profit and Loss Statement (P&L): measures the operating success and profitability of a business.

Property: the term for the physical hotel or restaurant.

Rate: the dollar amount paid by a customer to receive a product or service provided by a business.

Retention or flow-through: the amount of incremental revenue dollars that become incremental profit dollars. It is expressed as a percentage.

Revenue: the monetary amount that customers pay to purchase a product or service. It can be in the form of cash, checks, credit cards, accounts receivable, or electronic transfer.

Revenue per available room, RevPAR: an important measure of a hotel's ability to generate room revenue by measuring both average room rate and occupancy percentage.

Statement of Cash Flows: measures the liquidity and flow of cash of a business.

Volume: the number of units sold, served, received, or bought by customers during a specific time frame.

Working capital: the amount of money utilized in the daily operations of a business. It includes using current assets and current liabilities as well as cash in producing a product or service.

Formulas

Average Rate

$$\frac{\text{Room Revenue}}{\text{Rooms Sold}}$$

Occupancy Percentage

$$\frac{\text{Rooms Sold}}{\text{Total Rooms}}$$

Revenue

$$\text{Rate} \times \text{Volume}$$

Profit Dollars

$$\text{Revenue} - \text{Expenses}$$

Profit Percent

$$\frac{\text{Profit Dollar}}{\text{Revenue Dollar}}$$

Market Capitalization

$$\text{Number of Outstanding Shares} \times \text{Stock Price}$$

Retention or Flow-through

$$\frac{\text{Change in Profit Dollars}}{\text{Change in Revenue Dollars}}$$

RevPAR

$$\frac{\text{Total Room Revenue}}{\text{Total Available Rooms}}, \text{ or Average Rate} \times \text{Occupancy Percentage}$$

Working Capital

$$\text{Current Assets} - \text{Current Liabilities}$$

Review Questions

1. Name and describe the three main financial statements of a business. Include the characteristics of each financial statement.

2. Define RevPAR and explain why it is so important as a revenue measurement for room revenues as well as total hotel financial performance.

3. Name and describe the four profit levels in a hotel.
4. What is the difference between capitalization and working capital? What is each used for in business operations?
5. Why is understanding accounting concepts and methods of financial analysis important to a hospitality manager?
6. What are the three key measurements of the overall success of a business?
7. Why is the P&L Statement the most important for a hospitality manager to understand?
8. What are the formulas for room revenue, occupancy percentage, RevPAR, profits, and retention/flow-through?

Practice Exercises

1. Match the following types of accounts to their balance sheet classification:

 ___Accounts Payable   A. Current Asset

 ___Cash   B. Current Liability

 ___Equipment   C. Long-Term Asset

 ___Inventory   D. Long-Term Liability

 ___Bank Loan   E. Owner Equity

 ___Accounts Receivable

 ___Retained Earnings

 ___Taxes Payable

 ___Initial Capital Accounts

 ___Common Stock

2. Match these equations

 ___Revenues − Expenses   A. Working Capital

 ___Current Assets − Current Liabilities   B. Profit Formula

 ___Revenues − Cost of Sales + Wages + Benefits + Operating Expenses   C. RevPAR

 $\dfrac{\text{Wage Cost}}{\text{Revenues}}$ D. Cost Percent

 $\dfrac{\text{Profit Dollars}}{\text{Revenue Dollars}}$ E. Retention/Flow-through

 $\dfrac{\text{Room Revenues}}{\text{Total Rooms}}$ F. Department Profit

 $\dfrac{\text{Change in Profit Dollars}}{\text{Change in Revenue Dollars}}$ G. Profit Percent

3. Match the financial statement with the description

___Has opening and ending balances   A. P&L

___Is the same as an A&L Statement   B. Balance Sheet

___Closes out accounts at the end of an accounting C. Statement of Cash Flows
  cycle

___Is the same as a Source and Use of Funds
  Statement

___Is the same as an Income Statement

___Shows the value or net worth of a company

___Measures the operating success of a company

___Shows the liquidity of a company

2

Foundations
of Financial Analysis

LEARNING OBJECTIVES

- To learn about the fundamental methods of financial analysis.
- To understand the Financial Management Cycle.
- To understand the importance of comparing numbers to give them meaning (e.g., comparing the actual financial performance of a business to previously established measures or goals).

- To understand the importance of measuring change and what it tells about the financial performance of a business.
- To learn how percentages are used in financial analysis to measure financial performance.
- To be able to identify trends and understand their importance to financial analysis.

CHAPTER OUTLINE

INTRODUCTION

This chapter presents some of the fundamental accounting concepts and methods of financial analysis that will be used throughout the book and also throughout the career of any hospitality manager. These are not only fundamental accounting concepts but also important management tools to help operate a business on a daily basis.

The concepts and terms are explained in a direct and fundamental way. The typical detailed and complicated accounting explanations are missing because they will do no good if they are not understood. The information in this chapter will form a solid financial foundation, one that will enable students to build on in terms of knowledge and application as they work through problems and deal with business situations. It focuses on hospitality industry operations, but the methods of financial analysis presented here are useful and applicable to any business operation.

FUNDAMENTAL METHODS OF FINANCIAL ANALYSIS

Analyzing financial reports and statements requires a fundamental understanding of where numbers come from, how they are organized and presented, what they mean, what they measure, and how they are used. This section will discuss two concepts of working with numbers to analyze financial statements.

Two Important Tools

First, we will talk about two important ways numbers are used in business. They are used to measure financial performance and to provide a management tool to use in operating the business.

TO MEASURE FINANCIAL PERFORMANCE   Numbers provide a way to determine how a business is performing. Measuring financial performance is historical in nature and uses the actual numbers or results from business operations. It tells us what the business has produced and compares and evaluates that performance using specific measures. It is like looking back through the rearview mirror at operations. The three main financial statements are used in measuring financial performance.

The P&L Statement shows the revenues, expenses, and profits for a specified time period. Each month, quarter, or year, the numbers produced by an operation are recorded in the P&L Statement which shows whether the business revenue and profits are improving, declining, or remaining the same.

The Balance Sheet shows the value or net worth of a business based on assets, liabilities, and owner equity at a specific time. These numbers tell us whether the business is getting financially stronger by increasing assets or owner equity or if it is struggling and increasing liabilities. The numbers also tell us how the business is capitalized or started—with more debt than owner equity or more owner equity than debt.

Cash flow and liquidity are critical to the success of a business. The Statement of Cash Flows shows how much cash is generated by a business and how effectively it is being used in operating the business over a specified time period.

TO PROVIDE A MANAGEMENT TOOL   Numbers provide a way for managers to plan for varying levels of business volume. This can take the form of forecasting revenues, scheduling wages, implementing cost controls, expanding business operations, or developing the annual budget. Numbers give managers feedback on their operations and assist them in making appropriate changes.

This aspect of using numbers is very valuable to a business because it is the process of taking the information that numbers provide and applying them back to operating the business.

The Financial Management Cycle

Second, is the **Financial Management Cycle**. It is important to understand this process and how numbers are generated and used in business operations. This cycle deals with the flow and use of numbers in business operations.

1. *Operations produce the numbers.*   All the activities involved in the daily operations produce the numbers that measure performance. In a hotel, the daily operations provide products and services to guests, including the rooms department, food and beverage outlets, gift shop, and any other department that produces a sales transaction with the guest. Numbers used in financial analysis have to come from somewhere and that is the daily operations of the business.
2. *Accounting prepares the numbers and provides management reports and financial statements.*   At the end of the day, week, or month, the numbers resulting from all operations and activities are collected, summarized, and reported by the accounting department. These reports describe the operations and activities of the week, month, or year and are distributed to the appropriate managers for their review and use.
3. *Accounting and operations analyze the numbers.*   Operations management and accounting management work together to review and analyze management reports and financial statements. They look for changes, the cause of the change, and the result of the change to understand operations and determine ways to change and improve. Together they have

operational and financial analysis experience and should be able to identify any changes or improvements that need to be made to ensure that productive operations continue.

4. *Operations apply the numbers back to the business.*   After reviews and discussions, it is the operations managers that make any necessary changes to operations to correct or improve them. The ability to analyze quickly and accurately and then make any necessary changes is an important part of any business operation. It enables the business to constantly improve by being more productive or creating more value in the products and services that it provides.

COMPARING NUMBERS TO GIVE THEM MEANING

Numbers need to be compared to other numbers to have any meaning. **Comparison** is to examine or note the likeness or difference between two numbers. A hotel has monthly sales of $1,000,000. All this tells us is the sales level. How do we know if this is good or bad, up or down, or acceptable or not acceptable? A fundamental concept of financial analysis is to compare a number produced by operations to an established number that will tell us if there was an increase or decrease. The most common comparisons are with (1) budget, (2) forecast, (3) performance of last year, (4) performance of previous month or period, (5) pro forma, or (6) any other established goal.

Budget

Actual financial results for a month, quarter, or year are compared to the established budget. The **budget** is the formal one-year financial operating plan for a company. Budgets include planned increases in revenues and profits, and productivity improvements in costs and expenses. Comparing actual results to the budget shows whether the business is moving in the direction planned and budgeted and how close it is in meeting, exceeding, or missing the budgeted numbers.

Forecast

A **forecast** updates the budget. Whereas the budget is generally done once for the entire year, forecasts are done continually to adjust or relate to current business conditions. Forecasts can be weekly, monthly, quarterly, once in six months or the number of months until the end of the year. They are very important because they are more current and help project business performance reflecting current market conditions compared to the budget.

Last Year

Comparing actual financial results with last year's actual results will be very useful. The first evaluation of financial operations is to know if operations are better than last year. The best results are if the actual operations for the current year are better than that of the last year and the budget. Similarly, the results are worse if the performance of the current year is worse than that of the last year and the budget.

Previous Month or Period

These comparisons are very important because they identify trends in operations. The goal of any business is to continually improve. Examining month-to-month performance tells us the trend and direction of our operations. They can show improvements that hopefully are the results of corrective action implemented by management to keep the company moving in the right direction.

Pro Forma

A new business does not have any historical operating information. Therefore, management, developers, and bankers prepare a pro forma based on market conditions and expected financial returns. A **pro forma** is the estimate or projection of how they think the business will perform in the first year of operations. The pro forma is used for the first year of business operations and is then replaced by the budget, which is prepared based on the first year's actual performance. Pro formas are used to establish and identify initial business revenues and profits that will generate the cash flow necessary to repay loans and investments.

Other Goals

Occasionally, a business will establish other goals or benchmarks to compare with the actual performance. Examples are improving profit margins to meet an established goal, achieving specific revenue levels, or entering new markets.

Let's use our example to give meaning to the $1,000,000 in monthly sales. If last year we did monthly sales of $950,000, this year we increased that by $50,000, that is, to $1,000,000, which is good—sales are increasing. If the budget was $1,100,000, we missed the budget by $100,000, which is not good—our sales did not increase as much as we had planned in the budget.

Now let's analyze our $1,000,000 monthly sales performance. We know we increased sales by $50,000 over last year but we missed the budget by $100,000. Was our performance good or bad? The answer is both. It is good because we improved by $50,000 over last year. It was bad because we missed the budget by $100,000. The next question we have to ask is, "Was the budget set too high?" Comparing the budget of $1,100,000 to last year's actual of $950,000 tells us that we expected (or budgeted) sales to increase by $150,000. We can also measure this increase in percentages by dividing the $150,000 increase by last year's sales of $950,000 to get a budget percent increase of 15.8%. That is a very aggressive budget increase. If I were the manager of this business, I would be very happy to have the $50,000 increase over last year (a 5.3% increase). I would also review the reasons we thought we could increase by 15.8% and analyze why that didn't happen.

Comparing numbers to something concrete is essential to give any meaning to the number. This is particularly important for the P&L statements. The Balance Sheet and the Statement of Cash Flows are analyzed more with respect to changes from previous statements or to goals or benchmarks than to budgets. Typically, there is no budget for these two financial statements. That is why they are compared to the previous month or period or to a goal.

Remember to compare the numbers in any financial report to that of the last year, last month, budget, forecast, pro forma, or with the goal to give it meaning. Only then can we tell whether operations are improving or not.

MEASURING CHANGE TO EXPLAIN PERFORMANCE

One of the most important elements of financial analysis is to be able to identify where changes occur and what caused the change. **Change** refers to the difference in two numbers. In a large business with many products and departments, an effective financial analysis of the financial reports must locate the department that is changing and identify the causes of that change. Is it in revenues—volume or rate? Is it in expenses—cost of sales, wages, benefits, or direct operating expenses? Is it a direct or indirect, fixed or variable expense? One or many departments may be impacting operations with positive or negative changes.

Changes are identified by comparing actual performance to previous performance or to a specific goal or measure. These changes can be for a month, quarter, or year. The more the information that is obtained about the changes, the better the chance is that good decisions can be made to respond to the changes.

Changes, both positive and negative, are measured in terms of units, dollars, and percentages. These three measurements can tell us a lot about the performance of a business. From our $1,000,000 monthly sales example, we have already looked at the dollar *increase* (+$50,000 over last year) and the percentage *increase* (+5.3% over last year). We know that we have $50,000 more sales dollars, a positive change. We know that we increased sales by 5.3%, also a positive change.

Performing the same financial analysis process, our $1,000,000 is $100,000 *below* the budget of $1,100,000 and 9.1% *below* the budget. We know that we have $100,000 less sales dollars than budgeted, a negative result. Our 9.1% is also a negative result from our budget.

The final measurement is units. If the entire $1,000,000 in monthly sales was from room revenues, our unit will be the number of rooms sold. Our accounting reports would tell us how many rooms were sold and what the average room rate was. Let's assume the average room rate was $80. We can now calculate the number of rooms sold by dividing total room sales of $1,000,000 by the average room rate of $80 and that gives us 12,500 rooms sold. This should match with the number of rooms sold on our accounting report.

Now we have the units or volume—12,500 rooms sold, but we don't know if this is better or worse than last year's monthly sales of $950,000. The answer will come from last year's accounting reports. If the report tells us that the average rate for last year was $78 and 12,180 rooms were sold, we can multiply these together and get the monthly sales of $950,000. Now we can compare our actual 12,500 rooms sold this year to that of last year's 12,180. We can also compare this year's average rate of $80 to last year's average rate of $78.

Take a minute to calculate the increases from last year in dollars, units, and percentages for this year's monthly sales of $1,000,000 in Table 2.1.

TABLE 2.1   Comparison: Actual to Last Year

	Sales	Rooms Sold	Average Rate
This Year	$1,000,000	12,500	$80
Last Year	$ 950,000	12,180	$78
Dollar Difference			
Percentage Difference			

The Answers to Table 2.1
Comparison: Actual to Last Year

	Sales	Rooms Sold	Average Rate
This Year	$1,000,000	12,500	$80
Last Year	$ 950,000	12,180	$78
Dollar Difference	$ 50,000	320	$ 2
Percentage Difference	+5.3%	+2.6%	+2.6%

USING PERCENTAGES IN FINANCIAL ANALYSIS

Percentages are one of the three ways numbers are used to measure financial performance. **Percentages** are a share or proportion in relation to the whole. They provide an additional dimension or perspective in financial analysis. Percentages measure relationships and changes and always involve two numbers.

Calculating Percentages

Percentages are the result of combining two numbers that define a relationship. A change in one number changes the resulting percentage. Both numbers can also change. When a percentage changes, it is important to know which number in the relationship changed and what caused the change. For example,

$$\text{Wage Cost Percentage} = \frac{\text{Wage Expense Dollars}}{\text{The Associated Revenue Dollars}}$$

If our department wage expense is $350 and revenue is $1,000, our wage cost percentage is 35% ($350/$1,000).

Wage cost percent can go up or down in two ways. An increased wage cost percent would result from our actual wage expense increasing or our revenues decreasing. Continuing our example,

$$1. \ \frac{\$400 \text{ wage expense}}{\$1,000 \text{ department revenue}} = 40\% \text{ wage cost percentage}$$

$$2. \ \frac{\$350 \text{ wage expense}}{\$875 \text{ department revenue}} = 40\% \text{ wage cost percentage}$$

If our wage cost expense went up, we would analyze the labor numbers to see where the increase was and what caused the increase. In our first example, our wage expense went up $50 to $400 but our department revenue of $1,000 remained the same. This is not good because we spent $50 more on wages but did not increase our output or revenues. The business operation was *less productive.*

In our second example, our wage cost remained constant at $350 but our department revenue went down from $125 to $875. This is also not good because we spent the same amount of $400 on wages but it resulted in less sales—$875. Again, our business operation was *less productive.*

After identifying where the changes have occurred, you can look for the causes of the changes and make any necessary adjustments to improve operations. Our corrective action will be different in each example. In the first example, we would look at our work schedule to make scheduling changes to get back to 35% wage cost. In our second example, we would look to the sales department to see what caused the drop in sales to $875 and how we can correct it. In either case, it is an important part of financial analysis to make any necessary changes in our work schedule to adjust to the forecasted production volumes and their corresponding sales.

What Percentages Measure

Percentages measure relationships and *changes.* An example of relationships is the wage cost example mentioned in the previous section. A 35% wage cost means that 35 cents out of every revenue dollar is used to pay the wage cost associated with producing that revenue dollar. Another example is food cost percentage. An actual food cost percentage of 40% means that 40 cents out of every food revenue dollar is used to pay for the associated food cost to produce that one food revenue dollar.

The food cost percentage will go up or down based on changes in food costs or food revenues. To become more productive and profitable, the actual food expense that results in a sale would have to decline or stay the same but the food revenue would increase. To become less productive, our food cost would have to remain the same while food revenues go down or our food cost would have to increase while food revenues remain the same. By looking at each number and identifying any changes, we analyze the numbers and identify what changed and how that affects our operational performance.

Let's look at another example of percentages and change. If our revenues increase from $1,000 to $1,200, the resulting dollar change is an increase of $200. To calculate the associated percentage change, divide the $200 increase by the original $1,000 revenue and the result is a 20% increase in revenues. *The amount of change is always divided by the base, beginning or original number, never by the actual number!* Percentage change can be calculated for changes in revenues, expenses, profits, assets, liabilities, owner equity, units, or any other specific account.

Using percentages in the process of financial analysis includes three steps: first, identifying and measuring the change; second, identifying the cause of the change; and third, developing and implementing corrective action into daily operations.

FOUR TYPES OF PERCENTAGES USED IN FINANCIAL ANALYSIS

Cost or Expense Percentages

Cost or expense percentages tell us what dollar amounts of expenses are associated with corresponding revenues or sales. The previous examples of wage cost and food cost demonstrate cost percentages. Cost percentages can be calculated for any expense account or type that has a specific dollar cost associated with it. The formula for cost percentage is expense dollars divided by corresponding revenue dollars. Examples:

Room Revenues for January are $40,000. Wage cost are $5,000; benefit costs are $2,000; reservation costs are $4,000; and linen costs are $1,500. Our expense formula is dollar cost/department revenue. Our cost percentages for January are as follows:

$$\text{Wage cost} = 12.5\% \left(\frac{\$5,000}{\$40,000} \right)$$

$$\text{Benefit cost} = 5.0\% \left(\frac{\$2,000}{\$40,000} \right)$$

$$\text{Reservation cost} = 10.0\% \left(\frac{\$4,000}{\$40,000} \right)$$

$$\text{Linen cost} = 3.8\% \left(\frac{\$1,500}{\$40,000} \right)$$

$$\text{Total Cost} = 31.3\% \left(\frac{\$12,500}{\$40,000} \right)$$

Profit Percentages

Profit percentages tell how much of the revenue dollar is remaining after all expenses are paid. Profits are measured in dollars and percentages. Dollar profit measures the absolute amount of dollars remaining as profit while percentage profit measures how much of the sales dollar is remaining as profit. Profit percentages can be applied to different levels of profit—department profits, house profits, or net house profits. Continuing our example, our January profit percent is

$$\text{Total profits} = 68.7\% \left(\frac{\$27,500}{\$40,000} \right)$$

Department profit percentages are important because each department that is a Profit Center has a different cost structure and profit percent resulting in different department profitability. For example, the rooms department typically has a department profit range of 65%–75%, the banquet or catering department typically 30%–40%, lounges and retail shops 25%–35%, and restaurants 0–10%. It is also possible for some restaurants to operate at a loss, thereby having a negative percentage referred to as department loss percent rather than department profit percent. In this case, the dollar expense costs are greater than the revenue dollars.

Mix Percentages

Mix percentages tells us how much of a total comes from different departments or how much each department is of the total. Mix percentages can be measured in units or dollars. They are useful because they provide a quantified measure of each part to the whole.

Sales mix percent identifies the portion or amount that each department sales is of total sales. Following is an example of a hotel sales mix:

Department	Sales Dollars	Sales Mix Percentage
Rooms Sales	$1,000	50%
Restaurant Sales	300	15%
Beverage Sales	200	10%
Banquet Sales	500	25%
Total Sales	$2,000	100%

If each department has the same profit percentage, the sales mix percent is not very helpful. In this case, the same amount of profit will result from each revenue dollar regardless of the department. However, the actual department profit percents are very different, as demonstrated in the previous section. Let's add department profit percent to our example.

Department	Profit Percentage	Sales Dollars	Sales Mix Percentage	Profit Dollars	Profit Mix Percentage
Rooms Sales	70%	$1,000	50%	$700	70.7%
Restaurant Sales	10%	300	15%	30	3.0%
Beverage Sales	30%	200	10%	60	6.1%
Banquet Sales	40%	500	25%	200	20.2%
Total Sales/Profit		$2,000	100%	$990	100.0%

Now we can draw some additional conclusions about the monthly sales and profits.

The Rooms Department generated 50% of sales but 70.7% of total profit dollars.

The Restaurant Department generated 15% of sales but only 3.0% of total profit dollars.

The Beverage Department generated 10% of sales but only 6.1% of total profit dollars.

The Banquet Department generated 25% of sales and 20.2% of total profit dollars.

This information tells us that the Rooms Department is the main contributor to both sales and profits. This department should be our main priority. The Banquet Department is the next highest profit contributor in dollars and percentages. It is still important to focus on Restaurant and Beverage operations, but they do not account for a significant portion of profits—9.1% combined even though they have a combined 25% of sales.

These data have given us examples of sales dollars and profit dollars mix percentages. We can also calculate a mix percentage for units sold, market segment, meal periods, or any other unit that we measure and record. Following are examples of rooms sold market segment mix and restaurant meal period mix. These are in units, rooms sold, or customer counts.

Rooms Sold Market Segments			**Restaurant Meal Periods**		
	Rooms Sold	**Mix Percentage**	**Meal Period**	**Customers**	**Mix Percentage**
Transient	1,500	60.0%	Breakfast	325	41.7%
Group	700	28.0%	Lunch	190	24.3%
Contract	300	12.0%	Dinner	265	34.0%
Total	2,500	100.0%	Total	780	100.0%

Percentage Change

Percentage **change** is very important because it measures progress or lack of progress. Have our restaurant sales increased or decreased compared to last month? Which meal period showed the most improvement—breakfast, lunch, or dinner? Are the sales up because we had an increase in customers served or because our average check increased? The percentage change gives us this information.

Percentage change is calculated by dividing the change in dollars (increase or decrease) by the base or original amount. In our example, the change or difference would be calculated by subtracting the previous month's results from the current month's results. This change amount would then be divided by the base or in this example, the previous month's results. For example, this month's sales of $4,800 compared to last month's sales of $4,500. Our percentage change is calculated by subtracting the previous month's sales of $4,500 from this month's sales of $4,800 resulting in a *difference* of $300. This is where it is important to relate the numbers to actual operations. This calculation results in a $300 difference. We then know that this is a positive difference because our current month sales of $4,800 is larger than the previous month's sales of $4,500. We can now calculate the sales percentage change: $300/$4,500 = +6.7%

Red Lobster

The first Red Lobster Restaurant opened in 1968 in Florida. There are now over 650 Red Lobster restaurants in the United States and Canada. Their market share of the Casual Dining Seafood market is just under 50% and annual revenues are over $2 billion making it one of the world's largest casual dining restaurant concepts.

The average annual sales per Red Lobster restaurant were approximately $3,800,000 in 2007 and $3,900,000 in 2008 and each restaurant serves 150,000–225,000 customers per year. A typical Red Lobster restaurant includes 4–5 managers and 60–100 hourly employees referred to as crew members. Operating departments include Service, Culinary, and Beverage Hospitality. A Red Lobster manager will rotate through each of these departments as they develop their careers. As a Red Lobster manager, you will be responsible for managing about 10–20 crew members per shift to serve customers and achieve established sales and profit objectives. Refer to the following Web site for more information: www.redlobster.com.

From the above, calculate the following assuming 365 days per year:

1. Average sales per day
2. Average customers served per day
3. The percentage increase in average sales per restaurant from 2007 to 2008?

Photo Courtesy of Darden Restaurants, Inc.

TRENDS IN FINANCIAL ANALYSIS

Trends are defined as a general inclination or tendency and are important because they show the direction of movement of business operations, industry, and national and international economies. Understanding the different types of trends and how they affect the operations of a business is an important part of financial analysis. We will discuss four types of trends that affect a business.

Short- and Long-Term Trends

It is important to look at both short-term and long-term trends. Short-term trends (less than 90 days) often involve seasonality or the expected cycles of a business or industry. A business that is slowing down because of seasonality or an industry cycle should be evaluated differently than a business that is slowing down because of increased competition, product or service quality, or pricing issues. A long-term trend is a better evaluator of the success of products or services especially when compared to competitors and industry performance.

When looking at the month-to-month performance of a business, it is important to distinguish between one month of poor financial performance and several months of poor financial performance. It is typical for a business to have a slow period, a problem, or one-time event that results in performance below expectations for a month. One month by itself does not make a trend or signal a major or long-term problem. However, it is important to correct any poor performance to prevent it from becoming an ongoing problem.

If a business has several months of poor performance, that is a trend that could signal continuing major long-term problems. Management might have to make major evaluations and analysis to determine what is causing the ongoing poor performance and how it can be corrected. Correcting the cause of several months or years of poor performance is a much bigger task than correcting a problem affecting only one month.

Revenue, Expense, and Profit Trends

These trends are all shown in the P&L Statement. They are perhaps the most important trends because they reflect the current financial performance of the company and its management. Each individual trend is compared to the other two to determine if financial performance is improving or declining. For example, if revenue is trending up and expenses are staying flat, the profit trend should also be up. These are good trends and good relationships between revenues, expenses, and profits. However, if revenues are trending up but expenses are trending up at a faster rate, it will result in lower profits. That is not a good trend. Most important to note is whether revenues and expenses are trending to increase or decrease profits. Equally important is to know which one of the three trends is increasing or decreasing faster or slower than the other two. For example, if sales are increasing by 5% but expenses are increasing by 10%, profit margins will decrease. The best case for increasing profits is that sales are increasing and expenses are decreasing.

Favorable and unfavorable trends that affect productivity and profits are demonstrated as follows.

Trends that increase profits	Trends that decrease profits
Revenues increasing, expenses decreasing	Revenues decreasing, expenses increasing
Revenues increasing, expenses flat	Revenues flat, expenses increasing
Revenues increasing faster than expenses	Expenses increasing faster than revenues

Company and Industry Trends

It is important to compare the trend of a company with the trends of the industry and the general economy. Are the company trends the result of the success or failure of your business operations, the result of conditions that are affecting the entire industry, or the result of the general economic environment? Trends can result from any or all of these conditions and it is important to identify the causes of trends for the business and the industry. Then appropriate action can be implemented.

Some examples. If your business revenues are down by 10% from the previous year and the industry average is down by 8–12%, then you can safely say that your business revenues are down as a result of industry conditions and nothing specific to your business. However, if your revenues are down by 10% from the previous year and the industry average is up by 2%, then you can safely say that the reason your business revenues are down is the problems that you face or inferior performance of your business and not any industry factors. The causes of the 10% decrease in revenues are different than what is occurring in the industry and should be treated in different ways to correct problems and improve efficiencies of the company to get back to the desired revenue levels.

General Economic Trends—National and International

The world is indeed shrinking and problems in other countries or other parts of the United States can affect the performance of an individual business operation. Inflation rates, interest rates, unemployment rates, consumer confidence indexes, budget deficits, exchange rates, and social/political environments are all factors that may have major influences on a business. The most dramatic and tragic example of this is September 11, 2001, which changed the economic, political, military, and social environment for every country in the world. Each industry and business had to develop new policies, procedures, and strategies to survive in such a turbulent and negative environment.

Another example is the impact that the development activities in China had in the months leading up to the Olympics in 2008. Much of the world's raw materials and resources went to China to support the construction of the needed infrastructure. Significant amounts of cement, steel, copper, and other materials went to China, resulting in shortages of these materials in other countries, which in turn led to cost increases or construction delays. These are both negative economic trends and the cost increases often resulting in inflationary pressures and construction delays, reducing employment and expenditures.

The global recession of 2008–2009 is another example of the impact that national and international trends have on most countries and industries. During this period, businesses had to reevaluate their business models, their pricing schedules and cost structures, their market segments, and their customer base to determine how to survive in a declining economic environment. Since no one knew how long that recession would last, businesses had to make different plans assuming different lengths of time that the recession might last.

Another element of national economic influence is the understanding of business cycles. Economic growth, bull markets, and stable social and political environments do not go on forever. Neither do recessions, bear markets, and social and political instability last forever. There are business cycles as short as six months and as long as five years that occur in normal business and economic activities. Financial analysis can assist a business in identifying business cycles and their causes and determining best practices to permit the best possible operations in any economic environment.

Today's major impact player is China. It is such a large and undeveloped market that many major companies in the world are planning ways to tap into this new and emerging business market. Another major impact player is technology. Technological advancements are widely credited for the major gains in productivity experienced over the last 10 years. How it will affect business in the next few years is also a major factor for a business or industry to consider in their plans and strategies for the future.

An acronym to be considered in the future of all global businesses is BRIC: Brazil, Russia, India, and China. These are developing economies that are becoming major players in global markets. How they affect existing businesses will be an important factor to consider. Do these countries open up new markets for the products and services of a business or industry and therefore increase sales? Or do they produce another challenging competitor that has the potential to take away from the revenues of a business or industry.

Summary

This chapter has introduced important and useful accounting concepts and provided a framework for financial analysis by presenting key components of understanding and working with numbers. Analyzing management reports and financial statements provides ways to measure the financial performance of a business and provides information that can be used as a management tool to change or improve the operations of a business.

The four steps of the Financial Management Cycle show the flow of numbers as they are used in financial analysis. Operations produce the numbers, accounting prepares the numbers, both operations management and accounting analyze the numbers, and operations management applies the financial information to their daily operations to improve or change them.

Other key elements of financial analysis include (1) comparing actual financial results to other financial information such as last year's results, current year's budget or forecast, or a pro forma, (2) measuring and evaluating changes to other numbers, (3) understanding the importance of percentages in financial analysis, and (4) using trends to interpret financial performance.

Hospitality Manager Takeaways

1. There are four key ways in which numbers are used in measuring financial performance and as a management tool:
   (a) Numbers must be compared to other numbers or standards to have any meaning.
   (b) Numbers are used to identify the cause of change and to measure its impact.
   (c) Percentages are used to measure change and describe relationships.
   (d) Trends provide an important framework to evaluate financial performance.

2. The Financial Management Cycle describes the flow and use of numbers in a company or business. First, operations produce the numbers; second, accounting prepares the numbers; third, both accounting and operations analyze and evaluate the numbers; and fourth, operations apply the numbers to improve operations or solve problems.

3. Numbers are used in financial analysis as a management tool and a way to measure financial performance.

Key Terms

Budget: the formal business and financial plan for a business for one year.
Change: the difference between two numbers.
Comparison: to examine, to note the likeness or difference.
Financial Management Cycle: the process of producing, preparing, analyzing, and applying numbers to business operations.
Forecast: updates the budget weekly, monthly, or quarterly.
Last year: the official financial performance of the previous year.

Percentages: a share or proportion in relation to the whole or part.
  Change—measures the difference in percent between two numbers.
  Cost—measures the dollar cost or expense as a part of total applicable revenue.
  Mix—measures dollars or units as a part of a whole.
  Profit—measures the dollar profit as a part of total applicable revenues.
Pro forma: the projected first year of operations prepared before actual operations begin.
Trend: a general inclination or tendency.

Formulas

Change in Dollars   Actual Results − Previous Results

Change in Percentage $\dfrac{\text{Dollar Change}}{\text{Previous Results}}$

Cost Percent $\dfrac{\text{Expense Dollars}}{\text{Corresponding Revenue Dollars}}$

Mix Percent $\dfrac{\text{Individual or Department Amount}}{\text{Total}}$

Profit Percent $\dfrac{\text{Profit Dollars}}{\text{Corresponding Revenue Dollars}}$

Review Questions

1. What are the two ways numbers are used in financial analysis? Give examples.
2. Name the four steps in the Financial Management Cycle.
3. Name five reports or timeframes that actual financial performance is compared to.
4. What is the difference between an annual budget and a pro forma?
5. Discuss some of the important components of measuring change in financial analysis.
6. Name the four types of percentages used in financial analysis. Give examples.
7. Name the four types of trends used in financial analysis. Give examples.
8. Discuss in two paragraphs, why trends are important and how you would use them in analyzing the financial operations of a business.

Practice Exercises

1. Following are the financial results for January for the Lumberjack Hotel:

	Actual	Budget	Last Year
Room Revenue	$ 695,000	$ 680,000	$ 650,000
Room Profit	$ 500,000	$ 486,000	$ 460,000
Average Room Rate	$ 67.50	$ 68.00	$ 65.66
Rooms Sold	10,300	10,000	9,900
Occupancy Percent	83.1%	80.1%	79.8%
Restaurant Revenue	$ 126,000	$ 125,000	$ 124,000
Beverage Revenue	$ 48,000	$ 50,000	$ 47,000
Catering Revenue	$ 240,000	$ 250,000	$ 245,000
Total Food and Beverage Revenue	$ 414,000	$ 425,000	$ 416,000
Gift Shop Revenue	$ 23,000	$ 22,000	$ 21,000
Total Revenues	$1,132,000	$1,127,000	$1,087,000

Calculate the following:
A. Dollar change for room revenue—actual to budget and last year.
B. Percentage change in room revenue—actual to budget and last year.
C. Dollar and percentage change for rooms sold and average rate—actual to budget and last year.

	Budget	Last Year
Dollar Change		
Percentage Change		

D. Actual and budget sales mix percentages for room , total food & beverage, and gift shop revenues.

	Actual Mix Percentage	Budget Mix Percentage
Room Revenue		
Food & Beverage Revenue		
Gift Shop Revenue		

E. Actual and budget Food & Beverage sales mix percentages for restaurant, beverage, and catering revenues.

	Actual Mix Percentage	Budget Mix Percentage
Restaurant Revenue		
Beverage Revenue		
Catering Revenue		

2. The following financial information is from the Darden Restaurants Annual Report:

	Sales Dollars	Mix Percentage	No. of Restaurants	Mix Percentage
Red Lobster	$2,430,000,000		673	
Olive Garden	$1,990,000,000		524	
Bahama Breeze	$ 138,000,000		34	
Smokey Bones	$ 93,000,000		39	
Totals				

A. What was the total annual sales and the number of total restaurants for Darden?
B. Calculate the sales mix percentage for the different Darden Restaurants.
C. Calculate the restaurant unit mix percentage for the different Darden Restaurants.

3. Following is the Revenue (in millions) from Continuing Operations from a recent Marriott International Annual Report:

	This Year	Mix%	Last Year	Mix%
Full-Service	$5,876		$5,508	
Select Service	$1,000		$ 967	
Extended Stay	$ 557		$ 600	
Time Share	$1,279		$1,147	
Totals	$8,712		$8,222	

A. Calculate the sales mix percentage for each market segment for this year and last year.
B. Calculate the percentage change in revenue for each segment for this year compared to last year.
C. What is the total Marriott revenue growth (percentage change) for this year compared to last year?

4. Calculate each cost percentage and the profit (Earnings Before Taxes) percentage for General Electric for the following years:

	This Year ($)	Last Year (%)	This Year ($)	Last Year (%)
Total Revenues	$134,187		$132,210	
Cost of Goods Sold	37,189		38,833	
Cost of Services Sold	14,017		14,023	
Interest, Financial Charges	10,432		10,216	
Other Costs and Expenses	52,645		50,247	
Total Costs	$114,283		$113,319	
Earning Before Taxes	$ 19,904		$ 18,891	

5. Questions 1–4 represented the second step in the Financial Management Cycle. The following questions represent the third step—analyzing the numbers.
   A. For the Lumberjack Hotel, discuss the actual January performance including dollar and percentage change. Include comparisons of actual with both the budget and the last year and identify the operating departments that improved or did not improve.
   B. For Darden Restaurants, explain what the mix percentages tell about the sales amounts and number of units for each restaurant concept.
   C. For Marriott International, which market segment increased their sales mix percent the most and which, if any, had a decrease in their mix percent.
   D. For General Electric, list the cost areas that resulted in productivity improvements and any that resulted in productivity declines for this year. Comment on all four cost areas as well as total costs. Why did the earnings percentage go up? Is that good or bad?

Accounting Department Organization and Operations

LEARNING OBJECTIVES

- To understand organization charts and how they define operational and accounting responsibilities.
- To understand how hotel accounting departments are organized and operate.
- To understand how restaurant accounting is organized and operates.

- To understand the difference between on property accounting and regional or corporate accounting.
- To learn how hospitality managers work with accounting departments and corporate offices in the preparation of financial statements.

CHAPTER OUTLINE

Introduction

Organization Charts
    Full Service Hotels
    Accounting Department
    Smaller or Select Service Hotels

Accounting Operations
in Full Service Hotels
    Accounting Department Operations
    Hotel Department Operations and
        Relationships with Accounting
    Monthly Preparation of Financial
        Reports

Accounting Operations
in Restaurants and Smaller
Hotels
    Financial Statement Preparation
    Purchasing and Inventories
    Wage and Cost Controls

Summary

Hospitality Manager Takeaways

Key Terms

Review Questions

Practice Exercises

INTRODUCTION

This chapter will discuss accounting structures for large hotels, small hotels, and chain restaurants with a focus on the organization and operation of accounting departments in full service hotels. **Full service hotels** are defined as hotels having from 250 to over 2,000 rooms and in addition providing sleeping rooms, operates food and beverage outlets, catering functions, and meeting room rentals, gift shops, valet laundry, health workout facilities, bellmen, concierge, and other services and amenities that are typically included in larger hotels. There are a wide range of hotels that are included in the full service category such as corporate hotels, airport hotels, suburban hotels, convention hotels, and resorts. Because of the wide range of activities and the large amounts of revenues and profits generated, full service hotels have accounting departments in the hotel to take care of all the accounting responsibilities.

Because smaller hotels and select service hotels do not offer their guests such a wide range of amenities and services, they do not require an onsite accounting department. Their accounting functions are coordinated by a regional or corporate accounting structure that includes a centralized accounting department that handles the accounting activities of the individual hotels. These hotels provide information at the end of the day to the corporate accounting office, which then prepares reports and other information and sends them back the next morning to the individual hotels for their use and review.

The accounting operations of chain restaurants are very similar to those of smaller hotels. A regional or corporate accounting office provides the accounting services for each individual restaurant. It is the responsibility of each restaurant to provide the operating information at the end of the day to the corporate accounting office. This office then prepares the necessary accounting statements and reports for the restaurant and sends back to them the next morning.

Independent operators of small hotels and individually owned restaurants will either do their own accounting or hire an outside accounting company to handle all accounting requirements and to prepare financial reports.

ORGANIZATION CHARTS

An **organization chart** is a diagram of the structure and relationships of a specific business unit. It can include job titles, **direct reporting** relationships, areas of responsibility, and lines of communication among different job levels. We will discuss several organization charts as we describe the role and relationships of accounting departments.

Full Service Hotels

Exhibit 3.1 contains two examples of organization charts for a full service hotel and a resort. It includes four levels of responsibility divided into two main types of business activities: *operating departments* and *staff departments*.

GENERAL MANAGER   This is the top level of authority and responsibility. The **General Manager** is responsible for all the different activities and operations of

EXHIBIT 3.1
FULL SERVICE HOTEL ORGANIZATION CHART

Example 1

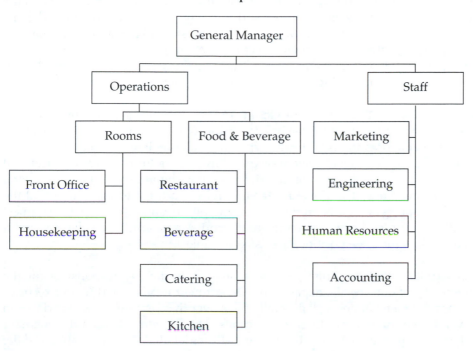

Example 2

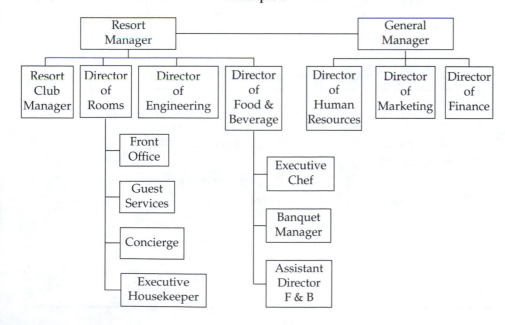

the hotel. The General Manager relies on specific senior managers to operate the separate and distinct operating departments in the hotel. These are divided into two areas. The **operating departments** have direct interaction with paying or external customers and generate revenue and profits for the hotel. There are generally two main departments in a full service hotel: the rooms department and the food and beverage department. A resort will have additional operating departments such as the golf course and the spa. The **staff departments** support the operating departments and their direct interaction is with internal customers—the operating department employees. Traditionally, there are four main departments: sales and marketing, human resources, engineering, and accounting.

EXECUTIVE COMMITTEE OR LEADERSHIP TEAM   The group of senior managers called the **Executive Committee** or Leadership Team has the direct responsibility for the overall operations of the departments under their leadership. They report to the General Manager. They are experts in their field of operations and will generally have over 10 years of experience of working in several hotels in several different positions. The General Manager relies on them to take care of all the detailed aspects of their operations including product and service delivery, guest relations, service levels, revenues and profits, and employee development. Typical titles for these positions are listed in Table 3.1.

DEPARTMENT HEADS   This group of managers is directly responsible for the operations of one specific department. **Department heads** report to an Executive Committee member and will generally have over five years of work experience in several hotels in several different positions. The Executive Committee member relies on department heads to take care of the detailed daily operations of the department. Examples of key hotel department heads are the Front Office Manager and Executive Housekeeper reporting to the Director of Rooms Operations and the Director of Restaurants and Director of Catering and Executive Chef reporting to the Director of Food and Beverage.

TABLE 3.1   Executive Committee Positions

Operations	Staff
Rooms	Sales & Marketing
Resident Manager or	Director of Sales & Marketing
Rooms Division Manager	Human Resources
Food & Beverage	Director of Human Resources
Food & Beverage Director	Engineering
	Director of Engineering or
	Chief Engineer
	Accounting
	Director of Finance or
	Controller

LINE MANAGERS   This group of managers actually run the departments. **Line managers** are the entry-level managers who have face-to-face interaction with the customers and are responsible for operating the different shifts of a hotel department and are divided into the a.m. or morning shift and the p.m. or afternoon/evening shift. They directly interact with the employees and the customers. They supervise and direct the employees in performing their specific responsibilities in taking care of and servicing guests. They also deal directly with guests in the normal department operations, take care of specific requests, and handle specific guest problems and complaints.

The line managers are typically entry-level managers or managers in their first management position. Part of their job responsibilities is to provide operational information to the accounting department such as wage schedules, payroll, purchasing, physical inventories, P&L statement critiques, and revenue forecasting. Examples of line managers are Assistant Front Desk Managers, Assistant Housekeeping Managers, Assistant Restaurant Managers, Assistant Catering Managers, and Kitchen Managers.

HOURLY EMPLOYEES OR ASSOCIATES   These are the employees who directly interact with paying or external customers to provide the expected products and services. Senior hourly employees can be promoted to Supervisory positions that give them added responsibilities. No group of employees is more important to an organization than the hourly employees who perform most of the work and ensure that organizational standards are met and processes are followed.

Hourly employees are often separated into employees who serve external customers and those who serve internal customers. **External customers** are paying customers who stay in hotels and eat in restaurants and pay for receiving those products and services. **Internal customers** are employees who receive the support of other company employees in performing their job responsibilities. Employees serving external customers interact directly with them providing the expected products and services. They also collect the money for the products and services provided and therefore deal with point of sale systems. Employees serving internal customers provide support to the employees who deal directly with paying customers. This support includes payroll and training, repair and maintenance, and accounting and financial functions.

The second example of a hotel organization chart shows a different example of the responsibilities and relationships in a resort. Note that the General Manager shares some of the primary operating responsibilities with the Resort Manager. The Resort Manager is responsible for the rooms, food and beverage, the main operating departments, resort club operations (time share or vacation club), and engineering. Note that there is also a difference in departments reporting to the Director of Rooms and Director of Food and Beverage. The Director of Human Resources, Director of Marketing, and Director of Finance along with the Resort Manager report directly to the General Manager.

This example offers a different way in which a hotel or resort can structure its operations. Each of these examples offers strengths and advantages depending on how the hotel chooses to operate. One is not necessarily better than the other, but just different.

Accounting Department

We will now discuss in detail the organization and structure of the Accounting Department. As we can see from the Hotel Organization Chart, the Accounting Department is one of the staff departments with the Director of Finance or Controller responsible for all accounting operations and reporting to the General Manager. The accounting staff includes both managers and hourly employees. Exhibit 3.2 is an Accounting Organization Chart for a typical full service hotel. Following are details about the positions and responsibilities of the accounting department.

DIRECTOR OF FINANCE/CONTROLLER   The Executive Committee member is responsible for all accounting department operations. While there is a group of employees who actually perform these responsibilities, the **Director of Finance** is responsible for ensuring that all accounting information for the hotel is accurate, correct, and conforms to generally accepted accounting principles. Specifically, the Director of Finance does the following:

1. Prepares the monthly financial statements, primarily the P&L Statement, and also reconciles the Balance Sheet (A&L) and the Statement of Cash Flows.
2. Supervises all activities of the different accounting functions.
3. Prepares the annual operating budget and the annual capital expenditure budget.
4. Analyzes and critiques all monthly financial statements and weekly revenue and wage forecasts.
5. Acts as a financial advisor to all hotel managers and their operations.
6. Coordinates all financial communications with regional and corporate accounting offices.
7. Prepares all financial statements and presentations for hotel owners.

ASSISTANT CONTROLLER INCOME AND OPERATIONS   The **Assistant Controller** is often a department head and oversees the various important aspects of accounting operations and their involvement with hotel department operations. His or her responsibilities include the following:

1. Assists the Director of Finance in hotel accounting activities including reconciling balance sheet accounts, preparing P&L critiques, capital expenditure accounting, weekly revenue and wage forecasts, productivity analysis, and any other activity requested by the Director of Finance.
2. Closes each month or accounting period and assists in the preparation of monthly P&L statements including adjusting balance sheet accounts, processing transfers, verifying physical inventories, and coordinating corporate entries.
3. Performs hotel audits.

EXHIBIT 3.2
ACCOUNTING OFFICE ORGANIZATION CHART

Example 1

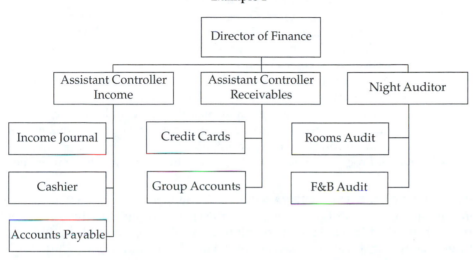

Example 2

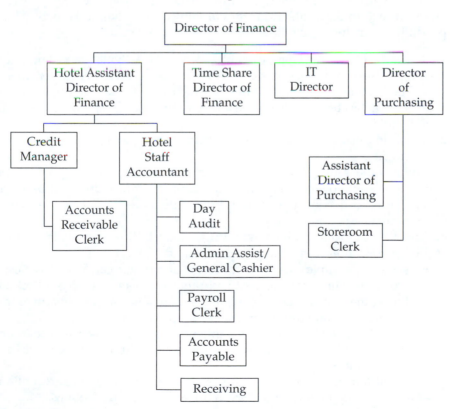

4. Assists Rooms and Food and Beverage operations managers.
5. Supervises accounting employees in the following activities:
   A. **Income Journal.** Records all hotel guest activity by revenues, customer counts, and average check for specific market segments and prepares daily, weekly, and monthly revenue reports.
   B. **General Cashier.** Handles all the cash operations of the hotel, including verifying department deposits, preparing daily hotel deposit, maintaining hotel change bank, assisting with department bank audits, and assisting with all cash handling activities.
   C. **Accounts Payable.** Processes the payment of all hotel purchases and invoices ensuring compliance with hotel purchasing procedures and coordination with operating departments. This includes proper coding of invoices to appropriate accounts, timely payments, maximizing discounts, and reconciling accounts payable balances.
   D. **Payroll.** Processes the payroll for hourly and management employees.

ASSISTANT CONTROLLER RECEIVABLES   This manager is responsible for the billing and collection of all revenues and accounts receivable due the hotel. **Accounts receivable** is the process of billing and collecting accounts settled after the guest or company has checked out of the hotel. It includes credit card billing and company direct billing.

They oversee several areas of billing and collection and are especially involved in group accounts at larger convention hotels and resorts. These responsibilities include the following:

1. Assists the Director of Finance in hotel accounting activities, including reconciling cash accounts (there could be many), reconciling credit card statements, and generating a positive cash flow for the hotel. These are very important responsibilities because they have a major impact on maximizing cash flow and liquidity for the hotel.
2. Assists in closing each month or accounting period and preparing financial statements.
3. Reviews the Aging Accounts to effectively manage current, 30–60-day, 60–90-day, and over 90-day accounts. Prepares information for bad debt write-offs and coordinates activities with collection agencies when necessary.
4. Coordinates group billings, including direct billing approvals, account preparation and review, and group account collection.
5. Supervises the employees in the following accounts receivable activities:
   A. Group Account Management including premeetings, account review during the group's stay in the hotel, and postmeetings to ensure proper authorization and processing of all group charges.
   B. Credit Card collection, including timely billing, processing, and collection of credit card payments. Reconciliation of all credit card charge backs and guest disputes.
   C. Credit Manager in proper credit review and approval for direct billing and preparing information for Credit and Write-Off Meetings.

NIGHT/DAY AUDITOR   The Night/Day Auditor is responsible for the processing and auditing of all accounting and operational information for each day. Traditionally, this function was performed on the all-night shift from 11:00 p.m. to 7:00 a.m. With the advances in technology, this function can now be completed in the morning by balancing POS information and running reports. They were also responsible for operating the all-night or 11:00 p.m.–7:00 a.m. front desk shift. These responsibilities include the following:

1. Records and balances all the day's transactions for each department of the hotel. This includes room revenues, food and beverage revenues, catering and meetings revenues, gift shop revenues, and any other revenue generated by other department.
2. Rolls the date after all accounting transactions are audited and in balance. This means closing all the information for the previous date and setting up all the information and systems for the next day.
3. Prepares daily management reports including daily revenue reports, discrepancy reports, and the next day guest reservations.
4. Ensures that all guests checking in and out of the hotel are taken care of efficiently.
5. Supervises the employees in the following auditing activities:
   A. Rooms revenue posting and auditing.
   B. Food, Beverage, and Banquet revenue posting and auditing.
   C. Front desk clerks in front desk operations.

Smaller or Select Service Hotels

Smaller hotels do not generate the volume and range of revenues and expenses as full-service hotels do and generally do not require an on property accounting office. If they are part of a national hotel chain, the General Manager or the owner will have the responsibility of providing daily operational information to the corporate accounting office, who will then process the information into reports and return to the hotel for their information and use.

If the hotel is privately owned, the owners will either assume the responsibility for all accounting information and reports or will hire an outside accounting service to provide these services for them. Because these are privately owned, they do not have many reporting requirements and regulations. They do need to meet state and local tax reporting requirements.

INDIVIDUAL RESTAURANTS   Individual restaurants that are part of national chains have similar accounting relationships and reporting procedures as small chain hotels. Each individual restaurant is responsible for providing daily operating and accounting information to the corporate office, which processes the information and returns the reports the following day to the restaurant for their use. It is the responsibility of the night restaurant manager to ensure that all revenue, payroll, and other operating information are transferred to the regional accounting office at the end of the day. It is the responsibility of the opening restaurant manager to ensure that the reports of the previous day have been received and to review those reports and ensure that they are accurate. With the privately owned restaurant, the same accounting responsibilities and relationships exist as that for individually owned restaurants.

Otesaga Hotel and Resort

The Otesaga Hotel and Resort is located in Cooperstown, New York, on the banks of Lake Otesego. It opened in 1909 with 179 guest rooms and now has 135 guest rooms, 5 food & beverage outlets, 13,000 square feet of meeting space, and an 18-hole golf course. The Otesaga offers meal packages that include breakfast and dinner in the room rate. The resort has very busy summer and fall seasons because of the Baseball Hall of Fame and the beauty of the surrounding mountains and lakes, especially in the fall with the color of the fall foliage. The Otesaga closes for approximately five months during the winter each year.

Visit the Otesaga website at www.otesaga.com and look at the different departments and activities that this resort offers. How will they be organized to cover operations and have financial accountability? Answer the following questions:

1. Draw the organization chart for the Otesaga Resort Hotel, including the Executive Committee that reports to the General Manager and the different department heads that report to the Executive Committee members.
2. With 135 rooms, would you recommend one Director of Operations or would you distribute those responsibilities between the Director of Rooms Operations and the Director of Food and Beverage? Why?
3. To whom would you have the Director of Golf reporting to and why?
4. What management positions do you think are for 12 months and what positions do you think will be seasonal or for 7 months only?

Photo Courtesy of the Otesaga Hotel, Cooperstown, New York.

ACCOUNTING OPERATIONS IN FULL SERVICE HOTELS

The **accounting department** is a staff department that supports all other staff and operating departments in the hotel with regard to accounting procedures and hotel operations. It works with these departments to provide services and information that will assist them in operating their departments on a daily basis.

Accounting Department Operations

The Accounting Department records and processes the previous day's hotel activities. Refer to the Accounting Office Organization Chart in Exhibit 3.2. Each day the individual sections within the Accounting Office receive the paperwork and record or process the information to update accounts and prepare reports. Consider the following examples:

INCOME ACCOUNTING   The **Income Journal** records the previous day's revenues in the appropriate account. Room revenues, rooms sold, and average room rates are recorded in individual accounts (or market segments) for Transient, Group, and Contract. This includes the previous day's revenue and rooms sold and the month-to-date revenue and rooms sold. The same process is used for recording Breakfast, Lunch and Dinner revenues; customer counts for a restaurant; and Breakfast, Lunch, Dinner, Coffee Breaks, Receptions, Meeting Room Rental, and

Audio Video for the Catering Department. Beverage revenues are recorded in Liquor, Beer, Wine, and Soft Drink accounts.

The Income Journal also records and balances the method of payment for each account. For example, Total Room Sales must equal or balance with cash receipts, credit card payments, and company or personal checks in payment of direct billings. This balancing function is very important because it ensures that the revenue recorded equals the money received.

Recorded Revenues	= Method of Payment
Transient Room Revenues	Cash Payments
+ Group Room Revenues	+ Credit Card Payments
+ Contract Room Revenues	+ Check Payments
	+ Direct Billing
= Total Room Revenues	= Total Receipts and Deposits

Here is an example for a typical day.

Transient Room Revenues	$12,500	Cash Receipts	$ 1,600
Group Room Revenues	$ 4,800	Credit Card Payments	$10,400
Contract Room Revenues	$ 1,200	Check Payments	$ 2,500
		Direct Billing	$ 4,000
= Total Room Revenues	$18,500	= Total Receipts/Deposits	$18,500

GENERAL CASHIER   The daily functions of the **General Cashier** are to collect, balance, and consolidate all the operating department deposits into one deposit for the hotel that goes to the bank each day. The General Cashier will balance all the cash and checks in each deposit to the same amounts posted for that day in the Income Journal account. In our example, the daily hotel deposit prepared by the General Cashier should be $4,100—the amount of cash and checks collected for the day (Cash receipts of $1,600 + Check payments of $2,500).

The credit card payments and direct billing are not part of the hotel deposit until the actual checks are received. In our example, the credit card sales of $10,400 for the day will generally be received within 24 hours via electronic transfer directly into the hotel's cash bank account and will not be a part of any hotel deposit. The direct billing of $4,000 should be received within 30 days and the actual check would then be added to the days deposit on the day that it is received.

The General Cashier also maintains a change bank for the hotel. This consists of keeping an adequate supply of coin and small currencies—$1, $5, and $10 bills to be used by the hotel departments in making change for their customers. The General Cashier will send a change order to the bank at the same time the deposit goes to the bank. This change order will include larger currencies of $20, $50, and $100 bills deposited by the hotel to the bank that will be exchanged for the smaller currencies and coins such as $1 and $5 bills and returned to the hotel the next day.

ACCOUNTS PAYABLE   Each day, the Accounts Payable Clerk will receive invoices to be paid. The procedures for paying invoices will include a manager's signature confirming the accuracy of the invoice and authorizing its payment, the amount to be paid, the due date that it needs to be paid by, and the account that it will be coded or charged to. It is the accounts payable clerk's responsibility to verify this information before writing the check.

Accounts payable checks are generally written during the week and mailed once a week or on a daily basis to take advantage of discounts and to meet due dates. Much of this process is now done electronically on computers and part of the accounts payable clerk's responsibility is to review and check the payments for accuracy and to ensure they balance to the backup documentation.

ACCOUNTS RECEIVABLE   Each day, the Accounts Receivable Clerk receives all the direct billing accounts to be processed for collection. Direct billing is when a company has been preapproved to have their bill sent to them at the end of the function, with payment being expected within 30 days from check-out. The two main categories of accounts receivable are credit cards and direct billing.

The credit card documentation for the day includes totals for each credit card. Individual guest room accounts are closed out or transferred to a credit card master account when the guest checks out. For example, the hotel might have 10 guests owing $1,800 who pay their accounts by American Express. These 10 individual room accounts are zeroed out and transferred to the American Express master account and sent to Accounts Receivable for processing. Another 15 guests might pay with Visa or Master Charge for $4,600 and $4,000, respectively. In our example the total credit card billings of $10,400 for the day become $10,400 of credit card receipts the following day when the funds electronically transferred from each credit card company are received directly into the hotel's bank account.

The direct billing of $4,000 will be monitored by accounts receivable personnel to ensure that there are no problems in the process and that the company being billed will review, approve, and issue the check for payment in a timely manner. When the check is received, it will be added to that day's deposit.

The accounts receivable department also handles guest disputes and problems. Credit card charge backs occur when a guest disputes the charge on his or her credit card. Accounts receivable will research the problem and provide proper documentation such as signatures and guest checks that verify that the charge is valid and correct and return to the credit card company so that they will rebill the customer.

NIGHT/DAY AUDIT   The Night/Day Auditor and his staff receive, audit, reconcile, and balance the day's transactions and prepare daily reports that report total revenues, update accounts, and ensure that all the day's transactions balance and are correct. A big challenge for the Night Auditor and his staff is to research and find problems or mistakes and properly correct them in a timely manner. They have to do this during the all-night shift when neither employees nor managers are available to answer questions or assist in finding and correcting mistakes. They must rely on their ability to research the paperwork and transactions to find out what actually happened and how to make the necessary corrections.

The advances in POS systems and accounting information systems have changed the role of night audit. The amount of detail, speed, and the ability to quickly and efficiently reconcile and balance accounting information that modern accounting systems provide have replaced the need for most night audit employees. Auditing and balancing functions are now completed by the accounting system and night audit has really become a day audit where the accounting reports and checklists are reviewed in the morning by the night auditor or other accounting staff members. Therefore, day audits are now a common occurrence.

Hotel Department Operations and Relationships with Accounting

Each operating department in the hotel has the responsibility of providing the required products and services to the customer following established hotel policies and procedures. The accounting department assists these departments in following appropriate procedures. Following are examples of how an operating department might interact with the accounting department:

FRONT OFFICE   Managers in the Front Office department will work with the Income Journal Clerk by reviewing the daily room revenue information recorded in the Income Journal. They can look at average room rates by market segment, rooms sold by market segments, and any adjustments to revenues in reviewing the previous day's operations. They can compare actual sales with forecasted, budgeted, and last year's sales. They constantly work with the General Cashier by requesting change for front desk cashiers, helping to research any cash handling problems such as shortages in banks or deposits, and processing or reimbursing petty cash requests. They work with the Accounts Payable Clerk by forwarding invoices for payments, checking on account numbers, researching invoice problems, and generally ensuring that all invoices approved for payment are correct. They handover the day's work to the Night Auditor at 11:00 p.m. to take care of any remaining guests to check in and to begin the process of auditing the day's work.

RESTAURANT AND CATERING   Managers in the restaurants and catering departments work with the accounting office in much the same way as the Front Office managers. Instead of market segments, these managers are interested in meal period information (breakfast, lunch, and dinner) to analyze their sales. The rest of their interactions are the same as the Front Office managers.

STAFF DEPARTMENTS   The Sales and Marketing, Human Resources, and Engineering departments primarily interact with the Accounts Payable Clerk in processing invoices for payment. Because these departments have no revenues, they do not have any direct interaction with the Income Journal Clerk or the General Cashier.

Monthly Preparation of Financial Reports

We need to refer back to the four steps in the Financial Analysis Cycle presented in Chapter 1.

1. Operations produce the numbers.
2. Accounting prepares the numbers.
3. Accounting and hotel management analyze the numbers.
4. Hotel management applies the numbers to operations to change and improve.

In the previous chapters we have discussed the first step: Operations produces the numbers. In this chapter we discuss the second step: Accounting prepares the numbers.

Hotels or restaurants will prepare either monthly or 28-day accounting period financial statements or operating reports. The process is the same for both. The difference is the time period covered. The monthly reports are prepared at the end of each month and include operating results for 28, 30, or 31 days depending on the month. While this makes for consistent comparison to the same month for a previous year, there are some problems with comparing results to the previous month as the compared month might be of greater or lesser number of days. For example, comparing February, March, and April results will involve 28 days, 31 days, and 30 days, respectively, of operating results. Comparing these three months will require some adjustment such as calculating daily averages to make the comparison more meaningful.

Accounting periods all have 28 days, 4 weeks, and start on the same day each period. There are 13 accounting periods in a year all with the same number of days in each period. This makes comparisons to previous periods or years consistent. Each week in an accounting period always begins on the same day, ends on the same day, and involves the same number of days. For example, a work week will begin on Saturday and end on Friday. However, monthly financial statements are more common. The 13 accounting periods include only 364 days, so there has to be an adjustment every seven years to get back to an end of the year close to December 31.

Regardless of whether a company is on a monthly or an accounting period basis, the process of closing the books and preparing the financial statements is generally the same. For consistency purposes, we will talk about monthly closings. The process of closing the month will include the following activities:

1. *Preclosing Information.*   Several days before the end of the month, invoices, physical inventories, and transfers documenting adjustment entries will be due to the accounting office. This gives everyone time to review and check the numbers reported for accuracy. If there is a problem, there is time to recheck the information.
2. *Month or Period End.*   This is the first day of the next month. The accounting office goes through a process of closing out all the hotel accounts and posts entries for the previous month. For example, in the Income Journal, the cumulative sales recorded for the month are totaled, balanced and verified, and then closed. The Income Journal for the next month will then be opened and all the income or revenue accounts will be set up for the new month. The accounts payable clerk will verify with hotel managers that all invoices that should be

paid for and charged to that month have been received, processed, and inventoried so that there will be a clean and consistent cut-off for the month.

Once the necessary operating information is received from all the departments, the accounting office verifies the information and enters it into the proper accounts on the proper reports. The main report is the monthly P&L Statement. All accounting entries that reflect hotel revenues and expenses for the month must be entered in the proper account on the monthly P&L statement. This includes entries to adjust accounts on the Balance Sheet so that the balances on the accounting books equal the balances of physical inventories or computer reports. The monthly P&L statement already has the budget and last year's information and the month end closing collects and reports the actual information for the current month.

3. *Post Closing Review.*   The first draft of the monthly P&L statement is available within one or two days. The Director of Finance and Assistant Controllers then review the information to correct mistakes or make allocations and adjust entries to finalize the information on the P&L statement. While this is primarily an accounting function, the accounting managers will be talking with hotel managers to ensure that any corrections that need to be made are proper and accurate. When these entries are completed and entered into the computer system, the final monthly P&L statement is generated. This P&L statement will include the current month results and Year-to-Date (YTD) financial results.

ACCOUNTING OPERATIONS IN RESTAURANTS AND SMALLER HOTELS

The accounting operations of restaurants and smaller, select service hotels are handled in a similar manner. Chain restaurants like Red Lobster and Chili's as well as select service hotels like Fairfield Inn and Hampton Inn are examples of this type of operation. The size and range of operations does not warrant an on-site accounting office. Therefore, these operations utilize regional or corporate accounting offices to provide required accounting functions.

The accounting process in these operations is based on daily communication with the **corporate accounting office,** which is a central location that provides accounting support and services for individual hotels or restaurants operated by the company. The operating results at the end of the day are transmitted to the corporate accounting office where it is processed and returned the next day in reports to the hotel or restaurant. It is the General Manager's responsibility to ensure that required operating information is submitted in a timely and accurate manner. While the General Manager can delegate this responsibility to his managers, it is ultimately his responsibility to see that all procedures are followed and that the transactions are processed correctly.

Financial Statement Preparation

At the end of each day, the restaurant or hotel will close out the day's operating information accumulated in their point-of-sale (POS) system. This will include meal period revenues, customer counts, wage costs, purchases, and any other expenses for the day. The P.M. or the closing manager has the responsibility of ensuring that all the day's operating information is sent at the end of each day. The corporate accounting office collects, summarizes, and reports the information and returns it to the restaurant the next morning. The next day, the A.M. or the opening manager will review the information for accuracy and completeness and make any necessary corrections. This daily information also includes month-to-date information, which is used by the restaurant managers in operating their restaurants.

A similar process is followed at the end of the month for the monthly closing. This process also involves taking physical inventories, verifying revenue and wage information, and ensuring the accuracy of the month-end cut-off date. The corporate accounting office prepares the monthly P&L statement and any other trend or summary reports and returns it to the restaurant generally in three to five days.

Customer counts and revenues are forecasted each week for the next two weeks. These forecasts update the budget for the upcoming weeks and are based on the current business conditions that the restaurant is experiencing. These forecasts are used to schedule wages and determine purchase quantities.

Purchasing and Inventories

Food, beverage, and operating supplies are generally ordered weekly through a centralized purchasing system. This computer program contains inventory level status, established par levels, and daily and weekly consumption amounts, prices, order quantities, and other pertinent purchasing information. The restaurant manager responsible for this function ensures that all the pricing and paperwork are complete and accurate, verifies delivery quantities, prices and invoices, conducts month end physical inventories, and processes invoices for payment.

While it is an advantage to have a sophisticated purchasing system to use, it is the manager's responsibility to ensure that all the information submitted is accurate. This requires a knowledge of restaurant standards and operations, accounting process, and the importance of current and ongoing communication with the corporate accounting office to ensure that the system is working as it is intended.

Wage and Cost Controls

Along with food costs, wage and benefit costs are the largest and most important expenses to be controlled in operating a restaurant. Wage costs are reviewed daily to ensure productivity standards are met and overtime and waste are minimized. This process starts with the preparation of the next week's wage schedule based on the average volumes and employee man-hours for the last several weeks. Relationships between guest counts and man-hours are established and used to schedule and control wage costs.

The wage department in a restaurant can be divided into service, bar and hostess, and kitchen or heart of the house. Wage standards are established for each of these departments and then the wage schedules are prepared for the next week based on forecasted customer counts. An additional part of managing wage costs is controlling overtime. Each overtime man-hour generally includes a 50% premium, or in other words, an overtime man-hour will cost 50% more than a regular man-hour. For example, a cook making $10.00 per hour will be paid $15.00 per hour for any hours worked above the typical 40-hour work week.

Another reason why controlling wage costs is so important is that for every wage dollar, there is an associated benefit expense. Most companies provide benefits to their hourly and management employees. This cost is split between the company and the employees. Typically, a company can pay 20%–40% in benefit cost for every wage dollar. This means that for every wage dollar paid, the restaurant will have to pay an additional 20–40 cents to pay the benefit costs to the employee. Unless a restaurant is effectively controlling wage costs, it will not be able to effectively control benefit costs.

Summary

The Accounting Department or Office in a hotel supports and assists the other staff departments and the operating departments. It interacts daily with these departments, exchanging information, assisting with problems, and preparing daily, weekly, and monthly management reports to be used by all the departments in their daily operations.

An organization chart presents and describes the responsibilities and relationships provided by a department or business unit. The Accounting Department Organization Chart shows the different management levels and the functions or activities that the departments are responsible for. The typical management structure in the accounting office for a full service hotel includes the Director of Finance, Assistant Controller, Night/Day Auditor, and the hourly employees. The accounting functions are divided into the income responsibilities, account receivable responsibilities, and night/day audit responsibilities.

The accounting department provides important assistance to the other departments in the hotel. The operating departments provide operating information to accounting and accounting prepares financial information for the use of other department managers. The relationship between accounting and operating departments can be linked back to the Financial Management Cycle. The first step is operations produce the numbers; in our industry, it is the rooms, food and beverage, and other staff departments. The second step is accounting prepares the numbers. And that is what we have talked about in this chapter. Without operations, accounting would have no information to prepare and report.

Small hotels and individual restaurants rely on corporate or regional accounting offices to provide all accounting services. Each hotel or restaurant sends operating information at the end of the day to the centralized Accounting Office, which records the information and prepares reports that are sent back the next day to the hotel or restaurant. Accurate and timely communications are essential to the successful operation of these systems.

Hospitality Manager Takeaways

1. The Accounting Office offers support and assistance to all hotel managers. Employees in the Accounting Office take the operational information from the hotel departments and prepare accounting reports and financial statements to be used as a management tool and to measure financial performance.
2. Hospitality managers have to know what operating information they need to provide the Accounting Department with so that the two departments can work together in analyzing and applying the financial information for improving hotel operations.
3. Hospitality managers need to understand how organization charts define operational and financial responsibilities.

Key Terms

Accounting department: a staff department that supports all other staff and operating departments in the hotel with regard to accounting procedures and hotel operations.

Accounts payable: the process of approving invoices and issuing checks in payment for products and goods received by a hotel or restaurant.

Accounting period: a 28-day time period that can be used instead of calendar months to prepare management reports and financial statements covering hotel operations.

Accounts receivable: the process of billing and collecting accounts settled after the guest or company has checked out of the hotel. It includes credit card billing and company direct billing.

Assistant Controller: a manager in the accounting office who reports to the Director of Finance and oversees specific functions in the accounting office, either Income Operations or Accounts Receivable.

Corporate Accounting Office: a central location that provides accounting support and services for individual hotels or restaurants operated by the company.

Department Head: a manager that has direct responsibility for the operations of a specific hotel department. Department Heads report to an Executive Committee Member and have line managers and supervisors reporting to them.

Direct report: the managers or positions that report directly to a specific management position.

Director of Finance: the Executive Committee Member directly responsible for all accounting operations in a hotel, sometimes referred to as the Controller.

Executive Committee: the members of senior management who report directly to the General Manager and have responsibility for several specific hotel departments. Department Heads report to an Executive Committee Member.

External customer: paying customers who stay in hotels and eat in restaurants and pay money for receiving those products and services.

Full service hotels: hotels with generally more than 200 rooms that operate food and beverage outlets, catering functions and meeting room rentals, gift shops, valet laundry, health workout facilities, bellmen, and other services and amenities.

General Cashier: the position that collects, balances, and consolidates all the operating department deposits into one deposit for the hotel that goes to the bank each day.

General Manager: the senior manager in the hotel who is responsible for all hotel operations. All positions and activities are the responsibility of this person.

Income journal: the section of the accounting office that is involved in recording income, processing deposits, paying expenses, and assisting other hotel managers.

Internal customers: employees who receive the support of other company employees in performing their job responsibilities. For example, all employees are internal customers for the human resource department, which administers benefits, processes payroll, and conducts training programs for their internal customers—all employees.

Line manager: the entry-level management position who has face-to-face interaction with the customers and is responsible for leading employees in operating the different shifts of a hotel department.

Operating department: a hotel department that records revenues and produces profits by providing products and services to paying customers or guests.

Organization chart: describes the reporting relationships, responsibilities, and operating activities for a department or business unit.

Staff Department: a hotel department that provides assistance and support to the hotel operating departments. They have internal customers.

Review Questions

1. Name the two operating departments and the four staff departments in a full service hotel.
2. Identify three areas of the accounting office and describe their duties and responsibilities.
3. Which specific management position is responsible for delivering products and services everyday to the guest?
4. Which management position is responsible for the overall operations of a hotel?
5. Describe the operations and responsibilities of a corporate accounting office.
6. Identify three types of operating/financial information that a corporate accounting office returns daily to a restaurant for their review and use.
7. Which is the most important financial report for hotel department managers that is prepared monthly by the accounting department?
8. Explain the differences, advantages, and disadvantages of monthly P&L statement to 28-day accounting period P&L statement.

Practice Exercises

1. Based on the examples provided, draw an organization chart for a 100-room select service hotel. To help yourself in this exercise, identify the different operations in a hotel of this size and then draw the organization chart based on these operations or departments.
2. Assume that you are going to open your own 100 seat restaurant and bar. Draw the organization chart that you would use to set up your restaurant. Be sure to identify specific departments, the different levels of management that would be responsible for these departments, and who they would report to.
3. What are the main differences in the organization chart of a 600-room full service hotel compared to a 100-room select service hotel?

CHAPTER

4

The Profit and Loss Statement (P&L)

LEARNING OBJECTIVES

- To understand the information contained in a Consolidated Profit and Loss (P&L) Statement.
  - A. Revenue and Profit Centers
  - B. Expense Centers or Support Costs
  - C. Fixed Expenses and Costs
  - D. Fees and Other Deductions
- To understand the different profit measures contained in a Consolidated P&L and a Department P&L and what they mean.

- To become familiar with the different formats for Consolidated P&Ls.
- To understand the information contained in Department P&Ls.
- To understand the four main expense categories of Department P&Ls.
- To understand how the financial information on a Consolidated P&L and a Departmental P&L is used as a management tool and to measure financial performance.

CHAPTER OUTLINE

INTRODUCTION

This is the most important chapter in the book for a hospitality manager. The Profit and Loss Statement (P&L) is the financial statement that hospitality managers need to understand completely. It is the financial statement that they will use to measure the financial performance of their department and use as a management tool to monitor and improve the daily operations of their departments. The Department P&L provides a way for the managers to measure specific components of the financial performance of their departments by comparing the actual monthly operations to the budget established for the month, to the most recent forecast, to last year's monthly performance, and to the previous month's performance.

The P&L is the financial report that involves hotel managers in all four steps of the Financial Management Cycle.

First, the department managers or **department heads** operate the departments that provide products and services to customers and produces the numbers—revenues, expenses, and profits. Second, the department managers ensure that the numbers that are submitted to accounting are accurate and consistent so that the financial reports prepared by accounting are accurate and useful. Third, the department managers must be able to understand, analyze, and discuss their department operating numbers to determine how well hotel operations are meeting the desired goals, including budgets and forecasts. This includes providing critiques and details of operations that can assist them and accounting managers in determining the best or the next course of action to be taken to correct or improve the operations of their departments. Fourth, the department managers are those who have the responsibility of applying the numbers back to operations by implementing changes for improvement or corrections to solve problems.

The P&L also provides information that is connected to both the Balance Sheet (A&L) and the Statement of Cash Flow. Hospitality managers who understand these relationships will be able to use these financial statements more effectively in operating their departments.

HOTEL CONSOLIDATED P&L STATEMENTS

The Consolidated P&L Statement or Income Statement for a hotel is a summary P&L that lists the department totals for Revenue Centers, Profit Centers, and Expense Centers. Only the department totals for revenues, profits, and expenses are included in the Consolidated P&L. It is a true summary report showing the important financial results for each department in the hotel.

Revenue Centers and Profit Centers

Both of these names refer to operating departments that produce revenues (sales) and profits. The terms *revenue* and *sales* are interchangeable. The terms revenue centers and profit centers are also interchangeable. **Revenue Centers** are operating departments that produce revenues by providing products and services directly to customers. It includes only revenues. **Profit Centers** are operating departments that produce revenues that result in a profit (or loss) by providing products and services to customers. It includes revenues, expenses, and profits. Specifically, these departments provide products and serviced to the customers who pay for these services. Employees record the sales on cash registers or point-of-sale computer systems (POS). That is why these operating departments are referred to as Revenue Centers. They receive and record revenues from customers. Examples of Revenue Centers in full-service hotels are the Rooms Department, Restaurants, Lounges, Catering and Banquets, Gift Shop, and Telephone Departments. Resorts have additional Revenue Centers such as golf, spas, tennis, and recreation. See Exhibit 4.1 for an example of Revenue Centers in a Consolidated P&L.

Exhibit 4.1 shows the revenue for the current period and year-to-date (YTD) for the Revenue Centers of the hotel. This part of the Consolidated P&L only records and reports revenues. A quick review of the financial results for the current period shows that the hotel actual sales of $161,000 was $2,000 over budget and $13,000 over last year. It is a good financial performance when actual results exceed the current budget and the last year's performance. The hotel's actual performance YTD is also exceeding the current budget and the last year's performance—actual revenue of $1,020,000 to a budget of $975,000 and last year's results of $950,000 YTD.

EXHIBIT 4.1
SAMPLE REVENUE CENTERS OF A CONSOLIDATED P&L

Flagstaff Hotel
Consolidated P&L Statement
June 30, 2009
(000)

Current Period*				Year-to-Date*		
Actual	Budget	Last Year		Actual	Budget	Last Year
$100	$102	$ 95	Room Revenues	$ 675	$640	$625
6	6	5	Telephone Revenues	34	35	34
8	7	7	Gift Shop Revenues	41	41	39
3	3	3	Miscellaneous Revenues	18	18	18
15	15	14	Restaurant Revenues	73	71	70
6	6	6	Beverage Revenues	29	30	29
23	20	18	Banquet Revenues	150	140	135
$ 44	$ 41	$ 38	Subtotal F&B Revenues	$ 252	$241	$234
$161	$159	$148	Total Hotel Revenues	$1,020	$975	$950

*Numbers are reported in thousands of dollars or (000).

The next section of the Consolidated P&L shows the profits generated by the Revenue Centers after all department operating expenses are paid. The direct costs of operating each Revenue Center are charged to each department and the detail is shown by line account in the Department P&L. The total expenses are subtracted from the total revenues to produce total department profit for each Revenue Center. The Consolidated P&L contains two entries for each Revenue Center: total revenues and total profits. That is why the two terms are interchangeable—revenue center or profit center. Both terms refer to operating departments that produce revenues and profits. In Exhibit 4.2, Department

EXHIBIT 4.2
SAMPLE REVENUE AND PROFIT CENTERS OF A CONSOLIDATED P&L

Flagstaff Hotel
Consolidated P&L Statement
June 30, 2009
(000)

Current Period*				Year-to-Date*		
Actual	Budget	Last Year		Actual	Budget	Last Year
$100	$102	$ 95	Room Revenues	$ 675	$640	$625
6	6	5	Telephone Revenues	34	35	34
8	7	7	Gift Shop Revenues	41	41	39
3	3	3	Miscellaneous Revenues	18	18	18
15	15	14	Restaurant Revenues	73	71	70
6	6	6	Beverage Revenues	29	30	29
23	20	18	Banquet Revenues	150	140	135
$ 44	$ 41	$ 38	Subtotal F&B Revenues	$ 252	$241	$234
$161	$159	$148	Total Hotel Revenues	$1,020	$975	$950

*Revenues are reported in thousands of dollars or (000).

Current Period*				Year-to-Date*		
Actual	Budget	Last Year		Actual	Budget	Last Year
			Department Profits			
$66	$67	$63	Rooms Profits	$439	$416	$406
1	1	1	Telephone Profits	6	6	6
2	2	2	Gift Shop Profits	11	10	10
3	3	3	Miscellaneous Profits	18	18	18
2	2	2	Restaurant Profits	12	12	11
2	2	2	Beverage Profits	12	12	12
8	7	6	Banquet Profits	53	49	47
$12	$11	$10	Subtotal F&B Profits	$ 77	$ 73	$ 70
$84	$84	$79	Total Hotel Department Profits	$551	$523	$510

*Numbers are reported in thousands of dollars or (000).

Profits are added to Department Revenues and are examples of how Department Profits are shown on a Hotel Consolidated P&L.

The profit section of the Consolidated P&L shows the Department Profit for each Revenue Center. The profit numbers include all revenues less expenses for each department for the current period and the YTD. A review of the Total Hotel Department Profits of $84,000 for the period shows that they are equal to the budget of $84,000 and $5,000 over last year's actual of $79,000. The amount of $551,000 of YTD profits is $28,000 over budget and $41,000 over last year. Again, these are good YTD financial results because the hotel's actual profits are over the budget and over that of last year's actual.

Expense Centers and Support Costs

Expense Centers are the staff departments in a hotel that support the hotel operating departments and include Sales & Marketing, Human Resources, Engineering, and Accounting. They can also be called **deductions from income** or **support costs**. These departments do not generate any revenue or profit. Their budget only includes expenses, which is why they are called Expense Centers. Also, they only include total department expenses on the Consolidated P&L. These expenses are the total of wage expenses, benefit expenses, and direct operating expenses for each staff department. Exhibit 4.3 is an example of the Expense Centers on a Consolidated P&L.

Three of these Expense Centers are based on allocations. They are Accidents, Training, and National Sales and Marketing. **Allocation** means that a set dollar amount or percent of sales dollar amount is charged to these departments each

EXHIBIT 4.3
SAMPLE EXPENSE CENTERS OF A CONSOLIDATED P&L

Flagstaff Hotel
Consolidated P&L Statement
June 30, 2009
(000)

Current Period*				Year-to-Date*		
Actual	Budget	Last Year		Actual	Budget	Last Year
$12	$12	$11	Administrative (G&A)	$ 71	$ 72	$ 71
7	7	6	Utilities	43	42	40
15	15	15	Repairs and Maintenance (R&M)	92	90	88
4	4	4	Accident Expense	25	25	24
2	2	2	Training and Relocation	12	12	12
21	20	19	Sales and Marketing	160	153	149
$61	$60	$57	Total Expense Center Costs or Total Supports Costs	$403	$394	$384

*Numbers are in thousands of dollars (000).

month. The money goes into a corporate account and is used to cover company or national programs. For example, in the Accident Department, a company might have one insurance policy that covers all hotels. The company allocates or charges each hotel the appropriate amount to cover both employees and guests insurance premiums, accident reserves, and the actual accident expenses for the specific hotel. Another example is the training allocation that pays for a Corporate Training Department that provides training to all the hotels. Also, the National Sales and Marketing allocation collects money from each hotel that is used at the corporate level to pay for national advertising and promotional campaigns and to pay for regional or national sales offices.

The rest of the Expense Centers include the wage, benefit, and direct operating expenses for the department. There is an Executive Committee Member in charge of each department and they are responsible for managing all department expenses and ensuring that they are productive and within the established budget (see organization charts in Chapter 3).

Fixed Costs, Fees, and Other Deductions

The last major expense category on the Consolidated P&L are the **Fixed Expenses**, also known as other **deductions**. These expenses are constant or fixed and are not affected by hotel volume levels or activity. They are the result of contracts, bank loans, fees, some taxes, and insurance policies. Often these costs are determined for the year and spread over each month in equal amounts. Examples of fixed accounts are lease expenses, bank loans, insurance costs, licenses and fees, and depreciation. Hotel management has very little, if any, control over these expenses. They are already set and have to be paid for out of hotel revenues regardless of whether the hotel is having a good month or year or a bad month or year.

These fixed amounts can be very large and difficult to pay unless the hotel is operating at high revenue levels. During slow months or low seasons, these amounts remain the same or fixed and must still be paid. These are the difficult times for a hotel. However, when a hotel is very busy and revenues and profits are increasing, these expenses do not go up but remain constant or fixed. So when the hotel is doing well, Fixed Expenses are more easily paid and should result in higher profits. When the hotel is not doing well, there is less money available to pay the Fixed Expenses and generally results in lower profits.

Hotel Profit Levels

There are several levels of profits in a hotel, each measuring a specific aspect of hotel performance. Each Executive Committee Member is responsible for specific departments and performances. The profit terms can change from company to company, but the concepts and formulas are the same. We will discuss Department Profits, Total Department Profit, House Profit, Net House Profit, and Profit after Taxes.

DEPARTMENT PROFITS The formula for **Department Profits** is revenue minus expenses equal profit. The Consolidated P&L records the revenues and profits for each operating department. The Resident Manager or Director of Rooms Operations is responsible for the overall operations of the Rooms Department and profit and the Director of Food & Beverage is responsible for overall operations of the Restaurant, Beverage, and Banquet Department and profit. A Department Head has the direct responsibility for the profits of his or her department. The Executive Committee Member and Department Head with his or her management and hourly employees can control and manage all the revenues and expenses for their departments.

TOTAL DEPARTMENT PROFITS   The formula for **Total Department Profits** is adding up and totaling the Department Profits for each operating department in the hotel. The Total Department Profits amount identifies the total profit dollars produced by the Profit Centers and in our example measures the management performance of the Resident Manager and Director of Food and Beverage in maximizing the profits for their departments. Total Department Profit is the dollar amount available to pay all other hotel expenses.

HOUSE PROFIT   Also called gross operating profit, the formula for **House Profit** is Total Department Profit minus Total Expense Center or support costs. The Expense Center costs represent the other costs incurred by the staff departments to support the operating departments in providing products and services to the guests. A specific Executive Committee Member is also responsible for each Expense Center and is expected to control costs and achieve productivity and budget standards for his/her department. Refer to Exhibit 3.1, and the departments listed in the Expense Centers section of this chapter to see the departments that make up Expense Centers and to identify the Executive Committee Member responsible for controlling that department expense.

House Profit or Gross Operating Profit is a very important profit measure because it identifies hotel management's ability to maximize revenues, control expenses, and maximize profits. The hotel profit measure is used to calculate management bonuses because the managers have the ability to affect and control procedures and operations to maximize profits and to minimize and control expenses. House Profit also identifies the profit or dollar amount that hotel operations turns over to the General Manager to pay hotel fixed costs.

NET HOUSE PROFIT OR ADJUSTED GROSS OPERATING PROFIT   The formula for **Net House Profit** is House Profit minus Fixed Expenses. This is the dollar amount or profit that remains after the hotel has recognized all revenues and paid for all variable and Fixed Expenses. It is the profit amount the hotel has produced that is available to pay all applicable taxes and to be divided among the hotel owner and hotel managers based on management contracts. Ownership accounting is important because it identifies which fixed expenses, reserve accounts, and taxes will be paid either by the owner, management company, or by any other investors or business entity having interest in the hotel. Exhibit 4.4 is a Consolidated P&L through Net House Profit.

EXHIBIT 4.4
CONSOLIDATED P&L

Flagstaff Hotel
Consolidated P&L Statement
June 30, 2009
(000)

Current Period*				Year-to-Date*		
Actual	**Budget**	**Last Year**		**Actual**	**Budget**	**Last Year**
$100	$102	$ 95	Room Revenues	$ 675	$640	$625
6	6	5	Telephone Revenues	34	35	34
8	7	7	Gift Shop Revenues	41	41	39
3	3	3	Miscellaneous Revenues	18	18	18
15	15	14	Restaurant Revenues	73	71	70
6	6	6	Beverage Revenues	29	30	29
<u>23</u>	<u>20</u>	<u>18</u>	Banquet Revenues	<u>150</u>	<u>140</u>	<u>135</u>
$ 44	$ 41	$ 38	**Subtotal F&B Revenues**	$ 252	$241	$234
$161	$159	$148	**Total Hotel Revenues**	$1,020	$975	$950
			Department Profits			
$66	$67	$63	Rooms Profits	$439	$416	$406
1	1	1	Telephone Profits	6	6	6
2	2	2	Gift Shop Profits	11	10	10
3	3	3	Miscellaneous Profits	18	18	18
2	2	2	Restaurant Profits	12	12	11
2	2	2	Beverage Profits	12	12	12
<u>8</u>	<u>7</u>	<u>6</u>	Banquet Profits	<u>53</u>	<u>49</u>	<u>47</u>
$12	$11	$10	**Subtotal F&B Profits**	$ 77	$ 73	$ 70
$84	$84	$79	**Total Hotel Department Profits**	$551	$523	$510
$12	$12	$11	Administrative (G&A)	$ 71	$ 72	$ 71
7	7	6	Utilities	43	42	40
15	15	15	Repairs and Maintenance (R&M)	92	90	88
4	4	4	Accident Expense	25	25	24
2	2	2	Training and Relocation	12	12	12
<u>21</u>	<u>20</u>	<u>19</u>	Sales and Marketing	<u>160</u>	<u>153</u>	<u>149</u>
$61	$60	$57	**Total Expense Center Costs**	$403	$394	$384
			or Total Supports Costs			
$23	$24	$22	**House Profit**	$148	$129	$126
$12	12	11	Fixed Expenses	72	72	66
$11	$12	$11	**Net House Profit**	$ 76	$ 57	$ 60

*Numbers are in thousands of dollars (000).

PROFIT BEFORE AND AFTER TAXES   Taxes are the last expense the hotel must pay. The term **Profit before Taxes** refers to the final dollar profit that has been recognized and accounted for all hotel revenues and expenses. This includes the payment of several different operational or sales taxes. The final expense is income taxes (or corporate taxes). Profit before Taxes is the profit amount that is subject to these taxes. The corporate tax is calculated and paid and the remaining amount is **Profit after Taxes**. This is the final profit amount that is divided up among the owners and management companies involved in operating the hotel. Exhibit 4.4 is an example of a complete Consolidated P&L.

Spring Hill Suites and Residence Inn Chicago Downtown River North Chicago, IL

The Residence Inn and the Spring Hill Suites by Marriott is the term used by Marriott Hotels for this property located in the heart of Downtown, Chicago, in the trendy River North area. Managed by White Lodging Services, these all suite hotels are just steps away from the Loop business district, world-class shopping on the Magnificent Mile, and favorite attractions and dining. The Spring Hill Suite offers 253 oversized guest suites each with a full kitchen and feature granite countertops and stainless steel appliances; perfect for extended stay guests. Both hotels offer a hot breakfast buffet. Guests can enjoy skyline views and a workout at the 27th floor exercise facility, the indoor pool, and the whirlpool.

Photo Courtesy of White Lodging Hotels.

These two properties complement each other by providing different experiences for travelers. Visit www.chicagorivernorthhotel.com to view more information on these new properties. Answer the following questions from the perspective of White Lodging.

1. Which property quoted the highest room rates?
2. Which property do you think would have the highest room profit margin and why?
3. What criteria would you use to put together the competitive set for each property and why?

FORMATS FOR CONSOLIDATED P&L STATEMENT

Exhibits 4.1–4.4 show the Consolidated P&L format used by Marriott Hotels. The P&L is arranged to present the financial information in a logical and clear format. We will look at the organization and format for Consolidated P&Ls in this section. There are three separate sections that make up the format of a P&L.

Titles

This is a basic but a very important part of any financial statement. The **title** gives the reader specific information about the financial statement so that the reader will know what the numbers represent. The title includes the following:

1. Name of the hotel or restaurant.
2. Type of financial statement—P&L Statement, Balance Sheet or Statement of Cash Flows.
3. Time period covered for the financial statement—monthly or accounting period.

The financial information in Exhibits 4.1–4.4 is for the Flagstaff Hotel and is the Consolidated P&L Statement for the time period June 30, 2009.

Horizontal Headings

The headings across the top of a P&L Statement tell how the financial information is arranged and organized according to time periods and type of financial information reported. The **horizontal headings** include the following:

1. The current accounting period or current month financial information.
2. The YTD financial information. This cumulates the financial information for all accounting periods or months as of the current date.
3. The actual numbers, budget numbers, and last year's numbers for the current accounting period or current month.
4. The actual numbers, budget numbers, and last year's numbers year-to-date.
5. Columns for the dollars and percentages for each of the above categories.

These horizontal headings arrange and organize the financial information so that it can be read logically and clearly.

Vertical Headings

The **vertical headings** in the middle or down the side of a P&L statement provide the names of the accounts or departments that the numbers will be organized into and reported for. The vertical headings include the following:

1. Revenue Centers for operating Department Revenues. This includes the revenues by market segment for individual departments such as Rooms and revenues by meal period for food & beverage and the total of the revenues for all the departments in the hotel.
2. Profit Centers for operating department profits. This includes the profits for individual departments such as Rooms and Food & Beverage and the total of the profits for all the operating departments in the hotel.
3. Expense Centers for the staff or supporting departments. This includes the total operating expenses for each department that is an Expense Center and the total costs of all the Expense Centers in the hotel.
4. Fixed Expenses are those expenses that do not change from month to month and are constant. These expenses can also be referred to as deductions from income.
5. Profit levels including Department Profit, Total Department Profits, House Profits, Net House Profits, and Profit before and after Taxes.

Examples of Consolidated P&L Statement

Following are examples of other formats that can be used for Consolidated P&L Statements. We will start with the format that we have used in this chapter. Note that Marriott has added a Key Statistics section at the bottom of the P&L to include key operational results in addition to revenues, expenses, and profits.

HOTEL P&L EXAMPLE 1
The Flagstaff Marriott
Title

Current Period or Month

Actual   Budget   Last Year
(in $ and as a %)

YTD Period or Month

Actual   Budget   Last Year
(in $ and as a %)

Revenue
Rooms
Telephone
Gift Shop
Restaurant
Lounge
Audio Visual
Banquet
Total Food & Beverage
Other Departments
Total Revenues
Department Profits
Rooms
Telephone
Gift Shop
Restaurant
Lounge
Audio Visual
Banquet
Kitchen Expense
Total Food & Beverage
Other Departments
Total Department Profits
Support Costs (Expense Centers)
Administrative
Utilities
Repairs and Maintenance
Central Training and Relocation
Accidents
Sales and Marketing

(*continued*)

Total Support Costs
House Profit
Base Management Fee
FF&E Escrow
Other Deductions
Net House Profit
Taxes
Profit After Tax
Key Statistics
Rooms Sold
Total Occupancy
Average Rate
Room RevPAR
Total RevPAR
HPPAR

In the second and third formats, note the different terminologies and see that they essentially show the same financial information for the same time periods. They all measure specific areas and types of financial results.

Our final example of a consolidated or summary P&L will be the format approved and recommended in the 10th revised edition of the *Uniform System of Accounts for the Lodging Industry* published in 2006. This format seeks to provide consistency in terminology and format in lodging summary P&L statements. Some of the more important changes are presented below.

Account titles have been altered to reflect typical lodging terminology, such as replacing the term "income after undistributed operating expenses" with "gross operating profit" and the term "income before interest, depreciation and amortization, and income taxes (EBITDA)" with "net operating income."

All undistributed operating expenses should be classified into one of the following four categories: administrative and general; sales and marketing; property operation and maintenance; and utilities. Human resources, information systems, and security are now listed as line items under Administrative and General.

Finally, the Summary Operating Statement is prepared for analytical purposes and is not in accordance with generally accepted accounting principles. It allows for only four sources of revenues: rooms, food and beverage, other operated departments, and rentals and other incomes. This again is meant to provide consistency in the formats so that P&Ls can be more easily compared and analyzed.

HOTEL P&L EXAMPLE 2
The Flagstaff Omni Hotel

	Current Period			Year-to-Date	
Actual	Budget	Last Year	Actual	Budget	Last Year
	(in $ and as a %)			(in $ and as a %)	

Total Hotel Rooms

Total Rooms Occupied

Revenue Occupancy %

Average Room Rate

RevPAR

Gross Operating Revenues

Room Revenue

Food Revenue

Beverage Revenue

Total Food & Beverage Revenue

Telephone Revenues

Other Revenues

Total Gross Operating Revenues

Department Profits

Rooms Department

Food Department

Beverage Department

Total Food & Beverage Department Profit

Telephone Department

Other Departments

Total Department Profits

Administrative and General

Management Fee

Advertising & Sales

Repairs & Maintenance

Heat, Light, Power

Total Deductions from Income

Gross Operating Profit

Fixed Expenses

EBITDA

Hotel P&L Example 3
The Flagstaff Four Seasons Hotel

	Month						Year-to-Date					
Actual ($)	Actual (%)	Budget ($)	Budget (%)	Last Year ($)	Last Year (%)	Actual ($)	Actual (%)	Budget ($)	Budget (%)	Last Year ($)	Last Year (%)

Occupancy Percentage

Total Average Rate

REVPAR

Total Rooms Revenue

Total Food Revenue

Total Beverage Revenue

Total F&B Revenue

Total Telephone Revenue

Total Other Departments Revenue

GROSS OPERATING REVENUE

Rooms Net Profit

F&B Net Profit

Telephone Net Profit

Total Other Departments Profit

TOTAL DEPARTMENT PROFITS

Administrative and General Department Total

Accidents Department Total

Repairs and Maintenance Department Total

Heat, Light, and Power Department Total

TOTAL DEDUCTIONS

Gross Operating Profit

Taxes and Insurance

PROFIT BEFORE FEES

Management Fees

Other Management Fees

Four Seasons Incentive Fees

NET OPERATING PROFIT

Rent Expense

Depreciation and Amortization

Other Expense

Gain/Loss Expense

Income Tax

NET PROFIT

<u>**HOTEL P&L EXAMPLE 4**</u>
Summary Operating Statement
10th Edition Uniform System of Accounts for the Hospitality Industry

	<u>Current Period</u>			<u>Year-to-Date</u>	
Actual	Forecast	Prior Year	Actual	Forecast	Prior Year
(in $ and as a %)			(in $ and as a %)		

Revenue

Rooms

Food and Beverage

Other Operated Departments

Rentals and Other Income

Total Revenue

Departmental Expenses

Rooms

Food and Beverage

Other Operated Departments

Total Departmental Expenses

Total Departmental Income

Undistributed Operating Expenses

Administrative and General

Sales and Marketing

Property Operations and Maintenance

Utilities

Total Undistributed Expenses

Gross Operating Profit

Management Fees

Income Before Fixed Charges

Fixed Charges

Rent

Property and Other Taxes

Insurance

Total Fixed Charges

Net Operating Income

Less: Replacement Reserves

ADJUSTED NET OPERATING INCOME   Note how this summary format clearly identifies the specific revenue departments and the type of expenses being reported in a line item. Management fees are reported in a specific line item as are replacement reserves. This format makes it clear to the reader of how these

---

RESTAURANT P&L EXAMPLE 1
The Flagstaff Restaurant

	Monthly Activity			Year-to-Date Activity			
2 Months Ago	1 Month Ago	Current Month Actual	Last Year	Current Year ($)	Per Guest	Last Year ($)	Per Guest
		Total Guests					
		Lunch					
		Dinner					
		Take-Out					
		Lunch Sales					
		Dinner Sales					
		Take-Out Sales					
		Total Food Sales					
		Total Beverage Sales					
		Total Add-On Sales					
		Total Sales					
		Food Cost					
		Non Food Cost					
		Beverage Cost					
		Other Cost					
		Total Cost of Sales					
		Hourly Wage Cost					
		Management Cost					
		Benefit Cost					
		Total Wage Compensation					
		Variable Expenses					
		Manageable Expenses					
		Utilities Expenses					
		Other Expenses					
		Total Manageable Expenses					
		Facilities Expense					
		Marketing Expense					
		Total Restaurant Earnings/Net Income					

expenses are being identified and recorded. It is important to understand the terms of a management agreement or contract that identifies the financial responsibilities of each party and how they will be recorded on financial statements. This Summary Operating Statement provides a recommended format that is consistent in its terminology and format.

RESTAURANT P&L STATEMENTS   Note how the horizontal headings in the following format for a restaurant P&L are arranged to show different time periods for financial results. This format focuses on the current monthly trends of financial results by comparing the current month to the two previous months. They also show some guest count information in addition to dollar information in the YTD section. The vertical headings are again found in the middle of the P&L to separate the current month activity from the YTD activity. This is just a different way to present the financial information.

These five different formats for hotel and restaurant P&L statements are examples of how the financial results of a business can be presented in different formats in a P&L so that readers can learn about the financial performance of a company or business. A company determines how it wants to organize the financial information in the P&L so that the information can be used both as a management tool and to measure financial performance. *A hospitality manager should be comfortable in reading and using a Consolidated P&L in any format.*

DEPARTMENT P&L STATEMENTS

Consolidated P&L Statements provide summary information of the financial operations of a hotel, including department totals for revenues, profits, and expenses. The **Department P&L** Statements provide detailed operating information for individual departments. They are the P&Ls that hotel managers use to measure the financial performance of revenues, profits and expenses, and use as a management tool to help them operate their departments more efficiently and productively. In addition to the revenues recorded on a Department P&L, there are four major **expense categories**—Cost of Sales, Wages, Benefits, and Direct Operating Expenses. We will now discuss these major expense categories as well as Department P&Ls for Profit and Expense Centers in more detail.

The Four Major Cost Categories

The financial information in Department P&L Statements for Profit Centers is arranged with Department Revenues at the top, Department Expenses in the middle, and Department Profits at the bottom. The terms referring to the "top line" as revenues and the "bottom line" as profits come from this format. We will explain in more detail how operating expenses are arranged in cost of sales, wages, benefits, and direct operating expense categories.

Cost of sales is a major variable expense for most profit departments. It can be defined as anything served to, sold to, or consumed by customers. Food cost can range between 25% and 35% in restaurants and banquet departments, beverage cost between 20% and 30% in restaurant and beverage departments, and cost of sales can range between 45% and 55% in gift shops. It is often the largest expense in terms of dollars and cost percentages in Department P&L Statements. Much attention is paid to understanding and controlling cost of sales by **department managers**. It includes controlling purchases, receiving and inspecting, verifying inventories and maintaining pars, and minimizing waste.

The rooms department does not have a cost of sales category. This is because guest rooms are constantly rerented. Guest rooms are available for occupancy the next day regardless of whether they were occupied or empty the night before. This is one of the main reasons why the rooms department has the highest profit margin of any profit department.

Salaries and wages is another a major variable expense category in both profit departments and expense departments. Major **line accounts** define the type of expense and collects the actual expenses for a time period and include management salaries, hourly wages, overtime, and any other payroll expenses. Management salaries are generally considered fixed in nature while hourly wages to be variable. As a result, department managers are expected to adjust hourly wage expenses to be consistent with forecasted business volumes. Higher forecasted revenues should result in an increase of hourly wages to take care of the increased business. Lower forecasted revenues should result in a reduction of hourly wages in recognition of lower business levels. Overtime is another expense and line item that department managers are expected to control. A successful manager in any department will be expected to understand and manage hourly wage costs to maintain expected profitability and profit margins.

Benefit cost has become a significant expense. It is closely related to wage costs and generally has a fixed relationship with it. Benefit costs will increase or decrease with an increase or decrease in the wage costs. If department managers do a good job in controlling wage costs, their benefit costs will be simultaneously controlled. Examples of benefit costs are health insurance premiums, vacation pay, sick pay, and employee meals.

Direct operating expenses are the remaining expenses that are essential in providing products and services to hotel guests and restaurant customers. There are many individual line accounts in each department. The following examples will illustrate some of the major expense accounts in a department P&L:

Rooms—reservation costs, guest supplies, cleaning supplies, office supplies, and uniforms

Restaurants—china, glass, silver, linen, cleaning supplies, paper supplies, and uniforms

Beverage—glass, paper supplies, uniforms, and menus

Gift Shop—paper supplies, office supplies, and freight

There can be as many as 30–40 individual line accounts in a department. A department manager should focus his or her attention on the largest expense categories and the ones with the largest variations in actual expenses compared to the budget, forecast, and last year's actual.

Revenue and Profit Department P&Ls

The Department P&Ls for Revenue Centers are composed of revenues, cost of sales, wages, benefits, and direct operating expenses. Exhibit 4.5 shows the format for a Department P&L. Note that the title and horizontal headings are the same as on the Consolidated P&L, only the vertical headings or accounts are different. In each major expense category, there are many individual line

EXHIBIT 4.5
DEPARTMENT P&L FORMAT

Flagstaff Hotel
Restaurant Department P&L
June 30, 2009

Current Period				Year-to-Date		
Actual	Budget	Last Year		Actual	Budget	Last Year

Revenues
Breakfast
Lunch
Dinner
TOTAL REVENUES
Food Cost
Hourly Wages
Management Wages
Other Wages
TOTAL WAGE COST
Medical Costs
Insurance Premiums
Vacation Pay
Employee Meals
TOTAL BENEFIT COST
China
Glass
Silver
Linen
Paper Supplies
Menu Expense
Sales & Promotion
General Expense
TOTAL DIRECT OPERATING EXPENSES
TOTAL RESTAURANT DEPARTMENT PROFIT

accounts that collect all the operating information for that particular expense. These are the same accounts that were discussed in the previous section. During the month, each expense incurred is classified or coded to the appropriate line account (expense account) in each department. At the end of the month, the accounting office collects, records, and reports all the operating information by line item or account. This is the financial information included in each account total on the Department P&L.

Expense Center Department P&Ls

The Department P&Ls for expense centers include wages, benefits, and direct operating expenses. Because they do not sell any products or provide any services to paying customers, there are no revenues or cost of sales. All other expense categories are the same as in the revenue centers. Expense center managers are expected to manage their expenses efficiently and stay within established budgets or forecasts to meet the expected productivities.

Fixed Cost Department P&Ls

There is only one expense category and that is Fixed Expenses. There are no revenues, cost of sales, wages, or benefits categories. Only single-line accounts that provide the total expenses such as loan payments, lease payments, insurance costs, depreciation expenses, and licenses and fees are contained in the Fixed Expense Department. Expenses for these line accounts are generally handled by the Accounting Department, which makes the journal entries or records the expenses each month or accounting period.

Exhibit 4.6 is an abbreviated example of a support Department P&L.

The individual Department P&Ls are directly connected to the organization charts that were presented in Chapter 3. There will be a specific manager in charge of each individual Department P&L. For example, in a large convention hotel or resort, the Food & Beverage Director will have final responsibility for many restaurant and bar outlets as well as the banquets and meetings departments. But he or she will have a Department Head directly responsible for all the restaurants. Examples of these department heads and their direct P&L responsibilities are shown below.

Director of Catering	Banquet and Meetings Department P&L
Restaurant Manager	Restaurant Department P&L
Room Service Manager	Room Service Department P&L
Beverage Manager	Lounge or Beverage Department P&L
Executive Chef	Kitchen P&L

The Food and Beverage Director will meet with each one of these Department Heads to review the operations and financial results for their departments and assist in any way he or she can. But it is up to the Department Head and his or her team of shift managers to operate their respective departments efficiently meeting the established goals, budgets, and forecasts.

EXHIBIT 4.6
DEPARTMENT P&L FORMAT

Flagstaff Hotel
Repairs and Maintenance Department P&L
June 30, 2009

	Current Period				Year-to-Date		
Actual	Budget	Last Year			Actual	Budget	Last Year
		Hourly Wages					
		Management Wages					
		Other Wages					
		Overtime					
		TOTAL WAGE COSTS					
		Medical Costs					
		Insurance Premiums					
		Vacation Pay					
		Employee Meals					
		TOTAL BENEFIT COST					
		General Building Repair					
		Kitchen Equipment and Repair					
		Maintenance Contracts					
		Electrical and Mechanical					
		Grounds Maintenance					
		Elevator Expense					
		Auto Expense					
		General Expense					
		TOTAL DIRECT OPERATING EXPENSE					
		TOTAL DEPARTMENT EXPENSE					

Analyzing Department P&L Statements

It is the responsibility of the managers in each department to ensure that the operating information for a month or accounting period that is submitted to the accounting department is accurate and timely. Operations managers need to understand the POS systems that record the revenues of their operations to ensure that revenues are recorded correctly and that revenue information is balanced after each shift. They need to understand the payroll systems that are used to record and control both hourly and management labor costs. This includes ensuring that wage departments, man-hours worked, current hourly wage rates, and overtime paid are correct for each employee each week.

Direct operating expenses can come from existing inventories or purchases from vendors and suppliers. Operations managers not only need to efficiently order materials and supplies so that inventories can be kept to a minimum but also need to ensure that necessary supplies are always available. It is a challenge to keep track of inventories and operating supplies such as uniforms, china, glass, and silver in the Restaurant Department or linen, cleaning supplies, and guest supplies in the Rooms Department. If budgeted productivities and profit margins are to be met each month, operations managers must be able to efficiently monitor and control all of their purchases, inventory levels, and expenses.

When the monthly Department P&L is prepared by the Accounting Department, there is time to review the information before the P&L is finalized and distributed. Generally, a preliminary P&L is prepared and then reviewed for problems or mistakes. This is when the department operations managers can review the P&L numbers with the accounting department to ensure that the numbers are correct. Corrections are made, adjusting entries completed, and the final P&L is submitted. When the final P&L is completed it is reviewed and any large variations in dollar amounts or percentages need to be explained in written P&L critiques. P&L critiques will include identifying where problems occurred, what caused them, and how they are to be corrected. Occasionally, an expense overrun will continue as the result of a vendor price increase or a change to a more expensive product. An important part of P&L critiques is identifying which problems or cost overruns will continue and which will be corrected.

Summary

P&Ls measure the financial performance of a business. There are two main types of P&Ls used by hotels—the Consolidated P&L and the Department P&L. The Consolidated P&L is mainly used to report and measure financial performance while the Department P&L is used as a management tool to provide more detailed financial information to managers, which they can use to operate their departments.

The Consolidated P&L is a hotel summary P&L that is arranged by Revenue Centers, Profit Centers, Expense Centers, and Fixed Costs. It also has several levels of profit measures. Total Department Profit measures the profitability of all the operating departments. House Profit measures the profits remaining after Expense Center costs are deducted from Total Department Profits. It reflects management's ability to successfully maximize revenues and minimize expenses. Net House Profit is the profit remaining after Fixed Expenses are paid from House

Profit and is a good measure of the financial profitability of a hotel.

The Department P&L provides specific financial information on the operations of each department. The six main categories on a department P&L are Revenues, Cost of Sales, Wage Expense, Benefit Expense, Direct Operating Expense, and Total Department Profit. There are specific line accounts within each of these main categories that further break down and identify expenses so that they can be measured and effectively controlled. Hospitality managers will spend a lot of time using their Department P&L to help them operate their departments.

The P&Ls are organized in a format that enables the reader to easily read and identify financial information contained in the P&L. The format can be different but the financial information contained in a P&L will generally be the same. Three main areas of the format of a P&L are the following: First, the title that identifies the report, time period, and company name. Second, the horizontal headings that include current month or period financial information organized into actual, budget, and last year and the year-to-date financial information also organized into actual, budget, and last year. Third, the vertical headings that identify the department's revenue, expense, and profit accounts and are organized with revenues at the top, expenses in the middle, and profits at the bottom.

Hospitality Manager Takeaways

1. The Consolidated P&L is a summary P&L for a hotel that reports total revenues, profits, or expenses for the departments in a hotel.
2. The Department P&L provides detailed operating information in specific line accounts for each individual department in a hotel. A specific department manager is directly responsible for the financial performance of each hotel department.
3. The total revenues and profits on each Department P&L are the same as the total revenues, profits, or expenses reported on the Consolidated P&L. In accounting terms, these numbers either tie in or balance each other on both P&Ls.
4. The Department P&L contains one revenue and four main expense categories (Cost of Sales, Wages, Benefits, and Direct Operating Expenses) and total department profit or expense. Each of the main expense categories contains individual line accounts that collect all the specific revenues or expenses for the month that are classified or coded to each specific account.
5. Both Consolidated P&L and Department P&L can have different formats that organize and report the financial results. Each company chooses the format that will work best for that particular company.
6. The managers of operating departments in a hotel are expected to critique and explain both favorable and unfavorable variations from budgeted or forecasted amounts.

Key Terms

Allocations: the portion of an expense charged to a specific hotel for services received in connection with expenses incurred at the corporate level on behalf of all the restaurants or hotels in the company.

Deductions from income: the same as Expense Centers. The direct expenses of staff departments that support the operating departments of a hotel in providing products and services to customers.

Department head: the senior operating manager for a specific department who is responsible for all aspects of that department's operations and financial performance.

Department manager: the shift manager and department head of a specific operating department who are responsible for the daily delivery of products and services to guests and for the financial performance of their department.

Department P&L: a P&L statement for one specific department that includes all revenues and expenses in detail that are involved in operating that department.

Department profits: the dollar amounts remaining in Revenue Centers/Profit Centers after the department recognizes all revenues and pays all expenses associated with operating that department for a specific time period.

Expense categories: the four major categories for collecting and reporting department expenses—Cost of Sales, Wages, Benefits, and Direct Operating Expenses.

Expense center: a staff department that supports the hotel operating departments—Sales & Marketing, Engineering, Human Resources and Accounting. It has no revenues or cost of sales, just wages, benefits, and direct operating expenses.

Fixed expenses: direct expenses of a hotel that are constant and do not change with different volume levels of hotel business.

Horizontal headings: the headings across the top of a P&L that identify the type, time, and amount of financial information.

House profit: the profit amount that includes all revenues and expenses controlled by hotel management and measures management's ability to operate the hotel profitably. It is calculated by subtracting Total Expense Center Costs from Total Department Profits.

Line account: a specific accounting code that collects and records all revenues or expenses classified within the description of the line account.

Net house profit: identifies the amount of profit remaining after all hotel revenues are recorded and all direct hotel expenses are paid. It is equal to House Profit minus Fixed Expenses.

Profit before taxes: the same as Net House Profit. The profit amount remaining after all hotel operating expenses have been paid.

Profit after taxes: the amount of profit remaining after corporate taxes are paid. It is divided among owners, management companies, and any other entities having interest in the hotel.

Profit center: an operating department that produces revenues that result in a profit (or loss) by providing products and services to customers. It includes revenues, expenses, and profits and is a term that is interchangeable with Revenue Center.

Revenue center: an operating department that produces revenues by providing products and services directly to customers. It includes only revenues.

Support costs: the same as expense centers and are costs that are deducted from Total Department Profits.

Titles: the top portion of a financial statement that tells the name of the company, type of report, and the time period covered.

Total department profits: the summation of the individual department profits of a hotel. It provides the amount of profit resulting from the operating departments of a hotel.

Vertical headings: the names of the departments, categories, and accounts that are on the side or center of a P&L that identify the type and amount of financial information recorded on the P&L.

Review Questions

1. Define and name the four main classifications of accounting information in a Consolidated P&L.
2. Define and name the five main revenue and expense categories in a Department P&L.
3. Name and describe four different profit levels in a Consolidated P&L. What do they measure?
4. Name the three sections of the format for a P&L.
5. Explain the differences between a Profit Center and Expense Center. Give examples.
6. What is a line account and why is it important in financial analysis?
7. Refer to the Hotel Organization Chart in Chapter 3. Identify at least one hotel department that each Executive Committee Member is responsible for.
8. Why do you think this is the most important chapter of this book?

Practice Exercises

1. Match the line account or classification to the appropriate P&L.

   A. ___ Hourly wage cost   1. Consolidated P&L
   B. ___ Linen expense   2. Department P&L
   C. ___ Revenue centers
   D. ___ Food cost
   E. ___ Fixed costs
   F. ___ House profit
   G. ___ Overtime
   H. ___ Total department profits

2. Draw the format for a Consolidated P&L using the three sections in review question 4.
3. Draw the format for a Department P&L using the three sections in review question 4.

The Balance Sheet (A&L) and Statement of Cash Flows

LEARNING OBJECTIVES

- To become familiar with other financial statements that are used to measure financial performance
- To understand the use of the Balance Sheet (also called the Asset and Liability Statement) by hospitality managers and accounting managers
- To understand how the Balance Sheet is used with the P&L Statement in managing operations
- To understand the difference between capitalization and working capital
- To understand the Statement of Cash Flow and its uses
- To understand the importance of liquidity and profitability

CHAPTER OUTLINE

INTRODUCTION

There are three financial statements that have the greatest value in measuring the operations and financial performance of a business: the Profit and Loss Statement (P&L), the Balance Sheet (A&L), and the Statement of Cash Flows. We discussed the P&L in Chapter 4. This chapter will discuss the Balance Sheet and the Statement of Cash Flows.

Whereas the P&L is mainly used by hotel managers as a management tool and a measure of financial performance, the Balance Sheet and Statement of Cash Flow are also used by owners, bankers, and other outside institutions or agencies that have a financial interest in the business. They want to understand the financial strength and stability of a business in terms of net worth and cash flow that will permit that business to operate successfully and profitably over time. The P&L measures financial performance and *the Balance Sheet and Statement of Cash Flows measure the ability of a business to sustain and produce profitable operations*. What resources does the business have, how effectively do they use them, and how sufficient are they in maintaining adequate cash balances to pay all expenses?

This chapter will discuss in detail the Balance Sheet and Statement of Cash Flows and how they are primarily used not only in measuring financial performance but also as a management tool. Hospitality managers should have a fundamental understanding of these two financial statements to go along with a strong and detailed knowledge of the P&L. This knowledge enables managers to discuss the financial aspects of their operations with senior management and to demonstrate the financial knowledge and skills presented in the Career Success Model discussed in Chapter 1.

THE BALANCE SHEET OR ASSET AND LIABILITY STATEMENT

The purpose of the **Balance Sheet** is to measure the financial status, value, and net worth of a business at a specific point in time. It is also referred to as the A&L Statement. It is prepared at the end of each month or accounting period as well as at the end of the year. The Director of Finance or the corporate accounting office is responsible for preparing the Balance Sheet each month and ensuring that the accounts are accurate and in balance.

Definition

The Balance Sheet measures the status or net worth of a business as of a specific date. It is like a snapshot in time. The Balance Sheet shows the amounts or balances in each account as of a specific date. It is called the Asset and Liability Statement (A&L) because it shows the balances in each of the asset and liability accounts as well as the owner equity accounts. It is called the Balance Sheet because, again, that is what it shows—the *balance* in each of the accounts at a specific time. Exhibit 5.1 is an example of the Balance Sheet for the Flagstaff Hotel.

The Balance Sheet measures the value or worth of a business. The key characteristics of the Balance Sheet are as follows:

1. It measures the value or worth of a company at a specific point in time. For example, a Balance Sheet might be prepared for the end of the year, December 31, 2009. It is a snapshot of account balances at a specific point in time that identifies what a company owns (assets), what it owes (liabilities), and how it is owned (owner equity).
2. The **Fundamental Accounting Equation** describes the Balance Sheet. This equation is

$$\text{Assets} = \text{Liabilities} + \text{Owner Equity}$$

3. It consists of accounts organized by asset, liability, or owner equity.
4. These accounts are divided into current accounts (less than one year obligations), also referred to as working capital, and long-term accounts (longer than one year obligations), which are referred to as capitalization.
5. Each account has a beginning balance, monthly activity, and an ending balance.
6. Unlike the P&L Statement, managers are not expected to provide critiques of monthly Balance Sheet activity. This is done by the Accounting Department.
7. Accounting Managers reconcile or balance monthly the accounts of a Balance Sheet.
8. Current accounts are used as working capital in operating the business. The definition of working capital is current assets (CAs) minus current liabilities (CLs).
9. Long-term Liability accounts and Owner Equity accounts are used as capitalization, which provides the money to start, renovate, or expand a business with purchases of long-term assets such as property, plant, and equipment.

It is important for hospitality managers to understand the Balance Sheet because they use the current assets and current liability accounts (working capital) in the daily operations of their business. They are expected to efficiently use the assets of a business to operate it profitably. Following are the definitions that describe important Balance Sheet accounts:

- **Current Assets**—Less than one year life
  - **Cash**—Money that is in the cash bank account and available for use in daily business operations. It can be in a savings or checking account. It is the most liquid form of an asset. It is available immediately.
  - **Accounts Receivable**—Dollar amounts that the company is owed for providing products and services to customers that is uncollected. These accounts go through a direct billing process and are expected to be paid generally within 30 days. Credit cards and direct billing to companies are the two major parts of accounts receivable. It is the next most liquid asset after cash.

- **Inventories**—Supplies or materials that the company has purchased but not used in order to provide products and services to its customers. Examples of important inventories for hospitality operations are food, beverage, china, glass, silver, linen, cleaning supplies, and guest supplies. The company has purchased and paid for the inventory but has not put it into use. Inventory is not considered very liquid because it must first be converted into a final product, then sold, and then the proceeds collected and deposited into the cash account.
- **Long-Term Assets**—More than one year useful life
  - **Property**—Land that is purchased to locate the building that will provide products and services to customers. This is the land that a hotel or restaurant is located on.
  - **Plant**—The physical structure or building that houses the business operation. This is the actual hotel or restaurant building.
  - **Equipment**—The machines and other assets that are used to produce the product or service. This is the kitchen equipment, guest room furniture and fixtures, restaurant tables and chairs, vehicles, washers and dryers, heat-light-power equipment, computers systems, and all other machines used in a hotel or restaurant.
- **Depreciation**—The portion of the total cost of property, plant, and equipment that is charged monthly to the actual operations of a business. It is calculated by dividing the total cost minus residual value by the number of years of useful production life to get the annual cost or depreciation charged to a specific year and spread or charged over 12 months.
- **Current Liabilities**—Less than one year obligations
  - **Accounts Payable**—Products or services received but not paid for that are due within one year. The invoices have been received, approved, and are in the process of payment.
  - **Wages Payable**—Wages owed but not paid to employees who have provided the products or services to customers. The employees have completed their work but the pay checks have not been distributed or cashed.
  - **Taxes Payable**—Taxes that have been collected but not paid to the appropriate tax agency. These are typically paid quarterly or annually.
  - **Advanced Deposits**—Funds received from customers before the arrival date to be applied as part of the payment for future sales of sleeping rooms, food and beverage, meeting space, and other products or services. This can be a major current liability for resorts and convention hotels.
  - **Accrued Liabilities/Expenses**—Amounts owed for purchases received but not paid for at the end of the month or end of the period cut-off date.
- **Long-Term Liabilities**—Longer than one year obligations
  - **Bank Loans**—Amounts owed to banks or other financial institutions that will be repaid over an extended number of years, generally from 5 to 30 years. Bank loans are used for capitalization, including start-up, renovation, or expansion.

- **Line of Credit**—A form of bank loan where a specific dollar amount is set aside for the business to use. The business may draw on or use these funds as needed. When used, they are repaid on similar terms as a bank loan.
- **Lease Obligations**—The land, building, or equipment that is leased, not purchased, that is recognized as a long-term liability according to the contract.
- **Owner Equity**—Investment in a company in the form of paid-in capital, common or preferred stock, and retained earnings. It is the excess of assets minus liabilities.
  - **Paid-in Capital**—The amount invested to start a company by the owners of a company or business. It is the dollar amount that they provide from their own financial resources.
  - **Common Stock**—The amount invested by other individuals or institutions by purchasing generally common stock and also the preferred stock in the company or business. The value of this investment is determined by the price of the company stock as it is traded on the open market.
  - **Retained Earnings**—The portion of annual operating profits that is kept or reinvested by a company. It should improve the strength of the Balance Sheet and the company as it increases each year.

The format of the Balance Sheet comes from the Fundamental Accounting Equation. The Fundamental Accounting Equation states that the dollar amount or value of assets must equal the dollar amounts or value of the liabilities plus owner equity used to purchase the assets. In other words, what you *own* should equal what you *owe* to financial institutions in the form of loans or to owners in the form of investment.

$$\text{Assets} = \text{Liabilities} + \text{Owner Equity}$$

- An *asset* is a resource. In business, it is all the property of a business that can be applied to covering liabilities (*Webster's Dictionary*).
- A *liability* is a debt. In business, it is something owed to another, a legal obligation (*Webster's Dictionary*).
- *Owner equity* is possession and value and is defined in two parts. To *own* is to have or possess and *equity* is the value of property beyond a liability (*Webster's Dictionary*).

The Fundamental Accounting Equation shows these relationships and defines them with dollar balances and values. The Asset total amount must equal the Liability and Owner Equity amount. This ensures that all funds and transactions are accounted for according to accounting rules and principles. The rules and procedures that govern accounting in business are called Generally Accepted Accounting Principles (GAAP). A business needs to collect, prepare, and report its accounting results in management reports or financial statements according to these principles in order for the numbers to be recognized as valid and accurate. Anyone who reads financial statements prepared in accordance with GAAP can have confidence in the accuracy and validity of the numbers contained in those statements. Exhibit 5.1 provides examples of Balance Sheets.

We will now apply the financial information in Exhibit 5.1 to the characteristics of the Balance Sheet as an example.

1. $\qquad$ Assets = Total Liabilities + Owner Equity, or

$$\$730 \text{ Total Assets} = \frac{\$350 \text{ total}}{\text{liabilities}} + \frac{\$380 \text{ owner}}{\text{equity,}} \quad \text{or} \quad \$730.$$

The Fundamental Accounting Equation is in balance because the $730 in Total Assets is equal to the $730 in total liabilities and owner equity.

EXHIBIT 5.1
BALANCE SHEET

(Equation Format)
Flagstaff Hotel
June 30, 2009
(000)

ASSETS		LIABILITIES	
Current		**Current**	
Cash	$ 75	Accounts Payable	$ 60
Accounts Receivable	40	Wages Payable	40
Inventories	90	Taxes Payable	25
Total Current Assets	$205	Total Current Liabilities	$125
Long Term		**Long Term**	
Property	$125	Bank Loans	$150
Plant	200	Line of Credit	50
Equipment	250	Lease Obligations	25
Less Deprecation	(50)	Other Long-Term Obligations	0
Total Long-Term Assets	$525	Total Long-Term Liabilities	$225
Total Assets	**$730**	**Total Liabilities**	**$350**
		OWNER EQUITY	
		Paid-in Capital	$200
		Capital Stock	100
		Retained Earnings	80
		Total Owner Equity	**$380**
Total Assets	**$730**	**Total Liabilities and Owner Equity**	**$730**

Balance Sheet
(Traditional Format)
Flagstaff Hotel
June 30, 2009
(000)

ASSETS

Current

Cash	$ 75
Accounts Receivable	40
Inventories	90
Total Current Assets	$205

Long Term

Property	$125
Plant	200
Equipment	250
Less Deprecation	(50)
Total Long-Term Assets	$525
Total Assets	**$730**

LIABILITIES

Current

Accounts Payable	$ 60
Wages Payable	40
Taxes Payable	25
Total Current Liabilities	$125

Long Term

Bank Loans	$150
Line of Credit	50
Lease Obligations	25
Other Long-Term Loans	0
Total Long-Term Liabilities	$225
Total Liabilities	**$350**

OWNER EQUITY

Paid-in Capital	$200
Capital Stock	100
Retained Earnings	80
Total Owner Equity	**$380**
Total Liabilities and Owner Equity	**$730**

2. Ending Balances as of June 30, 2009 are as follows (in $):

Current Assets	205	Current Liabilities	125
Long-term Assets	525	Long-term Liabilities	225
Total Assets	730	Total Liabilities	350
		Paid-in Capital	200
		Capital Stock	100
		Retained Earnings	80
		Total Owner Equity	380

These are the ending balances in the major accounts as of June 30, 2009. Anyone reading the Balance Sheet will rely on these numbers as being accurate as to the value or net worth of the Flagstaff Hotel as of this date.

3.

Current Accounts ($)		Long-Term Accounts ($)	
Current Assets	205	Long-Term Assets	525
Current Liabilities	125	Long-term Liabilities	225
		Owner Equity	380

The values or account balances in the current and the long-term Balance Sheet accounts are shown as of the specific date June 30, 2009.

4.   Working Capital = Current Assets − Current Liabilities
$80 Working Capital = $205 Current Assets − $125 Current Liabilities

The Flagstaff Hotel working capital is $80. This tells us that the Flagstaff Hotel has $80 left as working capital, reflected by the $205 already committed and invested in current assets and the $125 currently owed in current liabilities. The $80 is the remaining amount available for use in operating the business.

5.   Capitalization = Total Liabilities + Owner Equity, or
$730 Capitalization = $350 Liabilities + $380 Owner Equity

This tells us that the Flagstaff Hotel has total assets of $730 and that the hotel was financed by $350 in debt or long-term liabilities and $380 in equity.

Working Capital

Working capital is the dollar amount provided for the daily operations of a business. It is invested in the current assets of a business primarily in cash, accounts receivable, and inventory. The initial dollar amount invested as working capital is deposited in the cash account. Then it is invested in inventories as part of the process of providing products and services to customers (Exhibit 5.1). When a sale is made and the customer has not yet paid for the product or service, that dollar amount is identified as accounts receivable. When the credit card company sends electronic transfers as payment, or when individuals or companies send checks as payment, they are deposited directly into the cash account.

Working capital also involves the use of the current liabilities of a business primarily in accounts payable, wages payable, and taxes payable. When the company receives materials and supplies that are used in providing products and services but has not yet paid for them, they are recognized as accounts payable. As the invoices documenting amounts received and prices charged are approved by department heads or the Purchasing Department for payment, the accounts payable clerk processes a check and sends it out as payment. When the checks are mailed, the corresponding accounts payable is closed out (reduced to zero) and no longer recognized as a current liability. The same is true for wages owed to employees and taxes owed to government agencies. Wages owed to employees are accrued until the paychecks are distributed and cashed. Taxes are collected during a specified time period—quarterly or annually—and then paid. Until they are paid, they are recognized as accounts payable.

The definition of working capital is current assets minus current liabilities. Another term closely associated with working capital is liquidity. Liquidity is the ability of a business to pay its short-term financial obligations. The larger the cash balances of a business, the more liquid they are or the more capable they are of paying their financial obligations. A company cannot afford to invest too much in inventory by purchasing more than they need or let accounts receivable get too large by slow collection of accounts due. If that happens, it means that the company is taking longer to return the cash to the cash account after it has been used to purchase materials and supplies or that it is taking too long to collect accounts receivable from customers and convert these amounts into cash. That means that a company will have dollars tied up in large inventory and accounts receivable accounts rather than in the cash account where they can be used to pay the operating expenses of the business.

Capitalization

Capitalization identifies the way that a business obtains and uses money to start or expand a business by purchasing long-term assets. Capital is money or property that is used to create more money or property. Capitalization involves the use of long-term debt or owner equity (capital) as a way of obtaining the necessary funds or money to start or expand a business. Technically, capital refers to the funds contributed to a company by the owners or stockholders. Capital also describes the net worth of a company (*Webster's Dictionary*). We will include long-term debt as well as owner equity in our definition of capitalization because long-term debt is another source of obtaining the necessary money or finance to start a business.

Referring to our example in Exhibit 5.1 and point 5 above, the capitalization of the Flagstaff Hotel is $730. It was obtained with $350 in long-term liabilities and $380 in owner equity.

Capitalization can be in the form of three activities. First, the initial startup costs of establishing a company that involves purchasing mainly long-term assets to start a business. Second, the capital replacement of older long-term assets as they wear out or become inefficient or obsolete with new long-term assets. Third, the capital expansion, which is the use of capital to expand and grow the business. Capitalization provides the financial resources to invest in a business for a long term. These financial resources *should not* be used as working capital in the short term for the daily operations of a business. If a company has to use long-term capital to pay daily operating expenses, it is not generating sufficient revenues from daily operations to cover operating expenses. This demonstrates a major liquidity problem that could result in a company not being able to pay its bills and eventually going out of business.

THE RELATIONSHIP BETWEEN THE BALANCE SHEET AND THE P&L STATEMENT

Managers' Use of Balance Sheet Accounts in Daily Operations

Hospitality managers work primarily with the P&L Statement. It measures the financial performance of the department, hotel, or restaurant and is used as a management tool to help improve operations. Managers should be focused on effectively managing their operations to produce the budgeted or forecasted results. The P&L results for a month helps them review and evaluate actual performance and to plan for future performance.

Hospitality managers use the company's working capital (Balance Sheet amounts) in their daily operations. They primarily use the current assets of the company. They spend cash to purchase inventories (CA) or pay employee wages (CL) to produce products and services. They are expected to manage these accounts or expenditures according to budgets or company procedures. Working capital is the sum of the amount a Hotel or Restaurant Manager has to utilize in his or her daily operations and the amount or balance in the cash account that is not spent and is available for operations. Effectively managing the working capital in daily operations maximizes the working capital that is uncommitted and available for ongoing operations.

Business Operating Cycle

Figure 5.1 shows these relationships.

Follow the arrows to see the flow of "working capital" in daily operations. The working capital provides current assets to produce products and services for customers. This is shown on the right-hand side of the diagram. Note that everything starts with the cash Account. Current assets and operating expenses use cash. Inventory is a Balance Sheet current asset and wages and benefits are operating expenses on the P&L Statement. These accounts show how money is used to produce products and services. Production uses assets and incurs expenses.

When a sale occurs, the method of payment is recorded. This is shown on the left-hand side of the diagram. Cash payments get deposited directly into the cash account. Credit card sales go briefly into accounts receivable and then into the cash account when the electronic transfer of funds is received. Direct billing sales go to accounts receivable where they stay until the account is paid. Thirty day accounts are direct billing accounts that are expected to be paid within 30 days from billing date which is an acceptable time frame. Accounts that are unpaid between 30–60 days could represent a problem in collection. The customer is not paying his or her balance in a timely manner.

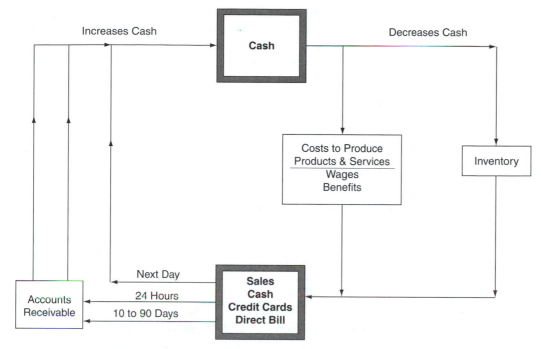

FIGURE 5.1 Business Operating Cycle.

Accounts between 60–90 days or over 90 days are problem accounts and tie up cash, put a strain on cash flow, and might not be collectable. A company expects payment within 30 days and can further stretch it to 60 days if it knows that billing questions are being answered, problems are resolved, and that chances are high that all or partial payment will be received. The more efficiently a company uses its assets and the quicker it collects its sales, the better the cash flow and financial soundness of the company.

Several of the accounts in Figure 5.1 are revenue and expense accounts that are part of the P&L Statement. For example, the amount of wages payable (CL) on the Balance Sheet is determined by the amount managers spend in management, hourly, and overtime labor costs. These costs are immediately recognized in the P&L Statement as expenses incurred in providing products and services to customers. The cost is recognized on the Balance Sheet as wages payable (CL) until the paychecks are written, issued, and cashed by employees. Once the check is cashed, wages payable and the cash account are decreased. So the time associated with an accounting transaction is different for the P&L and Balance Sheet; however, they will all be included in the same time period, usually the current month or accounting period. The wage expense on the P&L is *for the month or the accounting period* and the cash and accounts payable are *at the end of the month or the end of the accounting period.*

The same relationship exists for inventories and operating expenses. When a manager purchases guest supplies and linen for the Rooms Department, it will increase the guest supplies and linen inventory accounts when the supplies are received. The total expense is then recognized as accounts payable until the manager receives, approves, and sends the invoice to accounting for payment. When accounts payable sends out the check, the accounts payable and cash account will decrease. At this point, the transactions only affect the Balance Sheet accounts—inventory (CA) and accounts payable (CL).

Step 1: transaction is when inventory is purchased—increase inventory and increase accounts payable.

Step 2: transaction is when the invoice is paid—decrease accounts payable and decrease cash.

When the supplies are taken out of inventory and put into operations, the corresponding P&L expense accounts are charged. For example, if $2,000 in linen and $1,000 in guest supplies are taken out of inventory and put into operations, the inventory accounts are decreased by those amounts and $2,000 is charged to the linen operating expense account and $1,000 to the guest supply operating expense account on the Rooms Department P&L Statement.

Linen transaction	Decrease linen inventory account (CA)	−$2,000
	Increase linen expense account (P&L)	+$2,000
Guest supply transaction	Decrease guest supply inventory (CA)	−$1,000
	Increase guest supply expense account (P&L)	+$1,000

Similarities and Differences between the Balance Sheet and the P&L Statement

Let's take some time and review the characteristics and transactions that effect the P&L statement and the Balance Sheet.

SIMILARITIES

1. Both statements are subject to GAAP.
2. The Hotel Accounting Department or Corporate Accounting Department prepares both the financial statements.
3. Both statements have accounts that are a part of working capital and that will be used in the daily operations of the business.

Let's look at an example of how an Operations Manager uses Balance Sheet accounts in the operation of his or her department that produces actual financial results on the P&L Statement. A Housekeeping Manager is responsible for the linen, cleaning supplies, and guest supplies for the hotel. During the month, he or she may use products in each of these line accounts either by purchasing them from suppliers or taking them out of existing inventories.

For example, soap and shampoo are needed by the housekeepers. The Housekeeping Manager will first go to the housekeeping storeroom and obtain boxes of soap or shampoo from the existing inventories to issue to the housekeepers. If there are no boxes, the manager will order them from a supplier. **Par** amounts for each product are established to manage the inventory level and to determine when and how much to purchase. Pars are specific amounts of supplies and products needed to ensure the continuous availability of products and services used in operations. In our example of soap and shampoo, the operating par level for soap might be 12 boxes and shampoo 10 boxes. The reorder par for both might be four boxes. Our Housekeeping Manager would issue boxes of soap and shampoo until they get down to four boxes. The manager would then reorder 12 boxes of soap and 10 boxes of shampoo to reestablish the operating par levels. The four boxes left in the inventory at the time of placing the new order for soap and shampoo should be enough to last until the new order is received. If the hotel runs out of soap or shampoo before the new order is delivered, it should increase the reorder par to five or six cases to ensure supplies are available until the new order is received.

DIFFERENCES

1. The P&L shows financial performance *over a period of time* like a month or year. The Balance Sheet shows financial balances *at a specific time or date* like the end of the month, end of accounting period, or end of the year.
2. The P&L records revenues, expenses, and profit *amounts* incurred or spent during a specific month or accounting period. It also records Year-to-Date amounts for the same categories. The Balance Sheet records account *amounts or balances* at a specific time period such as the end of a month, end of accounting period, or end of a year.
3. The P&L *accumulates and totals* revenues received, expenses incurred, and the profit over the month or accounting period. A new month or accounting period starts with zero balances on the P&L. The Balance Sheet *records account activity* during the month or accounting period and the balance remaining at the end of the month. The ending balance for one month becomes the beginning balance for the next month.
4. The P&L has revenue, expense, and profit accounts, whereas the Balance Sheet has asset, liability, and owner equity accounts.
5. The P&L has actual, budget, and last year amounts, whereas the Balance Sheet has opening balances, activity, and ending balances.
6. The P&L is used by hospitality managers in operating their departments, and it measures the financial performance of the department. The Balance Sheet is used by hospitality managers in operating their department and it is also used by owners, investors, and outside financial institutions in evaluating the value and net worth of a business.

Pappadeaux Seafood Kitchen

Pappadeaux Seafood Kitchen is one of the nine restaurant concepts owned by Pappas Restaurants of Houston, Texas. Pappas operates over 90 restaurants in the United States with Pappadeaux having the largest number of restaurants and Texas having the largest number of Pappas restaurants. The menu includes Gulf Coast seafood and Louisiana-style favorites with a spicy Cajun flair.

(continued)

Photo Courtesy of Pappas Restaurants, Inc., Houston, TX.

A typical Pappadeaux Restaurant will have over 400 seats and include indoor and outdoor seating with a distinctive Dixieland feel. Take-out service is available and there are rooms for on-site catering functions. A selective wine list complements a large and well-stocked bar. Staffing generally includes 10–12 managers and over 100 employees. Visit the following Web site for more information www.pappadeaux.com.

Imagine you were a Pappadeaux manager and think about the following questions relating to your Balance Sheet and Statement of Cash Flows:

1. How is building and opening a 400+ seat Pappadeaux restaurant different from building a 150-seat Chili's or Olive Garden? Which Balance Sheet accounts would be most affected—current or long term? Explain why.
2. From a cash flow perspective, what are the main invoices and expenses that a Pappadeaux manager will need to plan for and pay daily, weekly, and monthly? Give some thought to this answer especially when you consider the purchasing of fresh food.
3. What do you think the two busiest and two slowest days of the week are for Pappadeaux sales? Explain your answer and tell how that affects cash inflows and outflows.

THE STATEMENT OF CASH FLOWS

The Statement of Cash Flows is the third financial statement that is used in measuring the financial performance of a company. It focuses on two areas of company operations. The first area is the cash account on the Balance Sheet. It identifies the movement of cash in and out of the cash account and the beginning and ending cash balances. Liquidity is the key term and measurement.

The second area is the source and use of funds generated by the company in using accounts on the Balance Sheet in daily operations. Working capital is the key term and measurement.

Definition

The **Statement of Cash Flows** measures the amount of cash a company has on hand and how cash flows through the company during the course of daily operations. The primary source of cash should be the revenues generated by the operations of a company or business. It should be sufficient to cover all expenses incurred in producing products, services, and profits. Key characteristics of the Statement of Cash Flows are as follows:

1. It involves the cash account of the Balance Sheet.
2. It has beginning and ending balances.
3. It shows how money is used in the daily operations of a business.
4. It measures liquidity.
5. It is a fundamental component of working capital.
6. It reflects the increases and decreases in Balance Sheet accounts.
7. It has three categories—operating, financing, and investing.

Cash Flow and Liquidity

There are several key elements of measuring and managing cash that are important for hospitality students to know and understand. A business must pay as much attention to managing cash and maintaining sufficient cash balances as it pays to making an operating profit.

CASH FLOW   The main reason that the cash account on the Balance Sheet is so important is that a company must maintain sufficient balance in its cash account to pay for all operating expenses in a timely and efficient manner. Purchases of supplies and materials from vendors, payment of wages to employees, and paying long-term obligations such as bank loans on time are critical to the success of a company. The Director of Finance of the hotel is responsible for managing the cash account so as to see that no disbursements are made in payment of obligations unless there is money in the cash account to cover these expenses and obligations.

Cash increases come through revenues recorded on the P&L Statement as a result of operating activities. Specifically, the cash account increases with the daily hotel or restaurant deposit of cash, traveler's checks, and individual or company checks received in payment of products and services provided by the hotel and directly billed to the customer. Each day, the hotel also receives electronic cash transfers directly into its cash account from the credit card companies in payment of guest accounts paid by credit card. Finally, specific accounts billed directly to individual guests or companies progress through the accounts receivable cycle until the bill is approved by the customer/company and a check is processed and mailed to the hotel in payment of amounts owed to the hotel.

Cash is a current asset on the Balance Sheet, so it will always have a beginning balance in the beginning of the month, activity during the month, and an ending balance at the end of the month. This activity in the cash account represents the cash flow of a company.

LIQUIDITY   *Liquidity* refers to the amount of cash or cash equivalents that a company has to cover its daily operating expenses and this is maintained in its cash or cash equivalent accounts on the Balance Sheet. This includes the length of time it will generally take to convert a Balance Sheet account to cash. A short conversion time period reflects a liquid asset. A long conversion time period reflects a nonliquid asset. Let's look at some examples of assets accounts on the Balance Sheet that illustrate liquidity.

- *Cash.*   Cash is the most liquid asset of all. It is available for immediate use.
- *Cash Equivalents.*   It is the next most liquid asset. These are current assets that can be converted to cash in a matter of hours, for example, 24–48 hours. Common stock, company and Treasury bonds, certificates of deposits (CDs), and overnight investments are examples of cash equivalents. They can be sold and the receipts are usually deposited in the cash account within a matter of days.
- *Liquid Asset.*   These are the accounts that are in process to be turned into cash. Accounts receivable is an example of a liquid asset. The sale has been made, the invoice has been sent to the buyer, and payment is in the process of being made. Receipt of payment and deposit in the cash account can be in a matter of days or weeks. The point to remember is that the next transaction of a liquid asset is that of being deposited into the cash account.
- *Nonliquid Asset.*   These are accounts that are not close to being turned into cash. Inventory is an example of a nonliquid current asset. The fact that money is tied up in inventory means that it has not been produced or sold yet. In fact, there are three categories of inventory reflecting three stages of production and, therefore, three stages of liquidity.

  Finished Goods.   Inventory of assembled and completed products at the manufacturing plant that are waiting to be shipped, on the shelves of a distributor ready to be shipped to retail outlets, or on the shelves of retail outlets ready to be sold to customers. Cars on dealership lots and on trains heading to dealerships are examples of finished goods inventory.

  Work-in-Process.   It is the inventory that is in the process of being assembled into a final product. It is no longer a raw material and will soon be converted into finished goods. Cars moving along the assembly line are examples of work-in-process inventory.

  Raw Materials.   It is the inventory that has not been used yet to produce a product. It is sitting on the shelves in the warehouse or in piles in the stockyard. It is a long way from being converted into cash. Steel at the automotive manufacturing plant is an example of raw material inventory.

Generally, no estimates are made of when inventory will be converted to cash because of the status and many variables involved in managing inventories.

Finished goods are much closer to being converted into sales and cash than work in process or raw materials. Finished goods are more liquid than raw materials or work in process.

- *Long-Term Assets.*   They are the assets that are not intended to be converted into cash but to be used in the daily operations of the company over an extended period of time. They are part of the capitalization of a company and represent assets that have a longer life, generally 1–50 years. They will only be sold or replaced when they are worn out or when they are outdated or fully depreciated.

It is important for a company to maintain acceptable levels of liquidity. Each industry has a standard that identifies the amount of cash or cash equivalents that a company should maintain to have acceptable levels of liquidity. Two of those measures are the working capital and the current ratio. Working capital is a dollar amount and is defined as current assets minus current liabilities. It implies that a company should have a higher amount of current assets than current liabilities. This means that the company owns more current assets than it owes current liabilities. It is important to look at the direction or trend of working capital from month to month. Is it getting larger and stronger or is it getting smaller and becoming a concern or problem?

The current ratio is a number and is defined as current assets divided by current liabilities. Again, a company would like a current ratio of more than 1 because it means that the company has more current assets than current liabilities. It is also important to look at the direction in which the current ratio is moving. Is it getting stronger or weaker? Is it high and safe or low and unsafe? Industry standards will be applied to a company's current ratio to determine if it is acceptable and moving in the right direction or it is a financial concern.

We will use the financial information in Exhibit 5.1 to illustrate the working capital and calculate the current ratio.

$$\text{Working Capital} = \text{Current Assets} - \text{Current Liabilities}$$
$$= 205 - 125$$
$$= \$80$$

$$\text{Current Ratio} = \frac{\text{Current Assets}}{\text{Current Liabilities}}$$
$$= \frac{205}{125}$$
$$= 1.64$$

Classifications of Cash Flow

Cash flow activities are classified into three main categories or **classifications of cash flow** that describe the nature of the cash inflow or outflow: (1) operating activities, (2) investing activities, and (3) financing activities. Hospitality managers are primarily involved in the operating activity but should have a good understanding of financing and investing activities.

Operating activities include *cash inflow* primarily from the sale of products and services to guests. This is the main reason for the existence of a company or business and is, therefore, the most important cash flow activity. Hospitality managers are directly involved in maximizing hotel and restaurant revenues. *Cash outflow* involving operating activities include the payment of wages and benefits to employees, the payment for supplies and materials to vendors, and the payment of taxes and other expenses to appropriate agencies. Hospitality managers, again, are directly involved in managing and controlling expenses to maximize profitability, which should also result in the creation of a strong positive cash flow.

Investing activities include cash outflow that involves purchasing long-term assets or investing in marketable securities. When these investments are reversed, *cash inflow* is created. For example, if older equipment or properties are sold, it results in cash being received and deposited in the cash account, therefore, this is a cash inflow. The same occurs when marketable securities are sold and cash is received and deposited in the cash account. The Director of Finance, along with corporate senior management is primarily involved with investing activities.

Financing activities involve the creation or use of cash for capitalization purposes. Cash inflow results from selling common stock or obtaining a bank loan. Therefore, cash account goes up. Cash outflow results from repurchasing common stock or the repayment of a bank loan. The cash account is decreased and the funds are used to buy the common stock or to repay the bank loan. Financing activities primarily involve the owner and management company working with the Director of Finance and General Manager in conducting financing activities.

Source and Use of Funds Statement

The **Source and Use of Funds Statement** is part of the Statement of Cash Flow and shows how cash is created or used among the different accounts on the Balance Sheet. It involves the changes in the balances of each account on the Balance Sheet. It will be helpful to refer back to the Fundamental Accounting Equation in discussing the changes in individual Balance Sheet accounts that result in a source of funds or a use of funds.

$$\text{Assets} = \text{Liabilities} + \text{Owner Equity}$$

Let's begin with the following table that separates sources and uses of funds and thereby demonstrates increases or decreases in the accounts:

Sources	Uses
1. Decrease in asset accounts	1. Increase in asset accounts
2. Increase in liability accounts	2. Decrease in liability accounts
3. Increase in owner equity accounts	3. Decrease in owner equity accounts

SOURCES OF CASH   A decrease in an asset account means that the asset balance has gone down or declined and less money is left in that account. For example, collecting $5,000 in accounts receivable (CA) means that accounts receivable is now lower by $5,000. The offsetting/balancing entry is cash (CA) increases by $5,000. The decrease in accounts receivable is a source of funds or source of cash. Another example is when food inventory (CA) is used to produce a menu item and the resulting sale of $3,000. The accounting entry is $3,000 decrease in food inventory that was sold and $3,000 increase in food cost on the P&L. Again the decrease in inventory creates a source of funds. In both these examples, money was freed up from a current asset account that generated a source of cash.

An increase in liabilities is also a source of cash and means that the amount owed by vendors or other companies has increased. Therefore, it is a source of cash because the actual cash disbursement has been delayed.

An increase in owner equity is also a source of cash. This means that owners have made additional contributions to the company in the paid-in capital account or that individual investors have bought more of the common stock of the company or that Retained Earnings have increased as a result of annual operating profits. All these transactions are a source of cash because the amount invested in the company in owner equity accounts has increased.

USES OF CASH   An increase in an asset account means that the balance in that account has gone up, which requires a cash outlay. For example, the company purchases and pays for $10,000 in materials that increase the inventory account. That is a use of funds because $10,000 has been taken out of cash flow and is "parked" in the inventory account. Therefore, cash flow is used in this transaction.

A decrease in liabilities is a use of cash and means the amount owed by vendors or other companies has decreased because the company has made payment to them. Using the same $10,000 inventory purchase example but not paying cash results in the following transactions:

Inventory + $10,000   Accounts Payable + $10,000

This part of the transaction is a source of funds because the company *has not paid the $10,000 invoice*. The second part of the transaction when the company pays the invoice is represented this way:

Accounts Payable − $10,000   Cash − $10,000

This is a use of cash. When the decrease in accounts payable occurs, the transaction is a use of funds.

A decrease in owner equity is a use of cash. This means that the paid-in capital account has decreased because one or several of the owners have taken money out of the account in the form of a cash disbursement. A decrease in the Common Stock account means that investors have sold the stock, resulting in a cash disbursement. The final activity is a decrease in retained earnings, which means that the company had an operating loss and money was taken from the retained earnings account to cover the loss. This is also a cash disbursement. In each of these owner equity transactions, the account value decreased requiring a corresponding decrease in cash as cash was disbursed or paid to cover the transaction.

Summary

The Balance Sheet is the financial statement that measures a company's value or net worth at a specific date. It is also called the A&L Statement. The Balance Sheet is organized according to the Fundamental Accounting Equation:

Assets = Liabilities + Owner Equity

Assets are resources or what a company owns

Liabilities are debts or obligations that a company owes

Owner Equity is who owns or how a company is owned

The main characteristics of a Balance Sheet are as follows:

1. It measures the value or net worth of a company at a specific date in time.
2. The Fundamental Accounting Equation describes the Balance Sheet

Assets = Liabilities + Owner Equity

3. It is made up of accounts organized by assets, liability, or owner equity.
4. These accounts are divided into current accounts (under one year obligations), referred to as working capital, and long-term accounts (more than one year obligations), referred to as capitalization.
5. Each account has a beginning balance, monthly activity, and an ending balance.
6. Unlike the P&L Statement, managers are not expected to provide critiques of monthly Balance Sheet activity. This is done by the Accounting Department.
7. Accounting managers reconcile or balance the accounts each month on the Balance Sheet.
8. Current accounts are used as working capital in operating the business. The definition of working capital is current assets minus current liabilities.
9. Long-term Liability accounts and Owner Equity accounts are used as capitalization, which provides the money to start, renovate, or expand a business.

Capitalization refers to the way a company or business obtains and uses money to start or expand a business. It involves obtaining long-term debt or raising funds from investors by way of paid-in capital or common stock to purchase long-term assets. Working Capital is the amount of funds used by a business in its daily operations and is defined as current assets minus current liabilities. Hospitality managers will be using the assets in the Balance Sheet accounts in the daily operations of their departments.

The Statement of Cash Flows identifies the movement of cash in and out of the cash account in the daily operations of a business. It measures the amount of cash available and identifies how it is used. The cash account is the most important current asset account because it is used to purchase the other assets required to produce the products and services and it is used to pay all operating expenses including the salaries and wages of employees making the products and services. Key characteristics of the Statement of Cash Flows are as follows:

1. It involves the cash account of the Balance Sheet.
2. It has beginning and ending balances.
3. It shows how money is used in the daily operations of a business.
4. It measures liquidity.
5. It is a fundamental component of working capital.
6. It reflects the increases and decreases in Balance Sheet accounts.
7. It has three main categories—operating, investing, and financing.

Cash flow activities are divided into three categories: operating activities, financing activities, and investing activities. Hospitality managers will be primarily involved in operating activities as they manage their departments.

Liquidity is an important measurement of cash flow. It is the amount of cash or cash equivalents that a company has to cover its daily operating expenses. The dollar amount available in the cash account is immediately available for use in company operations and requires no time for conversion into the Cash Account.

Hospitality Manager Takeaways

1. It is important for hospitality managers to have a general understanding of the Balance Sheet and Statement of Cash Flows. The daily operation of their department will effect both the statements.
2. Working capital is the accounts on the Balance Sheet that hospitality managers use on a daily basis—primarily cash, inventories, and accounts payable.
3. Hospitality managers must understand the importance of liquidity, which is the ability to maintain sufficient cash account balances to pay all debts and operating responsibilities.
4. It is important for hospitality managers to understand the basic characteristics of the Balance Sheet and Statement of Cash Flows and be able to have a positive impact on them through the daily operations of their departments.

Key Terms

Accounts receivable: what the company is owed for providing products and services to customers. Revenues recorded but uncollected.

Accounts payable: products or services received by a company but not paid for that are due within one year.

Assets: the resources owned by a company that are used in the production of products and services by that company.
   Current: assets that are used or consumed during a one-year time period.
   Long term: assets with a useful life of over one year.

Balance Sheet: the financial statement that measures the value or net worth of a business as of a specific date. Also called the A&L Statement.

Capitalization: identifies the way that a business obtains and uses money to start or expand a business by purchasing long-term assets.

Cash: funds that are in the cash account and available for use in daily business operations.

Classification of cash flow: operating activities, financial activities, and investment activities.

Fundamental Accounting Equation: Assets = Liabilities + Owner Equity.

Inventory: assets in the form of materials and supplies that the company has purchased but not yet used in the production of products and services.

Liabilities: obligations owed by a company.
   Current: obligations that are due within one year.
   Long term: obligations that are due for more than one year.

Owner Equity: the amount invested in a company by owners or investors, including Paid In Capital, Common Stock, and Retained Earnings.

Par: the specified amount of product that should be maintained in inventory to provide the necessary products and serviced to guests without interruption of service. This includes an order par amount that specifies when orders should be placed with suppliers to replenish inventories.

Source and Use of funds statement: a part of the Statement of Cash Flow that shows how cash is created (source) and disbursed (used) among the different accounts on the Balance Sheet.

Statement of Cash Flows: measures the liquidity and identifies the flow of cash in a company.

Working capital: the dollar amount provided for the daily operations of a business. It is invested in the current assets of a business primarily in cash, accounts receivable, and inventory.

Review Questions

1. Explain the financial information contained in a Balance Sheet and how it is used.
2. Describe working capital and capitalization and explain what each is used for. Include the Balance Sheet accounts that are used in each process.
3. What accounts on the Balance Sheet will hospitality managers generally use in the daily operations of their departments?
4. List five characteristics of the Balance Sheet.
5. Compare and contrast liquidity with profitability.

6. List five characteristics of the Statement of Cash Flows.

7. Name the three classifications of cash flow.

8. Name three changes in Balance Sheet accounts that are a source of funds and three that are a use of funds.

Practice Exercises

1. Which of the following accounts are part of working capital and which are a part of capitalization.

A. ___ Accounts payable

B. ___ Line of credit

C. ___ Laundry washers and dryers

D. ___ Inventory

E. ___ Cash

F. ___ Paid-in capital

1. Capitalization

2. Working capital

2. Following is the Balance Sheet in $ for the GTO Hotel:

Cash	250,000	Accounts Payable	175,000
Accounts Receivable	125,000	Wages Payable	145,000
Inventory	235, 000	Taxes Payable	80,000
Total Current Assets	**610,000**	**Total Current Liabilities**	**400,000**
Equipment	190,000	Bank Loan	500,000
Property	1,250,000		
Total Long-Term Assets	**2,050,000**	**Total Liabilities**	**900,000**
		Paid-in Capital	1,000,000
		Retained Earnings	760,000
		Total Owner Equity	**1,760,000**
Total Assets	**2,660,000**	**Total Liabilities and Owner Equity**	**2,660,000**

Answer the following:

_____ What is the working capital amount?

_____ What is the total capitalization amount?

_____ What is the liabilities capitalization percent?

_____ What is the Owner Equity capitalization percent?

CHAPTER

6

Hotel Management Reports

LEARNING OBJECTIVES

- To learn about internal hotel management reports
- To understand and be able to use Daily Revenue Reports
- To understand and be able to use Revenue Forecasting Reports
- To understand and be able to use Labor Productivity Reports
- To understand retention and flow-through—the relationship between revenue changes and profit changes

CHAPTER OUTLINE

Introduction

Internal Hotel Management Reports
    Definition
    Types and Uses

Daily Reports
    Daily Revenue Report
    Labor Productivity Report

Weekly Reports
    Weekly Revenue Forecast
    Weekly Wage and Cost Scheduling
    Profitability Forecasting

Monthly Internal Management Reports
    Monthly or Accounting Period P&L Statement
    Profitability, Retention, and Flow-through
    Monthly P&L Statement Critiques

Summary

Hospitality Manager Takeaways

Key Terms

Review Questions

Practice Exercises

INTRODUCTION

The three financial statements that we have discussed in previous chapters—the P&L Statement, Balance Sheet, and Statement of Cash Flow—are used by both management and outside parties in evaluating hotel operations. We will now talk about two types of internal financial and management reports that are used by hotel managers.

- One report summarizes and presents the operating results for the previous day or week.
- The second report forecasts or schedules operations and functions for the next day or next week.

Managers use these reports to understand and evaluate past operations and to plan their daily and weekly future operations. They will make any necessary changes to daily operations to achieve budgets and forecasts, or to respond to market or outside conditions.

Internal management reports are prepared by the Accounting Office and distributed to hotel managers for their use. Refer again to the Financial Management Cycle.

1. Operations produce the numbers
2. Accounting prepares the numbers
3. Operations and accounting analyze the numbers
4. Operations applies the numbers to change or improve operations

The reports that we will be discussing in this chapter are examples of the second step in the Financial Management Cycle. Operations produce the numbers, whether they are good or bad. It is the responsibility of the Accounts Department to collect and prepare management reports and financial statements from hotel or restaurant operations so that they can be used by managers to identify problems, evaluate operations, and come up with recommendations to improve operations. The management can then apply the information from these reports to the next day or next week's operations. The goals are to understand what happened, identify why it happened, and determine how it can be corrected or improved.

INTERNAL HOTEL MANAGEMENT REPORTS

Definition

An **internal management report** is a report that contains detailed operating information covering a specific time for a specific product, customer, department, or for the entire hotel or restaurant. It can contain the operational results for the previous day or week, or it can contain the information required to plan the next day or week. Daily and weekly reports are used internally as management tools, while the monthly reports are used for both as a management tool and to measure financial performance by reporting the monthly financial results for the three formal financial statements—the P&L Statement, Balance Sheet, and Statement of Cash Flow.

These internal management reports are extremely valuable to operations managers. They are a guide—a true management tool—for them to use in evaluating and managing their daily operations. They are even classified into a.m. or morning shift and p.m. or evening shift schedules or reports. The more a manager understands these reports, the better he or she will be able to use them to improve or change daily operations.

Types and Uses

Reports containing daily, weekly, monthly, and quarterly information are prepared. They include reports that provide actual operating results and financial information for previous time periods and reports that plan in detail for future weeks or months. Daily and weekly reports that provide the results of actual operations are used to forecast and schedule operations for the next day, week, month, or quarter. Table 6.1 illustrates the types and uses of internal management reports.

We will discuss the main reports in detail, including examples of the reports used by some of the major hotels and restaurant companies. Keep in mind that one type of report provides historical operating information (looking back) and the other type forecasts and schedules operations for the next week (looking forward).

TABLE 6.1   Internal Management Reports

	Daily	Weekly	Monthly	Quarterly	Annually
Performance Reports—The Past					
Daily Revenue Report	X				
Daily Labor Report	X				
Weekly Financial Report		X			
Monthly P&L			X		
Profitability Measurement			X	X	X
Planning Reports—The Future					
The Daily Room Count	X				
The Daily Banquet Schedule	X				
Weekly Revenue Forecast		X			
Weekly Labor Forecast		X			
Monthly Revenue Forecast			X		
Quarterly Revenue Forecast				X	
End of Year Revenue Forecast					X

DAILY REPORTS

The two most important daily reports provide information on revenues and labor costs. The names and formats of these reports can be different from company to company, but the content is the same. They focus on providing the actual operating results for the previous day and comparing those results with forecasts, budget, previous month, and last year information. These comparisons identify if operations are meeting expectations, not meeting expectations, or are exceeding expectations.

Daily Revenue Report

The **Daily Revenue Report** is prepared during the night audit shift and collects and reports actual revenue information of the previous day. It can be called the Sales and Occupancy Report, Daily Revenue Report, or Gross Revenue Report depending on the company. Each report contains virtually the same information. We will discuss a Daily Revenue Report that is organized into the following sections: (1) Hotel daily and month-to-date revenue by department, (2) Hotel daily and month-to-date room statistics, (3) Restaurant and Banquets Summary, and (4) Hotel market segment information.

The *daily revenue by department* is organized in a format similar to the P&L Statement. The *title* provides the name of the hotel, type of report, and date of the report. The *horizontal headings* provide revenue results for the previous day and compare those results with the budget and last year's actual revenues. It also provides month-to-date accumulated revenue for Actual, Budget, and Last Year. Managers can use this report to evaluate how their current financial results compare to the budget and last year for the previous day and month to date. The *vertical headings* show the individual revenue centers (or departments) for the hotel. Exhibits 6.1–6.3 are examples of the sections contained in a typical Daily Revenue Report.

Note how this section efficiently organizes the revenues by departments for the previous day and for the period-to-date or month-to-date. A manager can look at this report and determine whether his or her sales for the day met the budget, were below the budget, or were above the budget. He or she can also compare the sales for the day to last year's sales for the day. These comparisons will show if daily operations are producing the expected revenues along with where and why operations are producing the expected results. A manager can also compare his or her department revenues to the budget and last year's period to date results. This comparison will show the trends of sales as they are accumulated throughout the period or month. While a manager will be most interested in the revenues of his or her department, they will also be interested to know the revenues of the total hotel and how they compare to budget and last year for the day and for period to date.

The next section provides statistical information or results (Exhibit 6.2). It is also organized by *Today* and *Period to Date* and provides the Actual, Budget, and Last Year's results. The statistics reported can be room nights, average room rates, guests, or percentages.

EXHIBIT 6.1
HOTEL DAILY REVENUE REPORT: REVENUE SECTION

10th Day of 12th Period   Day of Week: Monday

	Today			Period to Date		
SALES	**Actual ($)**	**Budget ($)**	**Last Year ($)**	**Actual ($)**	**Budget ($)**	**Last Year ($)**
Transient Rooms	29,567	19,500	33,284	328,941	195,000	208,963
Group Rooms	56,235	51,000	18,493	314,683	510,000	267,844
Contract	483	500	0	3,194	5,000	0
Rooms Sales full day	**86,285**	**71,000**	**51,777**	**646,818**	**710,000**	**476,807**
GNS	1,243	600	245	4,712	6,000	5,749
Part-Day	0	200	125	1,386	2,000	1,738
Rebates	845	1,200	380	11,882	12,000	9,471
Net Room Sales	**86,683**	**70,600**	**51,767**	**641,034**	**706,000**	**474,823**
Telephone	1,285	1,500	415	14,581	15,000	6,418
Gift Shop	4,538	4,000	2,198	34,176	40,000	25,756
Restaurant	45,260	28,000	33,362	241,216	280,000	182,734
Room Service	1,248	1,500	843	17,863	15,000	13,294
Lounge	2,984	2,600	1,739	26,395	26,000	21,739
Catering	26,442	30,000	17,338	344,826	300,000	237,482
F&B Total	**75,934**	**62,100**	**53,282**	**630,300**	**621,000**	**455,249**
Total Hotel	**168,440**	**138,200**	**107,662**	**1,320,091**	**1,382,000**	**962,246**
Over/Under Budget	+30,240			(61,909)		

The first section on *room nights* reports the total number of rooms in the hotel, the number of rooms sold, rooms available for sale, out of order rooms, complimentary rooms, and vacant rooms. This section also reports the occupancy percent for rooms occupied to total rooms and rooms occupied to available rooms. A manager can use this information to determine if the previous day's rooms sold met, missed, or exceeded the established budget for the day and the actual results for the last year.

The next section reports the *average room rates* for different market segments as well as for the total hotel. The Front Office Department is directly responsible for the Transient rooms sold and Transient average room rate, while the Sales Department is directly responsible for the Group rooms sold and Group average room rate. The Full Day Average Room Rate reports the room rate for the day before any adjustments. The Net Average Room Rate reports the room rate after Part-Day Revenues and Guaranteed No-Show revenues have been added and after any rebates or adjustments of room accounts have been taken. And RevPAR

EXHIBIT 6.2
HOTEL DAILY REVENUE REPORT: STATISTICS SECTION

10th Day of 12th Period   Day of Week: Monday

Statistics	Today			Period to Date		
	Actual	Budget	Last Year	Actual	Budget	Last Year
Room Nights						
Total Rooms	453	453	427	4,077	4,077	3,859
Complimentary	6	12	10	90	91	125
Out of Order	1	0	5	19	0	27
Rooms Available	446	441	412	3,968	3,986	3,707
Rooms Sold	429	409	283	3,185	3,116	2,873
Rooms Vacant	17	32	129	783	870	834
Available Occupancy %	96.2	92.7	68.7	80.3	78.2	77.5
Total Occupancy %	94.7	90.3	66.2	78.1	76.4	74.4
Average Room Rates ($)						
Transient	302.39	229.55	206.48	276.50	229.59	213.46
Group	191.28	185.38	159.20	183.61	183.97	168.17
Contract						
Full Day Average Rate	199.94	175.43	168.08	206.67	186.53	172.14
Net Average Rate	200.88	168.47	167.89	204.41	178.93	170.71
RevPAR	190.18	152.04	111.21	159.78	136.83	123.27
Miscellaneous						
Total Guests	690			5,948		
Arrivals	102			1,078		
Departures	119			1,129		
Walk-Ins	3			33		
Guaranteed No-Shows	5			53		

reports how well the hotel management team maximized room rates as well as rooms sold in producing total room revenues for the day and period to date.

The last section reports useful miscellaneous statistics such as total number of guests in the hotel, number of arrival and departures, walk in guests (guests that did not make a reservation in advance), and the number of no-show guests. Managers will use these daily statistics to help plan for the next day's operations.

The final area of information is the Restaurant Summary (Exhibit 6.3). It reports the previous day's sales for all restaurants and beverage outlets and for the Catering Department. It is similar to the Sales and the Statistics areas in that it has an Actual, Budget, and Last Year's section to record the restaurant sales by

EXHIBIT 6.3
HOTEL DAILY REVENUE REPORT: RESTAURANT SUMMARY

Today

Outlets	Food Sales ($)			Food Customers			Food Average Check ($)	
	Actual	Budget	LYA	Actual	Budget		Actual	Budget
Restaurant	45,260	28,000	33,362	1,573	1,057		28.77	26.50
Room Service	1,248	1,500	843	58	68		21.43	22.00
Lounge	2,984	2,600	1,739	0	0		0	0
Subtotal Food & Beverage	49,492	32,100	35,944	1,631	1,125		28.52	26.22
Catering	26,442	30,000	17,338	685	715		38.60	42.00
Total Food & Beverage	75,934	62,100	53,282	2,316	1,840		32.79	33.75

Period to Date

Outlets	Food Sales ($)			Food Customers			Food Average Check ($)	
	Actual	Budget	LYA	Actual	Budget		Actual	Budget
Restaurant	241,216	280,000	182,734	8,196	10,560		29.42	26.50
Room Service	17,863	15,000	13,294	773	680		23.12	22.00
Lounge	26,395	26,000	21,739	0	0		0	0
Subtotal Food & Beverage	285,474	321,000	217,767	8,966	11,240		28.90	26.25
Catering	344,826	300,000	237,482	7,752	7,140		44.48	42.00
Total Food & Beverage	630,300	621,000	455,249	16,918	18,380		37.26	33.79

outlet for the previous day and period to date. Other helpful information for the restaurant manager is the actual average check and customer counts from the previous day's operations. Managers compare actual results to determine if sales for the day met the established goals and budgets and if they were more or less than last year's sales. They can identify the increase or decrease in the restaurant revenue compared to the budget and last year and determine if these changes are the result of higher or lower customer counts or higher or lower average checks compared to the budget and last year.

These reports contain a lot of information. They are complete and detailed. Each manager in the hotel will focus on the operating information for his or her department. The front office and housekeeping managers will focus on room sales and statistics. The restaurant, lounge, and catering managers will focus on food and beverage sales and statistics. Again, there is a lot of information on these reports, but each manager will focus on his or her own department and will be familiar with trends that will affect forecasts, the established budget, recent local and national events, and the status of the local economy. Working with the Daily Revenue Report each day will enable a hospitality manager to become familiar with and better understand the operational results contained in the Daily Revenue Report and how internal or external factors affect the results for his or her department and for the entire hotel.

Other hotel companies may choose to provide operating information such as labor costs and estimated profits for the day in addition to the revenues on its Daily Revenue Report. This additional expense information enables a manager to relate revenues for the day to the costs incurred to produce those revenues. If the manager sees problems with any of the costs, he or she can make changes and corrections immediately. For example, if sales were over the budget and above the forecast, what was the amount of any additional expenses incurred to support the higher level of sales. If sales were underbudget and less than that forecasted, did expenses decrease proportionately to maintain expected productivities, profit margins, and retention/flow-through standards.

It is important to go back to one of the fundamental financial analysis concepts—comparing actual results to other measures to establish a meaning. These daily reports provide the financial numbers that are produced from daily operations. These results are compared to the results from other operating time periods such as last month or last year to show if operations are improving, if revenues and profits are increasing, or if established budgets and forecasts are being met. After going through these daily reports, a department manager can adjust revenue forecasts, labor schedules, or make other operational changes if necessary. These daily reports can be a very effective management tool if understood and used consistently.

Labor Productivity Report

The second example of a Daily Revenue Report also includes daily labor productivity or wage cost information on the daily report. The managers in this hotel company have both revenue and labor information available to them on the same report. This is convenient, and by reviewing this report, they can make any necessary changes to labor schedules and costs that will improve operations and financial results.

The hotel company in the first example provides the labor and cost information in a separate daily or weekly labor report. The weekly labor report contains detailed information on sales and expenses and reports the labor expenses or wage cost for the previous day. These results are compared to budget or forecast numbers to determine if established labor guidelines and productivities are met. Each department manager will focus on his or her specific department results. Labor and wage costs are analyzed in two parts—labor hours that are referred to as man-hours in the hospitality industry and wage cost percentages. Both are important.

LABOR PRODUCTIVITY AND MAN-HOURS   This measure of productivity does not include any dollar cost information. It relates units of labor to units of output. More specifically, what amount of man-hours or labor hours are required to support a certain volume of business. A **man-hour** is defined as the number of hours one employee works in performing his or her job responsibilities. Typically, full-time employees are scheduled for an 8-hour work day and a 40-hour work week. Any additional hours during the week will result in overtime. So our basic unit of man-hour measurement is an 8-hour work day and a 40-hour work week. Examples of formulas and ratios used in the hotel and restaurant industry are as follows:

1. *Man-hours per room sold.*   The formula is total man-hours divided by total rooms sold. This measure is used by the front office and housekeeping departments to control man-hours in relation to business volumes. Each department has established labor productivity guidelines, such as man-hours per room sold, that are used in preparing budgets and forecasts. If actual results are different from these guidelines, managers are expected to identify what caused the difference or variations and then make any necessary corrections.

2. *Rooms cleaned per shift.*   The formula is total rooms cleaned divided by one 8-hour shift. This formula is used by housekeeping managers to schedule the number of housekeepers each day based on rooms occupied the previous night. The number of rooms cleaned by one housekeeper on an 8-hour shift can range from as low as 12 rooms at a resort to as high as 18 rooms at a full-service or limited service hotel. The guest rooms in a resort are typically larger with more amenities and services and, therefore, require more time to clean.

3. *Man-hours per customer.*   The formula is total man-hours used divided by total customers served in the restaurant. This relationship describes the amount of man-hours required to service or take care of a corresponding volume or level of customers served in the restaurant per meal period.

These formulas are used to calculate the number of man-hours required to work based on the forecasted number of rooms to be sold or customers to be served the next week. They are true measures of labor productivities because they relate labor input in man-hours to output in the form of products and services produced in terms of rooms sold or customers served. These labor measurements do not involve any cost dollars or revenue dollars.

Four Seasons Scottsdale

The Four Seasons Resort Scottsdale at Troon North is a 210-room luxury resort located in north Scottsdale, Arizona. Guest rooms are in one- or two-story casitas that either overlook the swimming pools, golf course, or Sonoran Desert. Each room includes a gas burning fireplace, generously proportioned bathroom, and outdoor terrace or balcony with magnificent desert views. Guests have several dining options, each with inside or outside seating. The 1265-seat Crescent Moon Restaurant offers breakfast, lunch, and dinner; the 100-seat Talavera Restaurant offers fine dining for dinner; and

(continued)

the 155-seat Saguaro Blossom offers poolside lunch, snacks, and cocktails. The Onyx Lounge offers beverages in a relaxing setting both indoors and outdoors. And finally, there is 24-hour in-casita dining.

Photo Courtesy of Four Seasons Scottsdale at Troon North.

For guests attending group functions, the Four Seasons Scottsdale includes over 17,000 and 10,000 square feet of indoor and outdoor meeting space, respectively, with multiple combinations to meet the needs of all sorts of meetings. Guests also have access to a 12,000-square-foot spa with 14 treatment rooms, golf at the two Troon North golf courses, or relaxing space at either of the two swimming pools. Visit the following Web site for more information www.fourseasons.con/scottsdale/.

As you read the material in this chapter, answer the following questions as it relates to the Four Seasons Scottsdale Resort.

1. How many Revenue Departments do you think are included in the Daily Revenue Report? Name them.
2. List the departments that prepare weekly wage forecasts that the Director of Rooms Operations is responsible for and also the departments that the Director of Food and Beverage is responsible for.
3. Which revenue center (rooms, restaurants, or banquets) do you think generates the highest sales? Explain why.

WAGE COST PERCENTAGE   This productivity measure compares the wage cost in dollars to the corresponding revenue in dollars. It converts the labor productivity in units to the labor cost in dollars and the revenue produced in dollars. The relationship now measures the dollar cost in wages incurred to the corresponding dollar revenue levels resulting from rooms sold or meals served. Examples of wage cost percentages are as follows:

1. *Wage Cost per Occupied Room.*   This formula has two steps. First, man-hours used times average hourly wage rate equals wage cost in dollars. Second, wage cost in dollars divided by rooms sold (same as rooms occupied) equals wage cost per occupied room. This shows how well managers are controlling labor dollar costs compared to actual rooms sold in the hotel.

2. *Front Office Wage Cost.*   The formula is total front office (front desk, reservations, bellmen, and concierge) wage cost in dollars divided by total room revenue in dollars. The resulting wage cost percentage measures the relationship in dollars between the wage cost incurred and that required to generate or support an expected level of revenue dollars. A hotel will have budget and forecast guidelines to achieve expected productivities and the actual wage cost percentage will be compared to the budgeted or forecasted wage cost to determine if expected productivities are achieved. The Front Office Manager is responsible for managing the Front Office wage cost percentage.

3. *Housekeeping Wage Cost.*   The formula is total housekeeping (housekeepers, housemen, public space, and supervisors) wage cost in dollars divided by total room revenue in dollars. This measures the housekeeping wage cost in relation to the number of rooms cleaned. The Director of Housekeeping is responsible for managing the Housekeeping wage cost percentage.

4. *Restaurant Wage Cost.*   The formula is total restaurant (servers, bussers, hostess, and cashier) wage cost in dollars divided by total restaurant revenue in dollars. The Restaurant Manager is responsible for managing the Restaurant wage cost percentage.

Labor productivities like man-hours per occupied room and man-hours per cover are the best measure of productivities because they measure labor input against labor output. It is the most important measure for managing wage costs. The next productivity measure identifies the dollar cost incurred to produce products and services and relates that cost to the dollar revenue resulting from the sale of products and services. This is the best measure of the financial relationship between expenses and revenues. Both measures—labor productivities and labor cost percentages—are essential in managing expenses in operating departments.

It really doesn't matter whether labor productivity is included in one report or in two separate reports. What is important is that the daily labor productivity reports are used and applied to department operations to enable them to run smoother and produce maximum revenues and profits.

WEEKLY REPORTS

The weekly reports are the primary reports used by managers to review and critique operations for the previous day and previous week and to forecast and prepare for the next week because operations are planned for in weekly time periods. Revenues are forecasted for the upcoming week, wages are scheduled for each day of the upcoming week, employee schedules are prepared for the upcoming week, and all operations for the upcoming week are planned in weekly planning meetings. Week is the key planning and measurement time period. Although managers are concerned with the daily operations, the planning generally involves planning each day in the upcoming week. The two most important weekly reports again are the revenue reports and the labor productivity reports.

There are two main uses of the weekly reports: forecasting to prepare for upcoming operations and critiquing the past week's operations. Some steps in the forecasting process are as follows: First, managers look at the budget that was prepared for the upcoming week. This will be the starting point for their weekly plan or forecast. Second, managers review recent results and business volume levels to see if adjustments need to be made to the budget because of the prevailing conditions. Third, managers prepare the revenue forecasts and wage schedules for the upcoming week based on this information. This becomes the weekly revenue forecast and will be the main planning document for each Revenue Department in the hotel. Hotel operations will be scheduled shift by shift and day by day based on this forecast. This part of the weekly report is about forecasting and planning.

The second use of weekly reports is analyzing or critiquing the previous week's performance to see how actual operations results compared with the budget or forecast. Following are the steps in the critiquing process: First, managers analyze the actual performance and compare it with the budget and forecast. Any differences or variations will be identified and critiqued to highlight both good and bad results. **Variation** is something different from another of the same type. In financial analysis, variation is the difference between a planned number and an actual number. If a problem exists and forecasted revenues or productivities are not achieved, it is important to identify if the entire week had problems or if there were big problems for a day or two. What caused the problem? Was the problem a result of lower revenues or higher costs? Was this expected for any reason?

Second, managers will evaluate how accurate their forecasts were for the week as compared to the actual results. Because a weekly forecast is prepared only several days before the week actually starts, it should be fairly accurate. Results from the previous week are available to help prepare as accurate a forecast as possible. It is important to evaluate the accuracy of the forecast as well as the actual performance because the weekly forecast is the main management tool or document that is used to prepare wage schedules and to plan the operating details of the next week's operations. Managers should be accurate in their weekly forecasts to establish reliability and credibility. A poor forecast can result in poor results, uncontrolled costs, and less revenues or profits. Third, managers will apply what they learned from the weekly operating results and use this information to forecast more accurately the next week's revenues and schedule appropriate wage and operating costs.

Weekly Revenue Forecast

As already discussed, the weekly revenue forecast is the first step in planning operations for the week. It is typical for hotel management to have a weekly selling strategy meeting on Monday or Tuesday to prepare a detailed, day-by-day forecast for the upcoming week that includes detailed daily revenue information such as daily rooms sold, daily arrivals and departures, daily average room rates, and daily revenues. The weekly room's forecast is then distributed to all managers for their use in planning the week. Food and beverage managers will then forecast their revenues for the week. All managers will look at the next month in more general terms to see if any significant changes are expected that will affect their weekly revenues.

Weekly Wage and Cost Scheduling

The next step is to take the weekly revenue forecast and schedule the appropriate man-hours including wage costs that will be necessary to support the forecasted revenue levels expected for each day. This is usually due on a Wednesday. Ratios and formulas are used to convert daily rooms sold or customer counts into daily wage schedules for each department. The man-hours and wage expenses for the week are then calculated and totaled and appropriate ratios are applied to ensure that the weekly productivities are maintained. Adjustments are made to get productivities in line. For example, if the housekeeping man-hours per room sold is too high, the Housekeeping Manager should determine which day or which Wage Department is above the wage standards and reduce the man-hours to get to the expected productivity levels for that day or for that Wage Department. If higher wage levels are required, the manager needs to document why and what work should be accomplished to justify that wage level.

Profitability Forecasting

With regard to profitability, the forecast is done by adding other operating expenses to it. These are generally based on historical averages or established formulas and ratios. Some costs are relatively fixed and may not be adjusted from week to week. Variable costs will need to be adjusted based on forecasted volume levels. Forecasted profits are calculated by subtracting all forecasted expenses from forecasted revenues. By completing profit forecasts for the week, the final weekly profit forecast can be compared to budgeted weekly profits to ensure that both revenue and expense forecasts are in line and will meet expected or budgeted productivities and profitability. How efficient management is in controlling expenses will be reflected in the retention or flow-through percentage which measures the change in profit dollars compared to the change to revenue dollars.

MONTHLY INTERNAL MANAGEMENT REPORTS

Everyone in the management team uses monthly reports, and that is why they are so important. We again focus on the monthly P&L Statement and how it is used by internal management, external investors, bankers, and other interested parties in evaluating financial performance. It is analyzed in great detail to measure financial performance and describe the operations for the month.

Monthly or Accounting Period P&L Statement

This is the financial statement that gets the closest scrutiny and is used the most in analyzing financial performance. This close analysis enables the monthly P&L Statement to become a very useful management tool. It describes not only the operational performance of a department compared to budget or last year but also the financial results produced by daily operations. The P&L Statement is the central point for discussion of financial performance because it is the financial statement that measures operating financial performance and that is used most by internal and external parties.

The monthly Consolidated P&L Statement provides a summary of each department's revenues and profits for the revenue centers and each department's total expenses for the expense centers. It is used to review the overall performance of a hotel at a large scale. Comparisons with the budget, previous month, or last year show if the financial performance of the hotel is improving, remaining the same, or declining. It also identifies which departments are underperforming and which are overperforming.

The monthly Department P&L Statements provide the detailed operating results by line item for each department. This is where the analysis of department operations begins. Department managers can see the financial results of the decisions and activities that they have made during the month in operating their department. Each line account in revenues and expenses can be examined to see if established operating plans and expected productivities were achieved. It is primarily the responsibility of the department managers to know and understand the operations that produced the numbers. They are assisted in evaluating their monthly Department P&L Statement by their Executive Committee Members, the Director of Finance, or any other member of the accounting office. This is the third step of the Financial Management Cycle—evaluate and analyze the numbers.

Profitability, Retention, and Flow-Through

This aspect of financial analysis is very important because it goes beyond comparing the monthly financial results of a department with the budget and forecast, or last month, or last year. It involves identifying revenue, expense, and profitability changes from budget or forecast. There is an expected relationship between increases and decreases in actual revenues from budgets or forecasts and its impacts on the increases or decreases in expenses and the resulting profits.

Refer back to the section on trends in Chapter 2. One important trend in financial analysis is to identify the relationship between revenue, expenses, and profits. Department managers are expected to be able to forecast increases and decreases in revenues compared to the budget and recent forecasts. They are also expected to be able to manage expenses in proportion to the change in revenues to maintain productivities and produce the maximum profit, given the forecasted change in revenues.

There are several important terms that we need to understand before we go on.

- **Incremental** refers to an increase, something gained or added. This term is used in financial analysis to describe revenues, expenses, or profits beyond what was expected. If sales increase, what are the corresponding increases in expenses and profits beyond what was expected. They should all increase in varying increments. Analyzing the incremental revenues, expenses, and profits will identify where the department did well and where it did not do well.
- **Fixed Expenses** refer to expenses that remain constant regardless of the volume and level of business. Fixed expenses do not change from month to month.
- **Variable Expenses** refer to expenses that increase or decrease directly with the volume and level of business. Variable expenses change each month based on business volume and managers are expected to control variable costs as revenue levels change.
- **Retention or Flow-Through** is the percentage or formula that identifies how expenses and profits are expected to change with the given changes in revenues. The formula expects higher levels of profits when higher levels of revenues occur and can be used to forecast expenses and profits that should result from incremental changes in revenues. Retention or flow-through are terms that measure how much profits go up or down as a percent of how much revenues go up or down.
- **Variation** refers to something that is different from another of the same type. In financial analysis, variation is the difference between two numbers. For example, the variation between actual sales and budget or actual sales to last year's sales.

To illustrate the concepts of retention or flow-through, we will use several examples. We will start with the Rooms Department forecast for a month. We will identify incremental revenues and its possible effects on expenses and profits at the new revenue level.

The forecast for the Rooms Department was $600,000 in room revenue and $523,000 in rooms department profit. The forecasted profit percent is 87.2%, which means that 0.872 cents out of every revenue dollar should be profit. Actual room revenue was $625,000 or $25,000 over forecast. Therefore, incremental revenue was $25,000. We can also calculate the percentage increase of the $25,000 incremental revenue, which is +4.2% ($25,000/$600,000). In other words, revenues were 4.2% higher than forecast.

Now let's look at the increase in expenses that resulted from the $25,000 increase in revenue. Fixed expenses did not change, so the incremental $25,000 in revenue incurred no additional fixed expense. Fixed expenses remained at $13,000. The fixed expense percentage will, therefore, decrease from 2.2% to 2.1%. This percentage decreases because the revenue increased without a

	Forecast		Actual		Difference/Variation	
	$	%	$	%	$	%
Room Revenue	600,000		625,000		+25,000	+4.2%
Management Wages (fixed expense)	11,000	1.8%	11,000	1.8%	0	0
Hourly Wages (variable expense)	36,000	6.0	37,000	5.9	+1,000	+2.8
Contract Cleaning (fixed expense)	2,000	0.3	2,000	0.3	0	0
Guest Supplies (variable expense)	8,000	1.3	8,400	1.3	+400	+5.0
Reservation Cost (variable expense)	20,000	3.3	20,500	3.3	+500	+2.5
Total Fixed Expense	13,000	2.2	13,000	2.1	0	0
Total Variable Expense	64,000	10.6	65,900	10.5	+1,900	+3.0
Total Expenses	77,000	12.8%	78,900	12.6	+1,900	+2.5
Total Profit	523,000	87.2%	546,100	87.4%	+23,100	+4.4%

Retention or Flow-Through = $23,100 or 92.4% ($23,100/$25,000).

corresponding increase in fixed expenses. We can, therefore, assume that for any incremental dollar increase in revenue, there will be no incremental increase in fixed expenses.

Variable expenses have a direct relationship with revenue levels—when revenue increases, variable expenses also increase, and when revenue decreases, variable expenses decrease. It is the responsibility of the Department Manager to control and manage variable expenses such as labor costs that can have a positive or negative effect on profits. In our example, variable expenses increased by $1,900 or 3.0%. This was the incremental amount of variable expenses incurred to support the $25,000 and 4.2% increase in room revenue. The variable cost percentage declines slightly from 10.6% to 10.5%.

The resulting profit increases by $23,100 from $523,000 to $546,100 or by 4.4%. The incremental revenue of $25,000 generated an incremental profit of $23,100. Stated in percent, 92.4% ($23,100/$25,000) of the incremental revenue of $25,000 made it through as incremental profit of $23,100. Therefore, retention or flow-through was 92.4%. This is a very high percentage and would indicate that the managers did a good job in controlling variable expenses.

The financial concept of retention or flow-through involves setting guidelines for the expected amount and percentage of incremental profit that will result from incremental revenue. Two examples of hospitality companies standards are a 60% retention of incremental profits at hotel gross operating profit and the other is 50% flow-through at hotel house profit. The 60% retention standard applied to the incremental of $25,000 in revenue would expect an incremental profit of $15,000 and that expected by the 50% flow-through standard would be $12,500.

Keep in mind that the retention and flow-through standards are for Gross Operating Profit or House Profit. There are specific department standards as well. For example, the Rooms Department retention standard is 80% and the Food and Beverage Department retention standard is 55% for one hotel company. The actual retention of 92.4% in our example exceeded the room retention standard of 80% for that hotel company.

All managers in a specific department have the responsibility of controlling and managing expenses to achieve guidelines and standards. It is equally important for the Director of Engineering to control the repairs and maintenance expenses as do the Restaurant Manager and Housekeeping managers to control the expenses of their departments. If each department does its part in managing expenses, the overall hotel productivity as measured by gross operating profit or house profits will achieve the set goals and standards.

Monthly P&L Statement Critiques

This refers to the process of analyzing the monthly Department and Consolidated P&L Statements to evaluate the financial performance of these departments and to determine what action to take next. The critiques should be prepared by department heads and line managers who are involved in the daily operations of departments and reviewed by the Director of Finance and Executive Committee Member. The objective is to analyze the numbers or financial results and explain what happened, why it happened, and what action will be taken as a result of the analysis. It is equally important to identify positive and negative changes in revenues and profits.

The Department P&L Critiques identify major variations explaining the causes of the variations in the accounts on the Department P&L Statement. The focus should be on the largest dollar accounts and variations from budget or forecast in terms of dollars and percentages. For example,

1. If revenues increased or decreased, which market segments or meal periods had the largest variations? Was it in rate or volume? Was it in one week or each week of the month? Or, was it on one or two very busy days or on one or two very slow days?
2. If food and beverage cost increased, was it in the full-service restaurant, specialty restaurant, room service, or banquet departments? What caused the cost increase and how will it be corrected?
3. If wage cost increased, was it in housekeeping or front office for the rooms department? Was it in the restaurant, banquets, or kitchen for the Food and Beverage Departments? Was it in increased man-hours or higher hourly wage rates? Which days or in which week did the increased wage costs occur? What was the cause of the increase?
4. If other operating costs increased, which account was it in? What caused the increase? How will it be corrected?

The Department P&L Critique will provide the explanations of what happened and how the department will improve operations in the coming months. It is important to remember that identifying the cause of increased revenues and profits is just as important as identifying the cause of problems that decrease profits. The Department Manager will want to know what actions produced the improvements and do what he or she can to keep those procedures or actions in place so that the improved operations will be achieved.

Summary

Internal management reports are essential to the successful operations of any hotel or restaurant. The entire hotel or restaurant management team uses these results to evaluate past performance and to determine appropriate action to take in the upcoming months to ensure acceptable performance in the future. This is the third step in the Financial Management Cycle—operations and accounting analyze the numbers. Department heads and line managers implement and critique these reports with the assistance of the Director of Finance and their Executive Committee Member.

Internal management reports cover two time periods. The first report contains actual operations from the previous day, week, or month. This looks back at actual operating results and describes what has happened. The second forecasts revenues, expenses and profits for the upcoming day, week, or month and is used to plan for expected business levels in the future. This one looks forward and forecasts what the managers plan and expect to happen.

There are daily, weekly, monthly, and quarterly reports. While operations are managed daily, they are planned for in weekly forecasts and schedules. The monthly reports are the main financial reports and are used by both internal managers and external parties or stakeholders in measuring the financial performance of the hotel operations.

It is extremely important to understand the concepts of incremental revenues and the expected impact that incremental changes in revenue will have on retention or flow-through to profits. These terms describe the guidelines set for managers to assist them in controlling expenses and maintaining expected productivities for different revenue levels. Because some expenses are fixed, there should be no increase in these expenses if revenues increase or decrease. Likewise, there is no decrease in fixed expenses if revenues decline. All department managers are expected to manage their variable expenses whether revenues increase or decrease. This is a critical factor in maintaining productivities and maximizing profits and retention/flow through.

Hospitality Manager Takeaways

1. The ability of hospitality managers to understand and use internal management reports is essential to the successful operations of any department.
2. The Daily Revenue Report summarizes the previous day's results and can include revenues, statistics, and labor productivities. This is one of the most important management tools that a manager can use in evaluating daily operations.
3. Weekly reports are used for planning and scheduling upcoming operations.
4. Retention and flow-through are essential financial concepts that identify management's ability to control expenses with the given incremental changes in revenues. This is a direct responsibility of managers in each department.
5. Managing variable wage costs is critical to maintaining productivities and maximizing retention or flow-through.

Key Terms

Daily Revenue Report: a report that is prepared during the night audit shift and collects and reports actual revenue information for the previous day. It can be called the Sales and Occupancy Report, Daily Revenue Report, or Gross Revenue Report depending on the company.

Fixed Expense: expenses that remain constant regardless of the volume and level of business.

Flow-Through: measures how much profit goes up or down as a percent of the change in revenue. Also referred to as **retention**.

Internal Management Report: a report that contains detailed operating information covering a specific time for a specific product, customer, department, or for the entire hotel or restaurant.

Incremental: an increase, something gained or added. In financial analysis it describes additional revenues, expenses, or profits beyond what was expected.

Man-hour: the number of hours an employee works in performing his or her job responsibilities. Typically, full-time employees are scheduled for an 8-hour work day and a 40-hour work week. Also known as *labor hour*.

Retention: measures how much profit goes up or down as a percent of the change in revenue. Also referred to as **flow-through**.

Variable Expense: expenses that increase or decrease directly with the volume and level of business.

Variation: something different from another of the same type. In financial analysis, variation is the difference between a planned number and an actual number. For example, the difference between actual results and the budget.

Review Questions

1. Compare the format of a P&L Statement with a Daily Revenue Report. What are the similarities and differences?

2. What information does the Daily Revenue Report contain and how does a hospitality manager use it?

3. Explain how fixed and variable wage expenses are used in maintaining labor productivity standards.

4. How are weekly revenue forecasts used to plan expenses for the upcoming week?

5. Define *retention* and *flow-through*. Why are they important?

6. How does a department manager use retention and flow-through to manage his or her department?

7. Define *incremental*. How is it used in financial analysis?

8. List three formulas for calculating labor productivities and three for calculating wage cost percentages.

Practice Exercises

1. Calculate the actual and budget department profit margins (remember profit margins are percentages) for the following hotel departments:

	Actual		Budget	
Room Revenues	$1,250,000		$1,200,000	
Restaurant Revenues	215,000		225,000	
Beverage Revenues	75,000		80,000	
Catering Revenues	480,000		450,000	
Total Hotel Revenues	$2,020,000		$1,955,000	
		%		%
Room Profit	$960,000	_____	$910,000	_____
Restaurant Profit	18,000	_____	20,000	_____
Beverage Profit	22,000	_____	25,000	_____
Catering Profit	170,000	_____	160,000	_____
Total Hotel Profit	$1,170,000	_____	$1,115,000	_____

2. Calculate the actual retention/flow-through in dollars and percent.

Actual retention/flow-through dollars _____

Actual retention/flow-through percent _____

Revenue Management

LEARNING OBJECTIVES

- To understand the importance of maximizing revenues
- To understand why RevPAR is so important to maximizing hotel revenues
- To understand the basic concepts of Revenue Management

- To understand how Revenue Management systems work in hotels
- To understand rate structures and selling strategies
- To be able to read, understand, and use Revenue Management reports

CHAPTER OUTLINE

INTRODUCTION

This chapter will discuss the importance of Revenue Management in operating a hotel. The two primary ways of maximizing profits are first to maximize revenues and second to control and minimize expenses. Understanding the policies, procedures, and tools that are available to maximize revenues and ability to use them effectively are valuable skills for any hospitality manager to possess, particularly in the Rooms Department. A hotel meeting or exceeding the revenue budgets is a much more enjoyable place to work and managers will find a better opportunity here to maximize profits because revenues are helping rather than hurting profitability. It is challenging for hospitality managers to maximize profits when a hotel is not meeting budgeted and forecasted revenue. The worldwide recession of 2008–2009 is a good example of the negative impact that declining sales have on profitability and cash flows. RevPAR is a key indicator of the direction of room revenues and hotel profitability.

Revenue Management relies on historical room revenue information stored and analyzed in a computer program called **yield systems** or **demand tracking**. Yield systems contain historical information organized by day of arrival (DOA) and compare the current years booking pace to the historical average. The booking pace compared to the historical average will show if reservations for the current year are being made at a faster or slower rate. It will also suggest appropriate selling strategies that a hotel can put in place to maximize room revenues for a specific DOA given the current market demand.

This chapter will cover the different aspects of Revenue Management, from understanding the supply and demand of micromarkets to the weekly or daily implementation of selling strategies. All managers need to have a good understanding of how their hotel generates revenues in different market segments and different market environments. It will help them understand the importance of maximizing revenues in the daily operations of a hotel.

RevPAR—REVENUE PER AVAILABLE ROOM

Definition

Revenue per Available Room (RevPAR) is total room revenue divided by total rooms available. It combines room occupancy and room rate information to measure a hotel's ability to maximize total room revenue. It is the best measurement of maximizing total room revenue because it identifies the hotel's ability to manage *both* occupancy (rooms sold) and room average rate in maximizing room revenues. A hotel must effectively manage both to maximize total room revenue.

There are two formulas for calculating RevPAR and either one can be used. The Tenth Revised Edition of the *Uniform System of Accounts for the Lodging Industry* prefers the formula Total Room Revenue divided by Total Available Rooms. The second formula is occupancy percentage times average room rate. The RevPAR calculated each way might be slightly different as a result of rounding off. Typically, occupancy percentage is rounded to one decimal—87.3%, for example. Average room rates are rounded to two decimals—$76.23, for example. Let's look at the formulas:

$$RevPAR = \text{Occupancy Percentage} \times \text{Average Room Rate} \quad \text{or}$$

$$= \frac{\text{Total Room Revenue}}{\text{Total Available Rooms}}$$

Applying the first formula to this example will result in a $66.55 RevPAR

$66.55 RevPAR = 87.3\%$ Occupancy Percentage $\times$ $76.23 Average Room Rate

Following are the characteristics of RevPAR that this example demonstrates:

1. RevPAR is measured in dollars and cents.
2. RevPAR will always be lower than the average room rate. The only exception is if the hotel is running 100% occupancy. Then RevPAR and average room rate will be the same. RevPAR can *never* be higher than the average room rate.
3. You need to know both the hotel occupancy percentage and the hotel average room rate to calculate RevPAR.
4. You need to know the total room revenue and the total available rooms in the hotel to calculate RevPAR. This leads to our second RevPAR formula:

$$RevPAR = \frac{\text{Total Room Revenue}}{\text{Total Available Rooms}}$$

To calculate RevPAR using this formula, we need to know the total room revenue (a variable) for the day and the total number of rooms in the hotel (a constant). Generally this information is provided in the daily revenue report or monthly P&L Statements. We can also calculate it. To continue our example, let's use a 400-room hotel. That is the only additional information that we need to calculate RevPAR with this formula. It will require three steps.

1. *Calculate rooms sold.* We need this number to calculate total room revenues. We can calculate rooms sold by applying our 87.3% occupancy percentage to our 400-room hotel.

    400 Total Rooms $\times$ 0.873 Occupancy Percentage = 349.2 Rooms Sold

    Because we cannot sell 0.2 of a room, we round to 349 rooms sold.
2. *Calculate total room revenue.* The formula is as follows:

    $$\text{Rooms Sold} \times \text{Average Room Rate} \quad \text{or}$$
    $$349 \text{ Rooms Sold} \times \$76.23 \text{ Average Room Rate}$$
    $$= \$26,604 \text{ Total Room Revenue}$$

3. *RevPAR = Total room revenue divided by total available rooms.* Make sure to use the 400 *total available rooms* in the hotel and not the 349 *rooms sold*. Our RevPAR is

$$\$66.51 \text{ RevPAR} = \frac{\$26,604 \text{ Total Room Revenue}}{400 \text{ Total Available Rooms}}$$

Let's compare our two RevPARs.

$66.55 RevPAR = 87.3% Occupancy Percentage × $76.23 Average Room Rate and

$$\$66.51 \text{ RevPAR} = \frac{\$26,604 \text{ Total Room Revenue}}{400 \text{ Total Available Rooms}}$$

There is a difference of 4 cents. Which one is right? The difference is the result of rounding off, so technically $66.51 is the best answer because it is calculated using total room revenues and total available rooms in the hotel. However, a 4 cent difference on a $66.51 RevPAR is insignificant, so either formula can be used. It is important to use the same RevPAR formula to be consistent and ensure that all RevPAR calculations are reliable and useful.

Why RevPAR Is Important

RevPAR measures both the ability to sell the most rooms (occupancy percentage) and the ability to achieve the highest average room rate. Therefore, RevPAR includes *two financial measures* and identifies how the hotel is combining the two strategies of maximizing rooms sold and maximizing the average room rate to maximize total room revenue. Together they are strong and very useful financial measures. They require the hotel management team to be good at managing *both measures*.

If a hotel's selling strategy focuses only on one of these measures, it can miss significant opportunities to maximize total room revenue with the other measures. For example, a hotel can focus on maximizing occupancy percentage and to accomplish this goal, managers might set low room rates to sell more rooms. If a hotel is running a 92% occupancy, which is very high compared to the industry average that typically is in the low 60% range, it probably dropped its room rates significantly lower than the other hotels in the area—its competitive set. If a hotel is running at $125 average rate and its competitive set at $165.00 average rate, the hotel is earning $40 less in average room rate. We refer to this as leaving money on the table. The important question for the hotel management is that can the hotel increase total room revenues by increasing its average rate and is it willing to run a lower occupancy percentage as some customers go elsewhere because of the higher average rate?

The same issue applies to average room rate. A hotel might set its room rates too high and lose customers as a result. Using the same example, if our hotel is achieving a $175 average room rate compared to the average room rate of $150 of the competitive sets, but running a 60% occupancy compared to the competitive sets average occupancy percent of 78%, then our hotel is probably not maximizing room revenue. Again, the hotel is leaving money on the table because of a high average rate that might turn away potential customers resulting in a lower occupancy percentage and lower room revenues.

In each of these examples, the hotel is doing well in only one of the revenue measurements. To accomplish this, it is probably not doing well on the other measurements. That is what makes RevPAR so important. RevPAR requires a hotel to be evaluated on its ability to *manage and maximize both rate and occupancy measurements*.

It is also important to understand the implications of RevPAR increases on total hotel profits. Generally, increases in RevPar as a result of higher average room rates will result in higher profits. This is because there are few, if any, incremental expenses as a result of achieving a higher room rate. Therefore, incremental revenues as a result of higher room rates should flow through to virtually the same amount of incremental room profits.

Increases in RevPAR as a result of higher occupancy or more rooms sold will also produce incremental variable costs such as the labor incurred in cleaning an occupied room, guest supplies and cleaning supplies used, and any other variable expenses incurred. Therefore, some of the incremental revenue resulting from more rooms sold will be used to pay incremental expenses resulting in a smaller amount of incremental room profits.

There is another financial impact of higher occupancies in a hotel. While it may result in higher expenses, it will also result in more guests in the hotel, implying that there are more potential customers to increase revenues in the Food and Beverage and other Revenue Departments. These increased revenues in other departments might generate more incremental profit than the incremental variable expenses incurred in the Rooms Department. The one constant is that any increase in RevPAR is a good financial accomplishment. A trend of consistently increasing RevPAR due to higher average room rates or higher room occupancies should always have a favorable effect on profits.

How RevPAR Is Used

RevPAR is used in several ways. It is used as a management tool that assists the hotel management team in maximizing room revenues. It is also used to measure financial performance by owners, management companies, franchisees, and outside investors in evaluating investments. It is contained in P&L Statements for a hotel and the annual reports for a corporation. *It is the most important measurement of how well a hotel is able to maximize room revenues and room profits.* If a hotel is maximizing room revenues as measured by improvements to past financial results and by comparisons to competitors, it makes it more possible for the hotel management team to efficiently manage expenses to maximize profits. Specific uses of RevPAR are as follows:

1. It is used as a measure of the hotel's management team's ability to maximize total room revenue.
2. It is used to compare the performance of the hotel to similar hotels in the same market area. This is called the hotel competitive set.
3. It is used to measure the progress of the hotel in consistently increasing total room revenue compared to previous year's results and the approved budget.
4. It is used by owners, outside investors, and other financial institutions to project future room revenues and cash flows.

Fairmont Maui Resort

The Fairmont Kea Lani in Maui, Hawaii, is a 450-room luxury all-suite and ocean villa resort. Each one-bedroom seaside suite includes a spacious living room, separate master bedroom, and elegant marble bathroom. The property encompasses 22 beachfront acres and includes four restaurants, three swimming pools, a spa, access to golf, and 30,000 square feet of meeting space. The Fairmont's meetings and events facilities can host groups from 12 to 750 and range from an indoor setting in the spectacular ballroom or a conference room to outdoors under swaying palm trees.

Visit the Fairmont Kea Lani Web site www.fairmont.com/kealani and view this property from the perspective of the Director of Revenue Management. Consider the seven core concepts of Revenue Management according to Robert Cross and answer the following questions:

1. What and why do you think the two biggest market segments are for this resort?
2. What effects will each of your market segments have on maximizing total resort revenue? Give at least one example for each of your main market segments.
3. Do you think average room rate or occupancy will have the greatest effect on RevPAR? Explain why.

Fairmont Maui. Photos Courtesy of Fairmont Hotels and Resorts, Toronto, Ontario, Canada.

RevPAR is used in many reports. It is calculated daily and included in the Daily Revenue Report. It is used in weekly forecasting. It is contained in monthly P&L Statements. It is used in preparing the annual operating budget. It is reported in corporate annual reports. This demonstrates RevPARs importance in the daily operations of individual hotels.

RATE STRUCTURES AND MARKET SEGMENTS

Definition

We defined *market segments* in Chapter 1 as customer groups defined by preferences, behaviors, buying patterns, and behavior patterns. These similar characteristics enable hotels to create promotions, packages, and rates that will meet the different expectations of each market segment. The hotel will identify market segments that it will be able to compete in and then advertise to attract customers in those market segments to the hotel.

Rate Structures are the range of room rates that a hotel determines for different market segments. They can be year-round or seasonal room rates. They are published and the hotel uses them to attract customers. Potential customers view the rates of a hotel and compare them with other hotels and choose a hotel to stay based on rate, experience, location, and the expected overall value of the service they will receive.

Establishing Rate Structures

Hotels use several factors in establishing room rates for their hotel. These include the following:

1. Room rates of their primary competitors
2. The age of the hotel, including recent room renovations and improvements
3. Perceived value of the products and services delivered by the hotel
4. Location
5. Cost of the hotel and the return on investment (ROI) required by investors
6. Any competitive advantages that the hotel might have over its competitors

Room rates are generally set for one year. They are determined based on last year's actual room rates, marketing studies, inflation rates, competitor's actions, renovations or improvements, and the expectation regarding increase in total room revenues each year. It is a detailed process to change the established rate structure and that is why room rates are generally set for a year at a time. The exception is seasonal properties such as a resort where a rate structure is established for each of the seasons of the year.

Establishing the room rate structure involves setting specific rates for specific market segments ranging from the highest to the lowest rates. Historically, the central point of room rate structures is the **regular rate**, which is also called the rack rate. This is the room rate that is available to all of the different reservation systems and channels selling rooms at a hotel, including travel agencies, airlines, car rental companies, and the Internet, and generally the first room rate quoted at central reservation centers (800 numbers).

All other rates are calculated based on increases or decreases from the rack rate. Let's look at a sample room rate structure for a full-service hotel and a limited or select service hotel:

	Full-Service Hotel	Select Service Hotel
Concierge (Upgraded Rooms and Service)	$249	Not Available (NA)
Regular or Rack Rate	$219	$125
Corporate Rate (Preference to Business Travelers)	$199	$109
Special Corporate Rate (Company Special Rates Based on Volume)	$190–$150	$105–$85
Discounts		
Super Saver	$139	$ 89
Weekend	$119	$ 75
Government/Military	$ 90	$ 50

These rates are examples of how a hotel might set its rate structure. The concierge rate is the highest rate because it includes special amenities and services similar to first class on an airline. It is an upgrade in service and amenities. The regular or rack rate is considered the standard room rate that the hotel would like to get for all of its rooms. Another room rate called the **bench rate** is the base room rate that a hotel wants to achieve and sell to the public.

All other room rates are forms of discounted rates from the rack rate. The corporate rate is a slightly discounted room rate extended to individual business travelers recognizing both the company and the individual's amount of time spent on the road on business. Often, the corporate rate has the highest rooms sold mix percentage especially for the full-service market segment. Special corporate rates are the next level of discounted rates and are negotiated directly with specific companies. The amount of the discount from the corporate rate is based on the number of room nights generated by that company annually. A company that produces 200 rooms annually might receive a slightly discounted rate of $190 at our full-service hotel example, whereas a company producing 1,000 room night annually might receive a larger discount and a $150 rate. The discount rate categories reflect lower rates that are available during low demand time periods. They involve the largest discounts because the hotel is generally running lower occupancies during this time. Our full-service hotel might run at 85% occupancy midweek but fall to 50% on weekends. The discounted weekend rates reflect a strategy to attract more rooms during slow times with a lower or discounted room rate.

In setting the room rates of a hotel, there is a logical relationship between all the various rates. Generally the discounted rates will be either a fixed dollar amount lower between each market segments such as a $10 or $25 discount or a fixed percentage discount lower such as a 10% or 15% discount. The rate structure is orderly and intended to accomplish two things that seem opposite of each other: maximize room revenue with higher rates on the upper end of the room rate structure and maximize room revenue with more rooms sold stimulated by lower room rates on the lower end of the room rate structure. Customers are looking for lower rates and lower rates generally do not maximize room revenues. This is the challenge for hotel management as they set room rates—how to balance maximizing room revenue and customer satisfaction.

At least once a year, hotels set new rates for the upcoming year. On occasion, they might change rates during the year based on new market conditions that would warrant new room rates. Also, if the hotel completes a room renovation and the hotel is refreshed and updated, it is typical for management to increase room rates at that time to reflect the better condition of the hotel and its facilities.

REVENUE MANAGEMENT

Definition

The objective of **Revenue Management** is to sell the right product to the right customer at the right time for the right price, thereby maximizing revenue from a company's products and services. This definition is contained in the well-renowned book *Revenue Management* by Robert Cross, Broadway Books, 1998. Revenue Management focuses on the market and current supply and demand characteristics as a way to best maximize total revenues. This replaces the historical cost-based pricing that established prices for customers based on the costs incurred to produce the product or service plus the profit amount that the company expects.

Market-based pricing suggests that the most effective way to set prices is to look at the external markets for a company's products and services and identify and measure the demand in different market segments. **Demand** is reflected by the customer's preferences and willingness to pay a specific price or rate for a product or service. This is a more important consideration than production costs in determining prices and rates. It is not ignoring costs but is focusing on the market and individual customers in setting prices and rates.

Seven Core Concepts of Revenue Management

Robert Cross identifies and explains seven core concepts in understanding Revenue Management. They are as follows:

1. *Focus on price rather than costs when balancing supply and demand.*   This means adjusting prices, not costs, should be the first action taken when trying to get the supply/demand balance right.
2. *Replace cost-based pricing with market-based pricing.*   This means focusing on demand and when demand is high, set prices higher. When demand is low, offer discounts or lower prices to maximize revenues. "The market (the consumer), establishes the price, and your job is to find the markets acceptable price point" (Cross, 1998, p. 70).

3. *Sell to segmented micromarkets, not mass markets.* Micromarkets or market segments are defined by demographics (e.g., age, sex, income, occupation, and education) or psychographics (e.g., attitude, personality, and lifestyle). "Different segments demand different prices. To maximize revenue and stay competitive, prices must vary to meet the price sensitivity of each market segment" (Cross, 1998, p. 77).

4. *Save your products for your most valuable customers.* This suggests that your products or services may have different values at different times. These different times could be weekdays or weekends, the short term in days versus the long term in weeks, or the availability of different levels of service. For example, a businessman might be willing to pay a higher price at the last minute because of a recent change in his or her travel plans. Saving seats for a flight or rooms at a hotel at higher rates for these customers enable the airline or hotel to maximize room revenues and satisfy the needs of a specific market segment.

5. *Make decisions based on knowledge, not supposition.* This means using accurate and current information to make decisions. Modern computer systems collect and analyze massive amounts of data and using this information will result in better decisions. "Forecast demand at the micro-market level to gain knowledge of subtle changes in consumer behavior patterns" (Cross, 1998, p. 85).

6. *Exploit each product's value cycle.* This means understanding the value cycle of your products or services and adjusting the pricing and availability to each market segment. For example, Super Bowl T-shirts of the winner have their highest value the days immediately after the team wins the Super Bowl. Weeks later, the same T-shirts will be significantly discounted.

7. *Continually reevaluate your revenue opportunities.* This means analyze your actual results and compare to expected results and make necessary changes to meet established goals and respond to changing market conditions.

These core concepts of Revenue Management provide a general understanding of the marketplace made up of potential customers in segmented markets (demand) and the different competitors (supply). To effectively maximize total revenues, a company must focus on the constantly changing marketplace and establish rate structures and selling strategies that provide the right product to the right customer at the right time for the right price.

Yield Systems

DEFINITION Revenue Management utilizes past historical information to project future room occupancies and revenues. They not only possess several years of historical room rate and rooms sold information, but also use computer programs that utilize this information to assist managers in projecting future demand and room sold. These programs are referred to as Yield Systems or Demand Tracking.

YIELD SYSTEM   We will use this term to describe computer programs used in collecting and reporting past rooms sold activity and trends and then projecting rooms sold for future dates. These computer systems collect, record, and analyze massive amounts of historical data. This includes the number and type of rooms sold every day in the past and the associated room rate. Generally the historical information of the hotel for the previous four to five years is collected and combined to provide historical averages and identify historical customer buying patterns.

WHAT YIELD SYSTEMS DO   Yield systems are the computer programs that organize a hotel's historical information by **Day of Arrival (DOA)**. The DOA is the focus point of yield management systems. The **historical average** is all past reservation information and trends for a specific arrival day in the future. This includes room rates, rooms sold, and room revenue by market segment. It tracks the number of rooms sold at a specific point in time for each arrival date in the future. Directors of Revenue Management can track the progress of reservations for any future DOA and compare it to the historical average for that date. The status of current reservations booked is called the **booking pace** and it is compared to the historical average for that DOA. Yield systems information determines whether the booking pace of this year's reservations for a specific DOA is ahead of or behind the historical average pace. Let's use an example to illustrate these points for a 400-room hotel. The yield system will provide the following information:

Day of arrival: June 1

Today's date: May 1

Number of days until the DOA: 31 days

Booking pace or the number of current reservations for the DOA: 275

Historical average of number of reservations 31 days before the DOA: 300

This information tells us that 31 days before the DOA of June 1, the hotel has 275 reservations booked compared to the historical average of 300 reservations booked 31 days before the DOA. The hotel booking pace is behind the historical average by 25 reservations. The selling strategy team will review this information and then decide what selling strategy to put in place to try and catch up and sell more rooms and maximize room revenues for the DOA. The team still has 31 days to affect the number of rooms sold. A typical strategy at this point will be to open up all discounted rates for the DOA in an attempt to stimulate reservations by making available lower, discounted room rates.

Now let's look at the yield systems information two weeks later:

DOA: June 1

Today's date: May 15

Number of days until the DOA: 16 days

Booking pace or number of current reservations booked for the DOA: 320

Historical average of number of reservations 16 days before the DOA: 325

This information tells us that 16 days before the DOA, the hotel lags behind by only five reservations from the historical average. The actual booking pace for the previous two weeks has been higher than the historical average, causing the hotel to lag behind only 5 rooms from the historical average. The current booking pace tells us that the hotel is catching up to the historical average of rooms sold. The selling strategy of keeping all discounts open or available at this time could remain the same, indicating that the hotel is willing to continue selling discount reservations in an effort to book more reservations to maximize room revenues. Or the selling strategy could change and restrict the lower discount rates but keep the higher discount rates open. The Director of Revenue Management will be the main person interpreting the information from the yield system and helping the other managers decide what selling strategy to implement.

One more example:

DOA: June 1

Today's date: May 25

Number of days until the DOA: 7 days

Booking pace or number of current reservations booked for the DOA: 350

Historical average of number of reservations 7 day before the DOA: 340

This information, gathered one week before the DOA of June 1, tells us that the booking pace for the hotel is now 10 reservations ahead of the historical average. The hotel has not only caught up to the historical average number of reservations seven days before the DOA of June 1 but has also booked 10 more reservations indicating stronger demand than historically. The selling strategy would now probably change and discount rates would be closed forcing remaining reservations to be booked at a higher rate. The hotel would choose this selling strategy because it has 10 more reservations booked indicating a higher demand than historical averages. Higher demand means a higher probability of selling out. The hotel will now implement a selling strategy of maximizing rates by closing discounts to maximize total room revenue. It could be more aggressive and require a two day minimum length of stay if the selling strategy team feels that this would be a good strategy to maximize total room revenues.

The yield systems historical averages for any DOA will reflect the historical average of the total number of actual rooms sold at a specific number of days before the DOA. It could be 400 rooms sold (a perfect sellout), or 375 rooms sold (a 93.8% occupancy, which is very good), or 200 rooms sold (a 50% occupancy, which is not good). The total number of rooms sold for the DOA will reflect the historical average for that DOA whether it is high or low, good or bad.

Figure 7.1 is an example of a yield management chart.

How Yield Systems Work

As the example shows, Yield Systems provide not only the number of actual reservations booked for a specific DOA but also the information that tells whether reservations are being booked at a faster or slower rate (the booking pace) than the historical average for any date before the DOA. This information

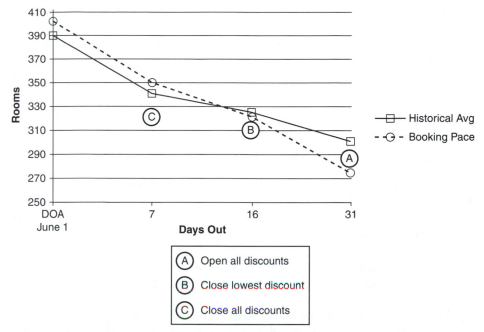

FIGURE 7.1 Revenue Management and Selling Strategies.

is very valuable for the hotel management as they determine the best selling strategy to implement to maximize total room revenue.

Yield systems provide a hotel with a historical number of reservations booked to compare with actual reservations booked at any point in time before the DOA. A Director of Revenue Management looks at the yield information on the computer daily to look for trends. He or she enters a specific DOA and compares the current booking pace to the historical average. Then he or she makes any appropriate changes to the selling strategy that will help maximize total room revenue for each DOA.

The fact that a hotel has 300 reservations on the books as of a specific number of days before a specific DOA has little meaning by itself. However, when it is compared to a historical average of 325 reservations or 275 reservations, the hotel knows whether it is booking reservations at a faster pace—325 rooms or a slower pace—275 rooms and can accordingly implement an appropriate selling strategy in either situation. Once again, financial analysis involves comparing current actual results with other numbers. In this example, the current actual information (the booking pace) is compared to historical information (the historical averages).

HOW YIELD SYSTEMS ARE USED Hotel management uses yield systems information as a tool to maximize total room revenue. It provides the hotel with a daily status of total room reservations made, the average room rate, expected room revenues, and the pace or progress at which reservations are being made for a specific future DOA. It reflects the current status of demand for hotel rooms. The reservation information contained in the booking pace shows the current demand and is compared with the reservation information of the historical averages that shows the historical demand. This information enables hotel management to consider room rates, rooms sold, and the reservation booking pace in managing reservations to maximize total room revenue. Managers can implement selling strategies to increase rooms sold or to increase room rates. They can change the selling strategy daily based on the updated information and room status that yield systems provide.

Using Revenue Management in Different Types of Hotels

All types of hotels in all types of markets and locations can use Revenue Management. This is because Revenue Management includes the historical and current information for any specific hotel. How that hotel uses the information can be very different. Let's look at some examples.

CORPORATE HOTELS (AIRPORTS AND SUBURBAN) The example we have just discussed is very similar to a corporate hotel. A significant portion of room reservations are booked within four to six weeks of the DOA. The main market segments are transient (business and pleasure) and then group. Group rooms at a corporate hotel tend to be smaller in number of rooms and length of stay. A training program for 20 rooms for 3 nights would be a typical example of a group block at an airport hotel.

The transient segments, especially business travelers (corporate and special corporate), tend to make their reservations within days rather than weeks or months out. That results in many room reservations being booked within the last two weeks before the DOA. It is typical for a corporate hotel to book 25% to 50% of their room reservations within the last two weeks before the DOA. The Director of Revenue Management can make changes to selling strategies several times a day during the week before the DOA to maximize room revenues.

GROUP HOTELS (DOWNTOWN OR SUBURBAN) These types of hotels are generally larger and group business makes up a significant part of their total rooms sold. It is typical that 60%–80% of total rooms sold are group rooms. These hotels sell a higher number of group rooms than transient rooms. Because groups require a block of sleeping rooms and a certain amount of meeting space, they require certain types of hotels. To ensure that groups can obtain the required number of sleeping rooms and meeting space, they book their reservations more in advance—typically 6–12 months out. These reservations are called **Group Room Blocks**, a signed contract that identifies the number and pattern of group rooms for each night and the total group rooms for that event. Group room blocks can include 5–300 rooms per night as an example for a 400-room hotel—a nice way to sell a large number of rooms. Group rooms generally have a lower average room rate because of the larger number of rooms sold as one piece of business. They also generate significant revenues for the Banquet and Food and Beverage Departments.

The booking time period for group hotels is very different from the corporate hotels. Because most of the rooms are booked more than three months before the DOA as group room blocks, less than 20% of reservations could be booked within the last two weeks before the DOA. If the location of the hotel is away from major highways and business areas, as little as 5%–10% of their rooms sold could be booked within the last three weeks of the DOA.

RESORTS AND CONVENTION HOTELS   These types of properties can book group blocks as far out as five to six years before the DOA. This is because many conventions are very large requiring 500–1,000 sleeping rooms per night and large amounts of meeting space and banquet functions (+50,000 square feet). To be able to secure this large amount of sleeping rooms and large amount of meeting space, large corporations and associations book their meetings two to six years in advance. The same is true for the resorts where the high or prime season includes only a couple of months. During these months, the demand is typically very high. Large corporate and association groups book five to six years in advance to ensure that they can conduct their meeting when and where they want and secure the necessary sleeping rooms and meeting space accommodations.

Even the group functions that require 100–300 sleeping rooms over several nights and a smaller area of meeting space book their functions one to three years in advance to ensure that they can conduct their meeting when and where they want. This is especially true at resorts during the prime seasons. The farther out from the meeting date a company books the rooms, the better the chances that they can meet when and where they want. It is possible for these groups to book within one year but only if demand is down, such as the recession of 2009, and there is greater risk that they might not be able to find a resort with the amount of sleeping rooms and meeting space required.

Revenue Management is used in a very different way for convention hotels and resorts. Historical averages for days of arrival are replaced with historical patterns of group room blocks. Group room blocks identify the number of rooms needed per night, length of stay, rates, and any other specific requirements. This information is organized by the number of years or months before the arrival date that the group confirms and signs a contract.

A hotel will have a typical pattern for the type, size, and rates for group room blocks booked months out, or more than one year out. The group room block will also identify the size and type of meeting space required for the meeting. This includes rooms for meetings, functions, and for meals.

The booking pace is replaced by the slippage or pickup of actual rooms compared to the group room block. **Slippage** is the difference between expected or blocked group rooms for each night in a group room block and the actual number of rooms sold for each night in a group room block. **Pickup** is the number of actual room reservations made by day for a group room block compared to the number of group rooms blocked for that night. A typical group room block will have the **peak night** with the largest number of required rooms. **Shoulder nights** are before and after the peak night and generally have fewer number of rooms blocked. The actual number of reservations made for each night of the group room block is referred to as pickup and will determine if the actual rooms reserved will be less, equal to, or more than the number of rooms blocked (slippage).

Revenue managers in resorts or group hotels will closely monitor the pick-up of rooms months in advance of the DOA to forecast the actual number of rooms expected to be occupied. If the pickup is lower than the group room block, some of the rooms could be released and made available to sell to other groups or individual travelers. If the pickup is higher than the room block, the hotel will increase the size of the group room block if rooms are available. A cut-off date from three to six months before the DOA is established for each group room block and that is the date that the group guarantees the number of rooms occupied on each night of the group room block and submits the rooming list of all expected attendees. The cut-off date is an important date because it can release rooms that might not be occupied by the group and make them available for the hotel to sell to other groups or individuals.

SELLING STRATEGIES

We have mentioned *selling strategy* several times in this chapter. Let's talk about selling strategies—what they are and what they do.

Definition

The **selling strategy** is the actions and decisions of the senior management of a hotel in opening and closing room rates, arrival dates, and length of stay to maximize total hotel room revenues. It involves establishing restrictions or qualifications to obtain a discounted room rate. Selling strategy meetings are typically held once a week and that is where yield systems information, the status of group room block pickup, and other room revenue information is reviewed and discussed and the best selling strategy identified and implemented.

The Selling Strategy Process

The selling strategy process involves a team of managers consisting of the Director of Revenue Management (the specialist), Director of Sales and Marketing, Director of Finance, Director of Rooms Operations, Front Office Manager, and the General Manager. They will discuss all the current transient and group reservation information generated by the yield system and determine the best strategy to put in place to maximize room revenues.

Selling strategies typically do not involve changing rate structures but rather opening and closing specific rate categories, arrival dates, and length of stays to maximize total room revenue. All of these actions impact total room revenues by either increasing the number of rooms available for sale or increasing/decreasing the room rates of potential reservations to be booked. Yield systems provide the most current and detailed information used in determining selling strategies.

SELLING STRATEGY TOOLS

1. Open and close discounted room rates
2. Require a minimum length of stay, two or more nights
3. Shift the DOA to a different, lower demand day by opening discounts for that day.

For example, if the booking pace for a specific DOA is significantly behind the historical average, the selling strategy will probably be to open all discounts and do everything possible to sell additional rooms. This strategy should result in more rooms sold but at lower, discounted rates. This is okay because the booking pace is behind the historical average reflecting lower demand than typical. This generally means that the hotel will not be close to selling out and will probably have many unsold rooms. A room sold at a lower average rate is preferable to an unsold room that produces no revenues.

Let's look at another example where the booking pace is significantly higher than the historical average for a specific DOA. This means that the demand for hotel rooms is higher than the historical average and therefore there is a higher probability of more rooms being sold for the DOA and opportunity to increase room revenues. The selling strategy will probably be to close or restrict all discounted room rates and ensure that all future room reservations are booked at the higher corporate, rack, and concierge rates. This strategy should result in higher room rates and higher room revenues. This should be okay given the higher demand that will generally indicate that customers are willing to pay a higher room rate. The expectation is that the hotel will still be able to sell the remaining unsold rooms at the higher rate because of the stronger demand.

When the selling strategy is decided at the selling strategy meeting, the Director of Revenue Management is responsible for changing the inventory restrictions to ensure that the available rates to all agencies and organizations that have access to booking reservations from the hotel inventory are the same. They do this by closing out the discounted rates, requiring a minimum length of stay, or shifting the DOA. This means that travel agencies, central reservations office, hotel and car rental companies, the Internet, the hotel reservation staff, and the hotel front desk clerks can book room reservations only in the higher rate categories.

Let's look at how the proper selling strategy can maximize room revenues for a sold out night at our 400-room hotel. Let's assume that one week out from the DOA we have sold 350 rooms at an average rate of $175. Yield Management tells us that this booking pace is 25 rooms higher than the historical average and therefore we will almost certainly have a perfect sell out—400 occupied rooms for the DOA. We will now compare two revenue possibilities for selling the remaining 50 rooms.

First, let's assume we do not change our selling strategy and leave the discounted rooms open and available for sale. We can assume that the average room rate for the final 50 rooms will be the same $175 that the yield system has calculated for the 350 reservations already made. It includes both higher and discounted room rates. The expected incremental revenue will be $8,750, which is 50 rooms sold times $175 average rate.

Second, let's assume that we change our selling strategy to close all discounted room rates. The remaining 50 rooms will be sold at the corporate rate of $199 and rack rate of $219. The average rate of these 50 rooms will be somewhere between these two rates. Let's use $210 as an average. The expected incremental revenue for these 50 rooms sold increases to $10,500 or 50 rooms sold times $210 average rate. By closing the discounts, the hotel will increase its average room

TABLE 7.1   Selling Strategies and Revenue Streams

	Example 1	Example 2	Difference
Rooms Sold	50	50	None
Average Room Rate	$ 175	$ 210	+$ 35
Total Room Revenues	$8,750	$10,500	+$1,750

rate from $175 to $210 for the remaining 50 rooms thereby generating incremental room revenue of $1,750 (the difference between $8,750 and $10,500). Table 7.1 illustrates the different room revenues of the different selling strategies.

The value of dynamic selling strategies is that they can take advantage of current daily updates of market conditions and trends to change selling strategies to maximize room revenues for a specific DOA. In fact, during high demand times, a hotel might change its selling strategy several times during the day. The information provided by yield systems is the key to maximizing room revenues because of the detail of current reservation information that it provides. The Director of Revenue Management can pull up individual DOAs on his or her computer and implement appropriate selling strategies at any time during a day. Obviously, Revenue Management is most useful in high demand time periods, when it is extremely valuable in maximizing room revenues. But it is also important to understand that Revenue Management can also maximize room revenues in low demand and slow time periods by identifying lower demand early, so appropriate selling strategies can be put in place to produce the highest room revenue possible during slow times. It would be a major mistake for a hotel to have discount restrictions in place when the information provided by the yield systems of Revenue Management indicate soft demand and that the hotel is only going to achieve a 50% occupancy for a specific DOA. All discount rate should be open and other restrictions removed during slow times to maximize room revenue and ensure that no room reservations are lost or turned down. Once again, it is better to sell a room at a lower, discounted rate and generate some incremental revenue than to have it unsold—another example of leaving money on the table.

Revenue Management Critiques

The last step in the Revenue Management process is to evaluate the selling strategies implemented and the results they produced for a specific DOA or week. The critique process is the same as that of critiquing monthly P&L performance. Questions included in the critique might include the following:

1. Did the implemented selling strategies produce the desired results?
2. Were selling strategies quickly and efficiently communicated to all reservation outlets, distribution channels, and selling agencies?
3. Were there any reservation turndowns or lost revenue opportunities?
4. Were there any problems or surprises that need to be considered in the future?
5. Did the Revenue Management process work as intended?
6. Do any changes need to be made to the selling strategy process?

Summary

Maximizing total room revenues is a major priority for every hotel management team. It involves managing room rates and rooms sold in the best balance to maximizing total room revenue. It is also the first step and probably the most important step in maximizing total hotel profits. If a hotel is increasing total room revenue from year to year and is meeting budgeted and forecasted room revenue, it makes managing and controlling hotel operating expenses much easier for department managers.

The process of maximizing total room revenues involves four important processes: First is effectively managing RevPAR. RevPAR is total room revenue divided by total available rooms in the hotel. This means doing a good job of managing average rates and maximizing total rooms sold.

Second is developing a competitive yet profitable room rate structure for a hotel. Establishing the different rates offered to each market segment is very important in maximizing total rooms sold and total room revenue. Rates should be competitive in the market, reflect a good value to customers, reflect the investment in the hotel and operating cost requirements, and take into consideration any competitive advantage that the hotel might have.

Third is Revenue Management process that utilizes a yield system to collect historical data and provides current reservation information that will assist in maximizing total room revenue. Yield systems are computer programs that compare the current years booking pace of reservations for a specific day of arrival (DOA) to the historical average booking pace for the DOA.

Fourth is developing and implementing successful selling strategies that will assist all reservation partners and hotel employees in effectively using the hotel room rate structure and current status of room reservations to maximize total room revenues. Selling strategies are developed at weekly selling strategy meetings and changed daily to react to current market conditions and rooms sold status.

Effective room Revenue Management is one of the most important elements of successful hotel operations. Maximizing room revenues enables the hotel to have flexibility in controlling and managing expenses to meet the expected profit margins and cash flow projections. These increased revenues will also help maintain or improve the hotels physical structure and provide more services and better amenities for hotel guests. A hotel that consistently produces lower room revenues than budgeted will not have the revenue and cash flow necessary to pay all operating and fixed costs to keep the hotel in a strong competitive situation.

Hospitality Manager Takeaways

1. RevPAR is the most valuable measure for maximizing total room revenues. It requires hotel management to be efficient in both maximizing rooms sold and maximizing average room rate.
2. Revenue Management is a valuable tool used by hotel management to maximize total room revenue and total hotel revenue. It compares the current reservation booking pace to historical booking averages for a DOA and is used to decide on the best selling strategy to maximize the total room revenue. It also compares actual pickup of rooms to group room blocks.
3. Yield systems are the computer programs that collect and analyze historical operations data to assist management in implementing the most effective selling strategies to maximize hotel revenues.
4. The selling strategy team is responsible for reviewing all reservation information, including Revenue Management information and implementing the best strategy to maximize total room revenue.
5. Room rates for a hotel are generally set annually for specific rate categories based on the hotel's largest market segments.

Key Terms

Bench rate: the base room rate that a hotel wants to achieve and sell to the public.

Booking pace: the current rate at which reservations are being received for a specific DOA. The booking pace is compared to historical averages to determine if demand is stronger or weaker than historical averages for a specific DOA.

Day of arrival (DOA): the focus point of yield management systems. All historical reservation information and trends for a specific arrival day in the future.

Demand: this is reflected by the customer's preferences and willingness to pay a specific price or rate for a product or service.

Demand tracking: the part of Revenue Management utilizing computer programs to provide historical information of reservations booking patterns that provide historical averages and trends for a hotel. Also called yield systems.

Group room block: a signed contract that identifies the number and pattern of group rooms for each night and the total group rooms for that event. It also includes the room rate, VIPs, people authorized to sign for charges, and other detailed information about the group.

Historical average: average reservation information based on four or five years of hotel information.

Peak night: the night or nights in a group room block that has the largest number of occupied rooms.

Pickup: the number of actual room reservations made by day for a group room block compared to the number of group rooms blocked for that night. It also included the pace at which actual reservations are being made for a specific day and the percentage of actual room reservations made compared to the group room block for the day.

Rate structure: a list of the different room rates offered by a hotel.

Regular rate: the room rate that is available to all of the different reservation systems and channels selling rooms of a hotel, including travel agencies, airlines, car rental companies, and the Internet, and generally the first room rate quoted at central reservation centers (800 numbers). Also referred to as rack rate.

Revenue management: the process of selling the right product to the right customer at the right time at the right price, thereby maximizing revenue from a company's products and services.

Revenue per available room (RevPAR): total room revenue divided by total rooms available. It combines room occupancy and room rate information to measure a hotel's ability to maximize total room revenues.

Selling strategy: the actions and decisions of the senior management of a hotel in opening and closing room rates, arrival dates, and length of stay to maximize total hotel room revenues. It involves establishing restrictions or qualifications to obtain a discounted room rate.

Shoulder night: the number of group rooms sold per night before the peak night (front side) or after the peak night (back side).

Slippage: the difference between expected or blocked group rooms for each night in a group room block and the actual number of rooms sold for each night in a group room block.

Yield systems: the computer reservation tracking system that combines current reservation booking information with historical reservation booking information. It is used to implement selling strategies that will maximize the total hotel room revenue.

Review Questions

1. What are the two formulas for RevPAR?
2. Why is understanding and using RevPAR information so important to maximizing total room revenue?
3. Explain the relationship between room rates and market segments.
4. What is DOA and why is it such an important part of yield management?
5. How is the booking pace used with the historical average in yield management?
6. Who is on a hotel's selling strategy team? Which one is the most important?
7. What selling strategy should a hotel implement when the booking pace is under the historical average pace?
8. What selling strategy should a hotel implement when the booking pace is over the historical average pace?

Practice Exercises

1. The corporate rate at a 600-room downtown east coast hotel is currently $199. The owner would like to see a small increase in the room rates for next year. Put together a room rate structure with at least six different rates. Your corporate rate should show a slight increase and the other rate categories should have a logical relationship to the corporate rate.

2. For this same hotel and the rate structure that you developed in Question 1, answer the following questions:
   A. What days of the week do you think demand would be the strongest?
   B. For those dates, give examples of a day when your selling strategy would be (1) to close either one or all discounted rates, (2) when you would try and shift the day of arrival, (3) when you would require a two day minimum length of stay. Be specific on which days you would do what strategies. For example, which days would a minimum length of stay be appropriate and which days would shifting the day of arrival be appropriate?

3. Discuss at least three Revenue Management terms that would be used primarily in a 1,000 room convention hotel and three Revenue Management terms that would be used primarily in a 400-room airport corporate hotel.

Comparison Reports and Financial Analysis

LEARNING OBJECTIVES

- To understand the importance of hotel revenue and profit analysis and how they are explained and analyzed

- To understand what variation analysis is and how it is used

- To learn the key formulas and ratios and how they are used in variation analysis

- To understand the format and uses of the STAR Market Reports

- To understand and use internal and external financial reports

CHAPTER OUTLINE

INTRODUCTION

In the previous chapters we have focused on numbers and how they are used to measure financial performance. At this point, students should be forming a solid foundation of financial knowledge and a good understanding of what financial analysis is, what it tells you, and how it is used in explaining hotel operations. The next concepts that we will discuss are other financial reports and methods of financial analysis used to compare and analyze hotel operations, management reports, and financial statements.

Referring back to earlier chapters that presented basic accounting concepts and methods of financial analysis, we now proceed to learn about some helpful internal and external reports that can be used in analyzing and comparing operating results. Note that we always start with actual operating performance followed by the analysis of the financial results that operations produce.

Internal comparisons of actual results are made with company budgets and forecast, results of previous months or periods, and established goals or standards. External reports are market or economic reports that are useful in comparing hotel operations and financial results with a competitive set, industry average, or other external financial information.

PROFITABILITY: THE BEST MEASURE OF FINANCIAL PERFORMANCE

Definition

Profits are defined as revenues minus expenses—a rather simple formula that is very important in measuring financial performance. In actual hotel operations, this formula is used in a variety of ways that results in specific profitability measures. Profits can be measured at several levels of any business. Let's review some of the key profit levels that are included in hotel Profit and Loss Statements (P&Ls).

$$\text{Department Profit} = \frac{\text{All of a Department's}}{\text{Revenues}} - \frac{\text{All of a Department's}}{\text{Direct Expenses}}$$

$$\text{Total Department Profits} = \text{Sum of All Hotel Department Profits,}$$
$$\text{Which Is the Same as the Sum}$$
$$\text{of All Profit Centers}$$

$$\text{House Profit or} \atop \text{Gross Operating Profit} = {\text{Total Department} \atop \text{Profit}} - {\text{Total of All Expense} \atop \text{Departments,}} \quad \textbf{or}$$

$$= \text{Total Department Profits} - \text{Support Center Costs}$$

Net House Profit or
Gross Operating Profit $=$ House Profit $-$ Fixed Expenses

Profit is the best measure of financial performance because it includes the two major factors of financial performance: maximizing revenues and minimizing expenses. Maximizing total hotel revenues is very important, but it is only the first step. Controlling and minimizing expenses is also important and is the second step. Maximizing profits requires management to be efficient in both areas. Together, revenue and profit analysis explain virtually every aspect of the financial performance of a hotel or restaurant.

The Difference between Analyzing Profits and Analyzing Revenues

Analyzing revenues is totally focused on the relationship between rate and volume in an effort to maximize total hotel revenues. It involves establishing rate structures, setting selling strategies, and comparing rate and occupancy results with internal and external reports. It also includes analyzing different market segments such as group or transient and weekday or weekend. Generally, department heads are the hotel managers who have the direct responsibility for maximizing the revenues of their departments.

Analyzing profitability not only includes revenue analysis as discussed earlier but also expense analysis in all department expense line item accounts. Each specific expense category is evaluated on the effect it has on the hotel's ability to efficiently provide products and services for its customers. These expenses include fixed and variable expenses, direct and indirect expenses, and operating and overhead expenses. Specific hotel managers have the direct responsibility for managing specific revenue market segments and controlling specific expense line accounts to maximize the profits of their departments.

The most important expenses to be analyzed and controlled are food cost and wage cost. These are two big variable expense accounts that can become major problems and a drain on total profits if they are not properly managed and controlled. Wage costs are even more important because they directly affect benefit costs. If wage costs go up and are over budget, benefit costs will generally go up and be over budget. Likewise, if wage costs go down and are under budget, benefit costs will generally go down and be under budget.

Finally, there are more expense line accounts to be managed than revenue line accounts. This requires the attention of all hotel managers in every department of the hotel. Each must be efficient in managing and controlling expense accounts if hotel profits are to be maximized. If each manager effectively controls his or her department expenses, the total hotel expenses will be in line and total hotel profit goals will be met.

The Impact of Department Profits on Total Hotel Profits

As we have mentioned earlier, all department profit dollars are not created equally. This means that each department that is a profit center has a different expense structure. Some have more expenses, thereby resulting in lower department profits, while some have lower expenses, thereby resulting in higher department profit. The larger convention hotels and resorts have more profit centers than typical full-service hotels and, therefore, can generate a larger Total Department Profit.

Let's look at two examples of full-service hotels and identify the profits associated with each operating department. Remember that the terms *revenue center* and *profit center* can be used interchangeably. While the revenue centers record only revenues, the corresponding profit center will record revenues, expenses, and profits. They are two terms that describe operating departments that produce revenues and profits. Also, remember that the department profit percentage shows how much of a department revenue dollar will make it to the "bottom line" as a profit dollar. The following department profit percentages (also referred to as profit margins) assume that total kitchen costs are allocated to the food and beverage operating departments.

Profit Center	Full-Service Hotel	Convention Hotel
Rooms Department	65%–75%	70%–80%
Banquets/Catering Departments	25%–35%	30%–40%
Full-Service Restaurant	0%–10%	5%–15%
Specialty Restaurant	None	10%–20%
Bar and Lounges	30%–40%	30%–45%
Gift Shop	25%–30%	25%–35%
Golf Club	None	25%–35%
SPA	None	25%–35%

Let's examine the impact that these examples have on profitability.

1. The Rooms Department has the highest profit percentage primarily because there is no cost of sales. The rooms are re-rented every night, not consumed (like food and beverage items) or purchased (like gifts and clothing); therefore, there is no cost of sales. In other revenue departments, cost of sales can range from 25%–35% for food and about 50% for clothing, so it is a major expense category. This is one reason why the Rooms Department profit is much higher than the other profit departments.

2. The room rates of the Rooms Department are generally much higher than the average checks in the Restaurants Department or average sales in the

Gift Shop. The higher room rate increases the Rooms Department profit percentage.

3. Convention hotels and resorts generally have higher average room rates and higher food and beverage menu prices than typical corporate hotels that help to increase their department profit percentage.

4. The more the revenue departments in a hotel, the more the sources of profits to increase Total Department Profits, House Profits/Gross Operating Profit, and Net House Profit/Adjusted Gross Operating Profit. This helps resorts and convention hotels to increase total revenues and profits.

5. Restaurant Departments have the lowest profit percent because of the many expenses required to prepare and serve food. Both food and wage costs will run between 25%–35% each, benefits 10%–15%, and other direct operating costs 10%–15%. This leaves little room for error in managing expenses if the restaurant is to be profitable.

6. Specialty restaurants are generally more profitable because they have higher average checks and also include higher beverage sales.

7. It is financially beneficial for restaurants to serve liquor because liquor has lower wage costs and lower cost of sales, resulting in higher liquor profitability. This helps the overall financial performance of the total food and beverage outlets including banquets.

8. The Banquet or Catering Department generally has a higher profit percentage than a restaurant because their food functions can be planned with specific prices and customer counts, a set time for the meal that results in more efficient operations, and higher profitability. For example, a banquet dinner for 500 people with a set menu and $30 average check can be planned for and produced with greater efficiency and profitability than opening a restaurant for the evening and waiting to see how many customers come, what they will order, what the average check will be, and what the total revenues will be.

The Director of Finance and the General Manager of a full-service hotel will generally spend a great deal of their time on the rooms and food and beverage operations for two very different reasons. First, the Rooms Department is important because it generates most of the revenues and profits. A well-run Rooms Department means there will be higher sales and cash flow that produce more financial resources to operate the rest of the hotel successfully. The Rooms Department is a good example of an operating department that focuses on maximizing revenues first and then controlling expenses. Second, the Food and Beverage Departments are important because of the complexity and detail of its operations. Food and Beverage operations have to be well managed to control all the different expenses to achieve a profit. If these departments are not operated well, operations could produce a loss rather than a profit. Restaurant Departments are good examples of departments that focus first on controlling and minimizing expenses and then on maximizing revenues.

The different department profit percentages discussed here are a good example of mix percentages presented in Chapter 2. One dollar of revenue in each of the above departments will produce a different amount of department dollar profit. The management team of a well-operated hotel knows and understands this and plans daily operations to consider the department profit that will result from the forecasted department revenues of all departments for the week. *To maximize hotel profitability, expenses must be minimized and revenues maximized.*

Maximizing and Measuring Total Hotel Profitability

There is a partnership in a hotel that enables the hotel to use all the operating and financial resources available to maximize profitability. This partnership is between the staff departments and the operating departments. The goal of the four staff departments (Sales and Marketing, Repairs and Maintenance, Human Resources, and Accounting) is to provide specialized support for the operating departments (Rooms, Food and Beverage, Golf, Spas, Retail). The operating departments are responsible for taking care of guests and generating revenues and profits for the hotel. Their focus should be on providing the best products and services to the guests of the hotel and ensuring that the guests want to come back.

The partnership and support that the Accounting Office and the Director of Finance provide to the operating managers is extremely important in successful hotel operations. Because the accounting and financial process can become complicated and demanding, it is important that the Director of Finance provide these services and knowledge efficiently to both department managers and senior management. It is equally important that the department managers provide accurate numbers to the Director of Finance so that together they have all the knowledge and resources necessary to identify problems and trends, develop corrective action, and determine the best way to implement changes so that operating improvements are made and financial goals met. It is a true partnership, with specialized knowledge and experience brought to the relationship by each manager and department. A strong financial team and a strong operating team are essential to the successful operations of the hotel.

It is also important to understand the services and support the other staff departments contribute to the successful operations of a hotel. The Sales and Marketing Department works hard to establish competitive but profitable rate structures, implement successful selling strategies, attract profitable group business, and develop good marketing and advertising programs. The Repairs and Maintenance Department works constantly to ensure that the equipment in the hotel is working efficiently and that the hotel looks sharp both inside and out. This is a big job! The Human Resource Department ensures that good employees are hired, provides training and development, handles employee problems, and takes care of payroll and benefit administration. If each of these departments does its job, the hotel will be operating at a high level of efficiency and have a much better chance of meeting the goals and budgets established to measure hotel performance and profitability.

CHAPTER 2 REVIEW: FOUNDATIONS OF FINANCIAL ANALYSIS

Chapter 2 introduced fundamental accounting concepts and methods of financial analysis that are used to analyze numbers and results. We will now use this material and these methods in analyzing internal operations, including revenues, expenses, and profits. We are also able to use this information to compare individual company performance with industry standards and external reports.

In this chapter, we will now focus on *applying the foundations of financial analysis* presented in Chapter 2 to our company performance. Variation analysis utilizes all of these fundamentals. Let's review them again.

Comparing Numbers/Results to Give Them Meaning

Numbers need to be compared to a standard or to other numbers to give them meaning. Variation analysis expands this idea by providing ratios and formulas that assist in comparing a company's monthly, quarterly, or annual performance in two ways. First, it allows for an internal comparison of company performance with the last year's results, the previous month's results, or with the established plans such as the annual budget and current forecast. Second, it allows for an external comparison of performance with the averages of other like hotels in a company, with the industry standards and averages, or with the external reports such as the STAR Market Report published by Smith Travel Research.

Measuring and Evaluating Change in Financial Analysis

Changes in a company's operating results are identified by comparing actual performance to previous performance or with an established goal or measure. Variation analysis expands this definition by identifying changes in company performance in terms of dollars, units, or percentages. The comparisons mentioned in the previous paragraph identify and calculate the amount of both positive and negative changes. Companies plan on improving their operations and financial performance by increasing revenues and profits from year to year. Actual results are compared to these planned changes (budgets and forecasts).

Percentages as a Tool in Financial Analysis

Percentages measure relationships and changes in operating performance. They always involve two numbers and provide another measurement in financial analysis beside dollar or unit changes. Percentages identify the size of a change compared to a standard. This is very important information. For example, a $1,000 change in revenues compared to $50,000 in revenues is a 2% change ($1,000 divided by $50,000). That same $1,000 change in revenues compared to $200,000 in revenues is only a 0.5% change ($1,000 divided by $200,000). These percentages tell us that the $1,000 change in the first example is a larger and more significant change than the $1,000 change in the second example.

The four types of percentages used most often in financial analysis are cost percentage, profit percentage, mix percentage, and percentage change. Each of these percentages provides specific information about a company's operations and is an important part of variation analysis.

The Importance of Trends in Financial Analysis

Trends are important because they show the size, direction or movement of business activity, industry averages and standards, and national and world economies.

Hyatt Regency Scottsdale Resort and Spa at Gainey Ranch
Scottsdale, Arizona

The Hyatt Regency Scottsdale Resort and Spa at Gainey Ranch is a 492-room resort located in the fashionable area of Scottsdale, Arizona. Each of the guest rooms includes balconies or patios overlooking the resort courtyard and water complex. The Hyatt offers six different food and beverage outlets, 27 holes of golf, Spa Aviana featuring 19 treatment rooms, and a 2.5 acre "water playground" that redefined the water recreation experience at world class resorts with its 10 swimming pools and three-story water-slide. Meetings and convention facilities include over 70,000 square feet of indoor and outdoor meeting space with 33 breakout rooms and prefunction space that incorporates the unique resort environment with desert and mountain views. View more details and feel the resort ambience at the resort Web site at www.scottsdale.hyatt.com.

Photo Courtesy of Hyatt Regency Scottsdale Resort and Spa, Scottsdale, Arizona.

The Valley of the Sun in Phoenix/Scottsdale is one of the most well-known resort destinations in the world with over a dozen world class resorts. Think of the challenges that are faced by these resorts as they compete in the luxury group and leisure markets. Consider the following questions as you analyze the financial performance of the Hyatt Regency Scottsdale:

1. Name five resorts that you would include as the competitive set for the Hyatt and explain why.
2. How do you think the location of the Hyatt in expensive Scottsdale affects the wage costs for the operating departments? Give examples.
3. Which revenue department would you like to manage? List three important factors that you would use to analyze the revenues and profits of your department.

Variation analysis compares the operating and financial trends of a company with the trends of other hotels or restaurants in the company, industry trends, stock market trends, or national or world economy trends. Variation analysis also identifies both positive and negative changes in the operating and financial trends of a company. Particularly valuable is comparing a company's revenue, expense, and profit trends in seeking to improve operating results and financial performance. The deep recession of 2009 is an example of how trends change and how hotels and restaurants have to realize that past trends may or may not still apply to current market conditions and operations.

VARIATION ANALYSIS

Definition

Variation analysis involves identifying the difference between actual operating performance and established standards. These standards can be last year's actual performance, the previous month's actual performance, the budget for this year, or the most current forecast. Variation analysis relies on accurate financial information to identify both good and bad variations in operating activities. Therefore, variations can be positive, reflecting better performance than the standards, or they can be negative, reflecting worse performance than the standards.

Variation analysis also includes identifying and examining the causes of changes in operations. It identifies the variations of each line account that collects all the financial information for a specific expenses category. The variations in the operating results of a hotel or restaurant are described and measured in the line accounts contained in the financial statements produced each month or accounting period.

Variation analysis is used in identifying and analyzing the operating results in revenue, expense, and profit accounts. Some of these accounts have several variables, while others have just one variable. **Variables** are the different components involved in an account and can be revenue accounts or expense accounts. Two variables mean that two components can be managed and analyzed. Variation analysis shows the impact that each component has on the total of each account. For example, the two variables in room revenues are average room rates and number of rooms sold. The two variables in wage analysis are average wage rates and man-hours. Both include two variables. Let's look at some of the main accounts and other variables that are measured in analyzing revenue and expense accounts.

Account or Line Item	Variable
Room Revenue	Average room rates and rooms sold/occupancy percentage
	Market segments—transient, group, or contract
	Weekday and weekend
Restaurant Revenue	Average check and customer counts
	Meal periods—breakfast, lunch, and dinner
	Average capture rates
Wage Cost	Average wage rate and labor hours
	Management, hourly, and overtime wage categories
	Labor hours per occupied room or per customer

Most of the remaining expense accounts involve only one variable. Examples are food cost, china, glass, silver, guest supplies, linen, and so on. The total expenses in one variable accounts involve purchase amounts, inventory variation amounts, and transfer amounts in and out of an account. Larger line accounts such as food cost are more complicated with many entries and can be more difficult to manage and control. For example, analyzing total food cost for a restaurant could involve over 100 entries each month, including food purchases, department transfers, and inventory variations to accurately identify the total food cost for the month. Less complicated would be analyzing linen costs, which will probably have from five to ten entries for the month.

Formulas and Ratios Used in Variation Analysis

Ratios are formulas that define relationships between numbers and are used in financial analysis. Ratios are classified into five major classifications in financial analysis. Each classification involves financial information from one or more of the three financial statements—the P&L Statement, Balance Sheet, and the Statement of Cash Flows. There are a few ratios that involve information provided on two of these financial statements. The five classifications are as follows:

1. *Activity Ratios.*   A group of ratios that reflect hospitality management's ability to use the property's assets and resources. These ratios primarily involve dollars and statistics from the P&L Statement. Consider the following examples:

   A. Total Occupancy Percentage $= \dfrac{\text{Rooms Occupied}}{\text{Total Rooms}}$

   B. Available Occupancy Percentage $= \dfrac{\text{Rooms Occupied}}{\text{Total Available Rooms for Sale}}$

   C. Average Occupancy per Room $= \dfrac{\text{Total Guest}}{\text{Total Rooms Occupied}}$

   D. Food Inventory Turnover $= \dfrac{\text{Cost of Food Sold}}{\text{Average Food Inventory}}$

2. *Operating Ratios.* A group of ratios that assist in the analysis of the hospitality establishment's operations. These ratios are also primarily from the P&L Statement. Examples are as follows:

A. $\text{Average Room Rate} = \dfrac{\text{Total Room Revenue}}{\text{Total Rooms Sold}}$

B. $\text{RevPAR} = \dfrac{\text{Total Room Revenue}}{\text{Total Rooms}}$ or

$\quad\quad \text{Average Room Rate} \times \text{Occupancy Percentage}$

C. $\text{Average Food Check} = \dfrac{\text{Total Food Revenue}}{\text{Total Customers}}$

D. $\text{Food Cost Percentage} = \dfrac{\text{Total Food Cost}}{\text{Total Food Revenue}}$

E. $\text{Wage Cost Percentage} = \dfrac{\text{Department Wage Cost}}{\text{Department Revenue}}$

3. *Profitability Ratios.* A group of ratios that reflect the results of all areas of management's responsibilities. These ratios involve information from three areas: the P&L Statement, the Balance Sheet, and information from publicly traded stock exchanges. Examples are as follows:

A. $\text{Profit Margin} = \dfrac{\text{Profit Dollars}}{\text{Revenue Dollars}}$

$\quad\quad$ (This can be for a department or the entire hotel.)

B. $\text{Retention or Flow-Through} = \dfrac{\text{Change in Profit Dollars}}{\text{Change in Revenue Dollars}}$

C. EBIDTA = Earnings before interest, depreciation, taxes, and amortization

D. $\text{Return on Assets} = \dfrac{\text{Net Profit}}{\text{Average Total Assets}}$

E. $\text{Return on Owner Equity} = \dfrac{\text{Net Profit}}{\text{Average Owner Equity}}$

F. $\text{Earnings per Share} = \dfrac{\text{Net Profit}}{\text{Average Outstanding Common Shares}}$

G. $\text{Price Earnings Ratio} = \dfrac{\text{Stock Price per Share}}{\text{Earnings per Share}}$

4. *Liquidity Ratios.* A group of ratios that describe the ability of an establishment to meet its short-term obligations. These ratios are from the Balance Sheet and P&L Statement. Examples are as follows:

A. $\text{Current Ratio} = \dfrac{\text{Current Assets}}{\text{Current Liabilities}}$

B. Acid Test Ratio $= \dfrac{\text{Cash and Near Cash Assets}}{\text{Current Liabilities}}$

C. Accounts Receivable Turnover $= \dfrac{\text{Total Revenue}}{\text{Average Accounts Receivable}}$

5. *Solvency Ratios.* A group of ratios that measure the extent to which the hospitality operation has been financed or capitalized by debt and is able to meet its long-term financial obligations. These ratios are also from the Balance Sheet. Examples are as follows:

A. Solvency Ratio $= \dfrac{\text{Total Assets}}{\text{Total Liabilities}}$

B. Debt Equity Ratio $= \dfrac{\text{Total Liabilities}}{\text{Total Owner Equity}}$

Key Hotel Ratios that Measure Financial Performance

There are many ratios and formulas that are used in analyzing and evaluating the financial performance of a hotel. The main ratios will be divided into revenue, profit, and expense categories. We will discuss and prioritize the most important ones in each category. Note that most of these ratios have been mentioned in the five ratio classifications previously discussed.

REVENUE Variation analysis is used in examining two different aspects of the actual revenues generated by the hotel. It seeks to identify where differences occurred and what caused them. The first analyzes rate and volume. The second compares actual performance to another standard such as budget, forecast, last year, or last month. The three primary measurements used in revenue variation analysis are rooms sold or occupancy percent, average room rate, and RevPAR. Let's examine rate and volume.

1. *Rooms Sold or Occupancy Percentage.* This is the volume measurement of the revenue equation. Revenue $=$ Rate $\times$ Volume. Variation analysis measures the actual number of rooms sold each night compared to the budget, forecast, or last year's rooms sold. The difference between the actual number of rooms sold and the budgeted number of rooms sold, for example, is the rooms sold variation. In our 400-room hotel, if the budgeted number of rooms sold is 360 and the actual number of rooms sold is 375, the rooms sold variation is +15 over the budget. The hotel sold 15 rooms more than that budgeted, which is a positive variation.

   Rooms sold can also be stated in percentage terms, which is the occupancy percentage. In our example, the hotel budgeted rooms sold of 360 equates to a 90% budgeted occupancy. The actual rooms sold of 375 equates to a 93.8% occupancy (note that we round off to one decimal from the 93.75%). Our analysis of rooms sold variation now has a second measurement, 15 more rooms sold or 3.8% higher occupancy. We have now identified what part of any room revenue changes that were the result of volume and selling more rooms.

2. *Average Rate.*   This is the rate measurement of our revenue equation. Revenue = Rate × Volume. Variation analysis measures the actual average room rate compared to the budget, forecast, or last years average room rate. The difference between the actual average room rate and the budgeted average room rate is the room rate variation. In our 400-room hotel, if the budgeted average room rate is $175 and the actual average room rate is $174, the average room rate variation is $1.00. The hotel's average room rate is $1 lower than budgeted, which is a negative variation—lower average room rate than the budgeted average room rate. We have now identified what part of any room revenue changes that were the result of average room rate.

3. *RevPAR.*   Revenue per available room (RevPAR) combines both rate and volume into one measurement. It is the first operating and financial statistic that is examined when analyzing total room revenues because it includes both rate and volume—average room rate and rooms sold/ occupancy percent. The difference between the actual RevPAR and the budgeted RevPAR is the RevPAR variation.

Let's continue our analysis with the average room rate and occupancy percentage information from our previous examples.

	Actual	Budget	Variation
Rooms sold/Occupied	93.8%	90.0%	+3.8% points
Average room rate	$ 174	$ 175	−$1.00
RevPAR	$163.21	$157.50	+$5.71

An analysis of our example shows that the actual RevPAR of $163.21 was $5.71 above the budgeted RevPAR of $157.50. Stated as a percentage, the $5.71 variance is 3.6% over the budgeted RevPAR. That is a positive variation. The next step is to identify whether rate or volume or both contributed to this positive variation. In our example, there is a positive occupancy or volume variation but a negative average rate variation. The fact that the overall RevPAR variation is positive tells us that the positive occupancy variation of 3.8 percentage points has a larger impact on RevPAR than the negative average rate variation of −$1.00.

The second aspect is the comparison of actual performance to a standard. We already started this process in our example. The importance of comparing the actual occupancy percentage, average room rate, and RevPAR to a standard is that it describes the direction and degree of actual performance. Comparing actual to last year shows where and how much operations have improved or declined from the previous year's operations. It compares the actual financial results from year to year. Comparing actual results to the budget shows how actual results compare to the operating plan or budget for the year. It compares the actual performance to the planned or budgeted performance in the future. Comparing actual to forecast involves the most current operating plan that includes the current trend and current economic environment. The forecast updates the budget and is the most recent plan, hence should be the most accurate plan. It compares actual performance to the latest plan.

The best financial situation is to have actual operating results with the financial performance exceeding all three measures: last year, the budget, and the forecast. The next best situation is to have actual results exceed last year's results but not meet the budget. This comparison shows that operations have improved over last year's actual results, which is always important, but did not improve or increase as planned or as much to meet the budget. This could be because an aggressive budget was set or a difficult market emerged as in 2009. Another good situation is to meet or exceed the forecast. This is because the forecast represents the most current plan or projection. To meet or exceed last year's performance and the forecast is very good financial performance even if the budget is missed. It is important to show improvement in at least one comparison because that indicates operations are moving in a positive direction.

PROFIT   Variation analysis is used in examining hotel profits at several different levels. The formula for profit is revenue minus expenses. Revenues have already been analyzed at this point, so the focus of profit variation analysis will be on the expense accounts. There are three aspects of profit variation analysis. The first analyzes the impact of revenues and expenses on profit. The second defines what profit level is being analyzed—department profits, house profit or gross operating profit, and net house profit or adjusted gross operating profit. The third compares actual profit results to another standard such as last year, budget, or forecast.

The first step is to examine revenues and profits.

1. *Revenues.*   This part of profit analysis has already been completed in the previous section as rate, volume, and RevPAR are examined and compared. Refer to number 1 under "Revenues" for the details.
2. *Expenses.*   The next step of profit variation analysis involves examining the different expense categories and line accounts. The detail of operating expenses are included in the Department P&L and include the four major cost categories of cost of sales, wages, benefits, and direct operating expenses.

The second step is to define what profit level is being analyzed. Following are the different profit levels that are examined as a part of variation analysis:

1. *Department Profits.*   This is the dollar profit for the Revenue/Profit Centers and the formula is department revenues minus department expenses.
2. *Total Department Profits.*   This is the sum of the department profits for all the Revenue/Profit Centers in the hotel and the formula is to add up and total all the individual department profits.
3. *House Profit or Gross Operating Profit.*   This is the dollar profit that measures management's ability to control all the operating expenses in the hotel. The formula is Total Department Profits minus total support costs or total expense center costs.
4. *Net House Profit.*   This is the final profit measure that includes all hotel revenues and expenses. The only remaining expense is the payment of taxes and the distribution of profits between hotel owners and hotel management companies. The formula is house profit minus fixed or overhead expenses.

The third step is to compare the actual performance to a standard. This analysis is the same as described in the revenue section. The actual profit performance in terms of profit dollars and profit percent at each level is compared to last year, budget, and forecast. Any differences or variations are then identified. The revenue variations have already been identified in the revenue analysis, so the focus is on examining the differences in the expense categories of the different profit levels and the impact that it has on each of the profit measurements.

EXPENSE   In the "Profit" section, we have discussed how expenses are analyzed. Managing expenses is a critical part of any hospitality manager's job. Let's look at what they are expected to manage in each of the four major expense categories.

1. *Cost of Sales.*   Restaurant and Kitchen Managers will be expected to meet budgeted food cost in dollars and percentages each month and year to date. This will require that they effectively manage food and beverage purchases, assist in taking accurate physical inventories and reconciling these totals with the book inventory, oversee storeroom rotation to ensure quality and freshness, organize transfers to other food departments, and coordinate all numbers and financial information with the Accounting Department. The responsibilities will be the same for Beverage Managers, Retail Managers, and any other revenue center managers having products that are sold to or consumed by customers.

2. *Wage Cost.*   Managers will be expected to be able to forecast and control variable hourly wage expenses, given the weekly increases and decreases in forecasted revenue volumes. This includes maintaining productivity levels as well as consistently delivering acceptable and expected levels of customer service. The largest part of hourly wages is variable expenses and the ability to effectively manage and control hourly wage costs are critical to meeting expected department profit margins.

   Overtime is also an important variable wage expense to manage. Overtime that is a result of short staffing or unexpected increase in business volumes may be a necessary operating expense. However, overtime that is the result of poor scheduling, poor supervision, or employee inefficiency is not acceptable and should be minimized or eliminated.

3. *Benefit Cost.*   Managers control this major expense category by controlling management and hourly wages. Most benefit costs are calculated based on the wage costs of both management and hourly employees. Therefore, if a manager does a good job of controlling hourly wage costs, department benefits costs should also be in line.

4. *Direct Operating Expenses.*   This cost category can have many line accounts that managers must control. Controlling these variable expenses includes purchasing appropriate quantities, verifying, approving and processing invoices, taking physical inventories, processing transfers, and critiquing actual monthly operating expenses compared to budget. Examples of these accounts are china, glass, silver, linen, cleaning supplies, guest supplies, paper supplies, reservation costs, and general expense accounts.

A detailed understanding of how to control all expenses and the ability to adjust them up or down given business levels is an important management skill for any hospitality manager. There will always be pressure to maintain productivities and stay within budget. A manager's ability to skillfully manage and control expenses will have a major impact on department profits as well as his or her career advancement.

There are two other aspects of profit analysis that need to be discussed—profit margins and retention/flow-through. Since profits are described in profit dollars and profit percent, hospitality managers need to have a good understanding of profit margins and how they can improve profitability as measured by profit margins. **Profit margin** is profit percent. It improves or increases when the revenues go up or expenses go down, and vice versa. Managers affect profit margins by their daily actions in improving revenues and decreasing expenses. **Retention or flow-through** identifies the amount by which profit increases or decreases given an increase or decrease in revenues. It, therefore, measures a manager's ability to increase or decrease the variable expenses in relation to the change in business volumes. Understanding profit margins and retention/flow-through are essential skills for operating managers to have.

STAR MARKET REPORTS

Definition

STAR Market Reports are published monthly by the Smith Travel Research Company, an independent hospitality industry research company. It is now part of STR Global. For additional information, visit their Web site www.strglobal.com. STAR reports provide room rate, occupancy percentage, and RevPAR information for a specific hotel and that hotel's competitive set. These reports cover a one year time period and provide a hotel with information to compare its monthly results with its last year's results and the results of its competitive set. They provide valuable trend information as well as the opportunity to compare a specific hotel's performance with its competitive set.

The **competitive set** is a group of four or more hotels identified by a hotel that is considered **primary competition**. These hotels compete for the same customer and offer very similar room rates, products, and services. Hotels that are considered **secondary competition** are the ones that offer different room rates, products, and services.

Any hotel or company can subscribe with Smith Travel Research and choose the type of STAR report that they would like to receive and use to compare its operating results with their primary competitors.

Different Types of STAR Market Reports

The STAR Market Report contains confidential information regarding rooms sold, occupancy percentages, room rates, and RevPAR. This confidential information cannot be shared directly among competitors because of monopoly and price fixing laws. Smith Travel Research collects this confidential financial information monthly for a minimum of five hotels identified by a subscribing hotel and converts it into averages. This average information for the specific hotels is called the competitive set. The subscribing hotels can then compare their operating results and the actual results of their competitive set. Information on the hotel's market share percentage, penetration percentage, and index percentage of the hotel compared to the competitive set results is also provided. **Market Share** is the percentage of total room supply, room demand, or room revenue that a hotel has as a percent of some larger group.

STAR MARKET REPORT
Hotel Name
Report Name
Report Date

	Last 12 Months Average	Last 3 Months Average	YTD
Each Month January–December Actual Results			
<u>Specific Hotel</u>			
Occupancy %			
Average Room Rate			
RevPAR			
Room Supply Share			
Room Demand Share			
Room Sale Share			
Percent Change from Previous Year			
Occupancy %			
Average Room Rate			
RevPAR			
Room Supply Share			
Room Demand Share			
Room Sale Share			
<u>Market</u>			
Occupancy %			
Average Room Rate			
RevPAR			
Percent Change from Previous Year			
Occupancy %			
Average Room Rate			
RevPAR			

Any hotel can purchase this service from Smith Travel. A hotel subscribes for the type of report that it would like and identifies what hotels it wants to include in its competitive set and agrees to provide its own monthly actual rooms sold, occupancy percent, average room rate, and RevPAR information to Smith Travel to be included in the Smith Travel Research information database. Smith Travel Research then *combines and averages* the information for the total competitive set. The report that it sends back to the hotel will contain the specific information for the subscribing hotel and the average information for the competitive set. The hotel can then compare its operating results to the competitive set as well as its own past performance.

We will look at the format for the 12-month market share report. The format will contain the same three categories that P&L Statements contain: title, horizontal headings, and vertical headings.

This sample format shows the amount of information and the detail of the information that is available for hotel managers to use in evaluating their actual room operating performance. Note that this is only a room revenue report and does not include any food and beverage or banquet sales information. It also does not include any expense or profit information.

The members of the selling strategy team will review this report and look for trends and comparisons that will assist them in developing better strategies and make better decisions to maximize total room revenue.

The hotel will focus on two primary areas. First, it will compare its results of the current month with that of the previous month and with that of the quarterly and yearly averages. The hotel will focus on the size and direction of change from their previous results. Second, the hotel will compare its results for the current month with the results of the competitive set. The hotel will identify where its results are better or worse than the competitive set and if the difference is due to a single-month event or is an ongoing trend. If the hotel results are below the competitive set, managers will need to identify and discuss what improvements are being made, has any progress been identified, or is the hotel still underperforming compared to the competitive set? If the hotel results are above the competitive set, is the hotel maintaining, increasing, or decreasing its advantage? The hotel will be interested in both comparing its actual results to the competitive set and identifying if improvements are being made, reflecting good management of the hotel's room revenues.

How STAR Market Reports Are Used

A great deal of operating information is present in the monthly STAR Market Reports. There are many different types and formats of reports that provide very specific month to month and total year operating information. These include many trends and provide good comparative information. The hotel management team analyzes this information and compares its operating results to the competitive sets operating results. A hotel that is well run would expect its results to be better than the results of the competitive set.

Summary

The ability to effectively manage and critique revenues and expenses is an essential skill for all hospitality managers. Making or exceeding budgeted profits is equally important for maintaining customer satisfaction in the successful operations of a business. Both are important for maximizing profits. Profits are the most examined financial measurement used both internally by the senior management of a company and by owners, external investors, developers, and other financial agencies.

Variation analysis is the process of examining financial results to identify differences or variations from expected results and performance. Identifying where variation occurs and determining the size and cause of variations are important elements of financial analysis. Specific ratios and formulas are used to determine the effectiveness of actual operations to historical performance of established budgets or forecasts. Ratios can be divided into five different categories: (1) activity ratios, (2) operating ratios, (3) profitability ratios, (4) liquidity ratios, and (5) solvency ratios.

Variation analysis applies the methods of financial analysis presented in Chapter 2 to the actual performance of a company. These key methods of financial analysis are as follows:

1. comparing numbers to give them meaning,
2. measuring and evaluating the change in numbers and financial results,
3. using percentages as a tool in describing financial performance, and
4. utilizing trends to evaluate current financial performance.

Management is also expected to use external information in the evaluation of financial performance. This includes comparisons with other like hotels or restaurants within the company, comparisons to industry averages, and comparisons with competitive sets within their market. STAR Market Reports prepared by Smith Travel Research are an example of outside financial reports that include several different types of revenue management reports that enable a company to compare its performance with the average performance of competitors within their primary market. This is called the competitive set and provides a specific hotel with average operating information for a group of competitors in its market.

Hospitality Manager Takeaways

1. A hospitality manager must develop a solid understanding of department and hotel profits. This includes the ability to manage operations to maximize profits and the ability to identify and critique variations from budget and forecast.
2. A very important financial skill is the ability to use ratios and formulas in variation analysis. The manager who can effectively identify, explain, and correct operating results will have a major competitive advantage and will possess an important skill for maximizing profits.
3. Managers must be able to understand the different types of ratio classifications and know how and when to use them.
4. Understanding and applying external reports is essential for hospitality managers to effectively manage their operations. The STAR Market Report provides very valuable information about the operations of a specified hotel competitive set.

Key Terms

Competitive set: a group of five or more properties selected by individual hotel management. A competitive set enables hotel managers to compare actual results to the average results of its primary competitors.

Market share: is the percentage of total room supply, room demand, or room revenue that a hotel has as a percent of some larger group.

Primary competition: a group of similar hotels that compete for the same customer. Hotels that you lose business to are primary competition.

Profit margin: is profit percent calculated by dividing profit dollars by revenue dollars.

Ratios: formulas that define relationships between numbers and are used in financial analysis.

Retention or flow-through: identifies the amount that profit increases or decreases given an increase or decrease in revenues.

Secondary competition: a group of hotels that offer competition but provide different rates, services, and amenities and, therefore, are not considered direct or primary competition.

STAR Market Reports: monthly reports published by Smith Travel Research that provide a hotel with rate, occupancy, and RevPAR information for itself and for its competitive set.

Variables: the different components involved in an account and can be revenue accounts or expense accounts. Two variables mean that two components can be managed and analyzed. Variation analysis shows the impact that each component has on the total of each account.

Variation analysis: involves identifying the difference between actual operating performance and established standards. These standards can be last year's actual performance, the previous month's actual performance, the budget for this year, or the most current forecast.

Review Questions

1. Name two important variables for maximizing revenues.
2. Name two important variables for controlling expenses.
3. What is the impact of different department profit percentages on total hotel profits?
4. Define variation analysis and explain why it is an important tool in financial analysis.
5. Name one important ratio from the five ratio classifications and explain why you think it is important in financial analysis.
6. Discuss the relationship between the four elements that make up the foundations of financial analysis and why are they an important part of variation analysis.
7. What key information is provided in STAR Reports?
8. How is STAR Report used in the operation of and financial analysis of a hotel?

Practice Exercises

Calculate the following ratios from the information sheet and balance sheet that are attached.

Flagstaff Hotel
Balance Sheet
June 30, 2008
(000)

ASSETS		LIABILITIES	
Current		**Current**	
Cash	$ 75	Accounts Payable	$ 60
Accounts Receivable	40	Wages Payable	40
Inventories	90	Taxes Payable	25
Total Current Assets	$205	Total Current Liabilities	$125
Long Term		**Long Term**	
Property	$125	Bank Loans	$150
Plant	200	Line of Credit	50
Equipment	150	Lease Obligations	25
Less Depreciation	50	Other Long-Term Obligations	0
Total Long-Term Assets	$525	Total Long-Term Liabilities	$225
Total Assets	$730	**Total Liabilities**	$350
		OWNER EQUITY	
		Paid In Capital	$200
		Capital Stock	100
		Retained Earnings	80
		Total Owner Equity	$380
Total Assets	$730	**Total Liabilities and Owner Equity**	$730

Flagstaff Hotel—600 Rooms
Operating Information
June 30, 2008

1. Total rooms $18,000 = 600 \times 30$ days in June
2. Total out of order and complimentary rooms = 75
3. Total rooms sold in June = 15,300
4. Total guests = 18,360
5. Total room revenue = $1,185,000
6. Total restaurant customers = 11,000
7. Total restaurant revenue = $125,000
8. Total food cost = $35,500
9. Total hotel profit (net profit) = $550,000
10. Number common shares outstanding = 1,000,000
11. Stock price = $12.00
12. Total hotel revenue = $1,575,000

ACTIVITY RATIOS

_____ Total occupancy %

_____ Available occupancy %

_____ Average guests per room

OPERATING RATIOS

_____ Average room rate

_____ Average food check

_____ RevPAR

_____ Food cost %

PROFITABILITY RATIOS

_____ Profit margin %

_____ Return on assets (use the balance for June 30)

_____ Return on owner Equity (use the balance for June 30)

_____ Earnings per share

_____ Price/earnings ratio (PE Ratio)

LIQUIDITY RATIOS

_____ Current ratio

_____ Accounts receivable turnover

SOLVENCY RATIOS

_____ Solvency ratio

_____ Debt equity ratio

Budgets

LEARNING OBJECTIVES

- To understand the four types of budgets
- To understand the importance of the operating budget in analyzing the financial performance for a company
- To learn the formulas and steps used to prepare a budget

- To be able to prepare an operating budget
- To understand how capital expenditure budgets affect hotel operations
- To understand construction and preopening budgets

CHAPTER OUTLINE

Summary   Key Terms
Hospitality Manager   Review Questions
Takeaways   Practice Exercises

INTRODUCTION

Budgets represent an integral part of the financial management of a company. A **budget** is the formal business and financial plan for a business for one year. It is a detailed operating plan for the coming year for a company that applies financial goals and measurements to business operations. Budgets, combined with the results from the previous year (last year), are the key measurements of financial success to which current actual financial results are compared.

The primary budget used by department managers is the **annual operating budget**. It contains the specific revenue goals, the specific expense amounts, and the profit objectives that each department is expected to meet for the year.

There are three other types of budgets. The **capital expenditure budget** identifies expenditures that are necessary to replace long-term assets, to renovate parts of the business, or to expand the business. It involves capitalization.

The **construction budget** establishes the cost to physically construct the hotel. It may also include the cost of the land. The **preopening budget** establishes dollar amounts that are expected to be spent by management to open a new hotel or restaurant. It is the dollar amount needed to cover all expenses incurred before the hotel or restaurant opens and starts to record revenues.

Operating managers must be knowledgeable about his or her department operating budgets as they manage their daily operations. The budget is both a management tool and a way to measure financial performance. Managers must also understand the capital expenditure budget and its process to enable them to plan for and obtain financial resources necessary to obtain long-term assets required in their operations.

THE USE OF BUDGETS IN BUSINESS OPERATIONS

The purpose of budgets is to provide a financial plan for a business for the next fiscal year. The annual budget generally includes an operating budget and a capital expenditure budget. Annual budgets are generally prepared based on the actual financial results for the previous year. Because a fundamental concept of business operations is that a business will grow from year to year, the annual budget will plan for growth and improvement in revenues, profits, and cash flow compared to previous year's financial results. These goals are included in the annual operating budget.

Definition

The annual operating budget is the formal business and financial plan for a business for one year. The operating budget contains the details of department operations including revenue goals by market segment that the business or department is expected to achieve for the upcoming year. It also includes the necessary or planned expense amounts that the business will require to attain the budgeted revenue for the coming year and also to produce the expected or budgeted profits and cash flow.

The Four Types of Budgets

Generally, there are four types of budgets used in business operations. The *annual operating budget* is the main budget used by department managers in daily operations and identifies expected revenue goals and expense amounts that can be used to support or achieve the revenue budget. Both revenues and expenditures are for one year of operations. Managers use the budgeted amounts as guidelines to operate their departments from month to month. The *capital expenditure budget* identifies expenditures necessary to purchase long-term assets. It is a form of capitalization. Capital expenditures are depreciated over the useful life of the asset purchased and a portion of their value is recorded in the depreciation account in the fixed expenses department.

The next budget is the *preopening budget*, which is used to identify and plan for necessary expenditures incurred before a business opens. It is separate from the construction budget and generally amortized over the first one to three years of operations. The final budget is the *construction budget*. It estimates the cost to construct the hotel. It includes architectural drawings, design and décor specifications, engineering fees, and all actual construction costs such as permits, licenses, fees, code compliance and inspections, materials, and labor.

The annual operating budget (also referred to as the **department budget**) contains the details and specifics of the financial operations of a business and its operating departments for one year. Characteristics of annual operating budgets are as follows:

1. It is a plan for the next year, therefore, a plan for future operations.
2. It is for one fiscal year.
3. It is generally based on the previous year's actual financial results.
4. It includes expected growth amounts and financial improvements over the previous year. This means increasing revenues and controlling expenses.
5. It includes dollar amounts, percentages, units, and statistics.
6. The budget column is included on monthly Profit and Loss Statements and actual financial results are compared to the budget amounts.
7. It starts with the hotel's current marketing plan.

Operating budgets are prepared for each department in a hotel and include the details for each month or accounting period. If a business operates on monthly P&L Statements, it will prepare a budget for each month of the year. Adding the department budgets for the 12 months will result in the operating budget for the year. If a business operates on 13 accounting periods, it will prepare a budget for each week of the four-week accounting period. Adding the department budgets for the 13 accounting periods will result in the annual operating budget for the year.

The Director of Finance of a hotel has the main responsibility for preparing the annual operating budget. This is because he or she is the financial expert of the hotel and not only prepares the monthly financial reports but also analyzes and critiques them with the operations managers. Each year, when the budget process starts, the Director of Finance will work with the appropriate Executive Committee Member and the department managers to prepare the budget for that department for the next year. The budget is then submitted to the General Manager for approval and is then forwarded to the corporate office or owners for final approval.

All of the department annual operating budgets are added together to make the **consolidated hotel budget** or *total hotel budget.* This budget summarizes all the revenues, expenses, and profits for the revenue departments and the total department costs for the expense departments.

For a company with a fiscal year ending December 31, the budgeting process will generally start in October and be completed by November. Final approval by senior management and owners should be received in December so that the budget is in place when the new fiscal year starts from January 1. Once the annual operating budget is approved, it is not changed. It represents the formal and final operating plan for the year. Weekly or monthly forecasts are used during the budget year to update the budget. As business conditions change, these forecasts are prepared to reflect these changes. Forecasts can increase or decrease revenues, expenses, or profits. Therefore, actual monthly financial performance can be compared to three important measurements: last year, the budget, and the most recent forecast.

Capital expenditure budgets are also prepared annually and identify the needs for replacing long-term assets of the business, renovating the business, or expanding the business. Capital expenditure budgets generally involve projects or equipment that cost a significant amount of money and that can be used for more than one year. This involves capitalization and not working capital. Characteristics of a capital expenditure budget are as follows:

1. It identifies purchases of specific pieces of equipment such as a laundry machine, airport van, kitchen oven, or mechanical motor.
2. It identifies projects that involve many pieces of equipment or activities such as room soft goods or hard goods redo, and restaurant renovations or expansions.
3. Budget items must have a useful life of more than one year.
4. Budget items must exceed a minimum cost established by a business.
5. Capital expenditure projects must contain the details of all expenditures necessary to complete the project.
6. Capital expenditure items and projects have different approval levels. For example, items costing under $5,000 might only require the approval of the General Manager while items costing over $5,000 might require corporate approval and owner approval.
7. Small capital expenditure items can be included in one list, totaled, and approved.
8. Large capital expenditure items or projects are itemized and approved one by one.

Capital expenditure budgets can be funded in several ways. First, owners contribute the amount necessary to purchase capital expenditure equipment or to complete capital expenditure projects. Second, the hotel contributes money from its annual operations (usually a percentage of total sales) to a capital expenditure **escrow** account that can be used to fund capital expenditure projects. Third, outside financing can be used such as obtaining bank loans, utilizing a line of credit, or obtaining a lease.

Preopening budgets are established to guide a new business as they prepare to open. This budget includes all the costs that will be incurred to get the business ready to open but before any revenues are recorded or guests checked in. Characteristics of a preopening budget include the following:

1. Wage expenses for all employees working before the business opens including training.
2. Advertising and promotional expenditures.
3. The costs of all the items necessary to furnish the hotel or restaurant such as guest room furniture and amenities, restaurant furniture and supplies, and kitchen equipment and supplies.
4. The total cost is established for all expenses before opening.
5. The total preopening costs are spread over or paid back over a predetermined time period.

Preopening budgets are prepared based on expected operations and expenses necessary to start up a new business. This can be tricky or difficult as generally there is no previous information or concrete information to base these budgets on. They are prepared based on assumptions about the market, competitors, and expected business volumes. These budgets are true estimates and often additional expenditures occur that need to be added to the original preopening budgeted amount, especially if there are construction delays.

Construction budgets are very complex and detailed. They include the cost of designing and planning the building, materials and equipment necessary to construct the building, and all the wage costs of the manpower required to build a hotel or restaurant. Many people are involved in preparing the construction budget such as architects, designers, engineers, cost estimators, developers, inspectors, and investors to identify as accurately as possible the cost of materials and labor to construct the project. Preparing these budgets generally involves the developers; the owners; the managers involved in a management contract; franchisees if appropriate; and any other parties involved in financing, developing, and building the project. Operations managers generally do not get involved with these budgets.

Radisson Fort McDowell Resort & Casino Fort McDowell, Arizona

The Radisson Fort McDowell Resort & Casino is tucked away in pristine Sonoran Desert surroundings on the Fort McDowell Indian reservation just east of Scottsdale, Arizona. The resort offers 246 spacious guest rooms and suites each beautifully decorated according to Native American traditions. The restaurant features local menu items and room service is offered 24 hours a day. With over 25,000 square feet of

Photo Courtesy of the Fort McDowell Yavapai Nation, Fort McDowell, Arizona.

meeting space indoor and outdoor and 15 breakout rooms, the resort can accommodate the needs of a wide range of meetings and activities.

Resort activities include golf at the Wekopa Golf Club, with both courses consistently rated in the top 10 golf courses in Arizona because of the natural beauty and unique challenges the golf course offer its players. The Fort McDowell Casino is a short walk and offers additional food and beverage outlets as well as a wide range of gaming opportunities. The Fort McDowell Adventures offers a distinctive southwestern experience of steak fries, horseback riding, and jeep tours in the natural beauty of the southwest desert. Visit the Web site www.fortmcdowelldestination.com to get a feel of this distinctive resort destination. Consider the following budget questions for Fort McDowell as the owner of these different operations:

1. From the above information and the Web site, list the revenue department budgets that you think the Radisson Resort Fort McDowell reviews each year. Be specific.
2. Make a list of at least five pieces of equipment that might be on a typical capital expenditure list for the Radisson Resort and five pieces of equipment for the Wekopa Golf Course. Remember the golf course is divided into golf shop, food and beverage, and golf course maintenance departments.
3. Name what you think might be the three biggest expense accounts for each of the following departments:
   A. Rooms operations
   B. Food and beverage operations, including banquets
   C. Golf clubhouse
   D. Golf course maintenance.

ANNUAL OPERATING BUDGETS

Consolidated Hotel Budget

The consolidated hotel budget contains the summary of the financial information of the entire hotel. Its main purpose is to present the key financial results for all of the hotel departments. Characteristics of consolidated budgets are as follows:

1. Contains the total revenues, expenses, and profits for operating departments in the hotel.
2. Contains the total expenses for the staff or supporting departments in the hotel.
3. Includes the hotel profit budgeted amount for Department Profit, Total Department Profits, House Profit, and Net House Profit.
4. It contains all of the pertinent summary financial information for the hotel stated in dollars, percentages, or units.
5. It does not contain detailed budget information for line accounts for any department.

The consolidated hotel budget is used by the senior management and owners to get a summary or overview of the planned financial results of a business generally on one page. When the budget is prepared, reviewed, and approved, it becomes the formal operating plan for the next year. It therefore shows what the financial expectations are for the coming year. The actual financial results are compared each month to the budget to determine if the budgeted operational and financial expectations are achieved.

Revenue and Expense Department Budgets

The Department Budgets contain the detailed budget information in line accounts for a specific department. These budget amounts provide operations managers specific financial guidelines that can be used as management tools in the daily operations of their departments. Department budgets can also be considered roadmaps of where the department operations should go and what financial results they should produce. Characteristics of department budgets are as follows:

1. Contains the detailed revenue budget for the department including market segments, average room rates or average guest checks, and volumes such as rooms sold and customer counts.
2. Contains the budget amount for expenses for each line account.
3. Contains detailed wage budget guidelines including man-hours, average wage rates, and total wage costs for specific wage departments.
4. Provides detailed operating information that is used as a management tool.
5. A specific Executive Committee Member along with the appropriate Department Head has the responsibility for specific department budgets.
6. A Department Head has the direct responsibility for meeting the daily department budget goals.

The department budget contains many pages compared to one page for the consolidated budget. This is because of the amount of detailed operating and financial information included in the department budget. Following are examples of the details that can be in a department operating budget.

REVENUE BUDGETS—MARKET SEGMENTS OR MEAL PERIODS In the Rooms Department budget, the market segments provide average room rates; number of rooms sold; and total revenue for transient, group, and contract market segments. In the Restaurant Department budget, the meal periods include average checks; customer counts; and total revenues for breakfast, lunch, and dinner. In a typical 600-room full-service hotel, the revenue budget for the Rooms and the Food and Beverage Departments will each be several pages long.

EXPENSE BUDGETS—WAGE DEPARTMENTS In the larger operating departments such as Housekeeping and Restaurants, hourly wages are separated into specific wage subdepartments or classifications that define specific job responsibilities for more effective control. Each one of these wage classifications contains the budget and actual average wage rates, man-hours, and total wage cost. For example, Housekeeping includes the following wage classifications: housekeepers, supervisors, housemen, and public space. The wage budget will include average wage rates, man-hours, and total wage costs for each of these wage classifications. In the Restaurant, the wage classifications might include servers, hostess, bussers, and cashier. In the Kitchen, the wage classifications might include station attendants, cooks, lead cooks, dish washers, and expeditors.

DIRECT OPERATING EXPENSE ACCOUNTS These line accounts are not as detailed because they do not involve rates or volumes. Rather, they include, collect and record all the costs of purchases, inventory consumption and expense, and transfer costs for a specific line account. For example, the guest supply account in the Rooms Department will include all the purchases from outside vendors, issues from hotel inventory, and transfers from other departments for guest supply items such as soap, shampoo, condenser, pens, stationery, and tissue. The total expenses for the china account, glass account, and silver account in the restaurant will include all the purchase costs from outside vendors, issues from inventory, and transfers from other departments during the month or accounting period.

PROFIT BUDGETS The profit budgets do not contain any line accounts or detailed information like the revenue and expense budgets because the profit budget is an amount calculated by subtracting total expenses from total revenues. This simple formula can involve many market segments and expense line accounts to finally get to the Total Department Profit. The budgeted Department Profit is typically considered the most important measurement of financial performance.

Fixed Expense Department Budgets

This budget generally includes only one department where all the fixed expenses for operating the hotel are recorded in individual line accounts. Expenses are identified by line accounts where entries are made to record the appropriate costs for the month or accounting period for that line account. For example, monthly bank loan payments are recorded in the bank loan line account, monthly insurance costs are recorded in the insurance line account, the monthly cost of annual licenses and fees are recorded in the licenses and fees line account. The detail is present in the depreciation account where fixed monthly depreciation costs are recorded in specific line accounts for property, plant, and equipment. For each piece of equipment, there are depreciation schedules that show the original purchase price, monthly depreciation amounts, and residual value.

Department managers do not get involved with managing fixed expense departments because these costs are predetermined and are not managed and do not change during the month. The Accounting Department generally records and reviews the costs in these departments.

FORMULAS AND STEPS IN PREPARING A BUDGET

It is important for hospitality managers to be involved in the preparation of their annual department operating budget. This will require a good understanding of both their daily operations, the accounting policies and concepts, and the methods of financial analysis that will be used to evaluate the financial performance of their departments.

The Goals of an Operating Budget

Goals are used to provide a financial guideline for measuring financial performance and to provide managers a management tool to help achieve expected financial results. The operating budget combines previous year's results with planned growth and improvements to project financial expectations for the next year. It is indeed a roadmap or game plan for operations for the next year. Actual operating results and financial performance are compared to the budget as well as previous year and any variations identified and explained.

When the budget is not met for a month or accounting period, operations management analyzes the operations to identify the problems and work on solutions to correct those problems so that improvements can be made. Variations from the budget identify problems and also the successes in operations and management can deal with each of these as appropriate. By identifying problems, budget variations red flag areas that management needs to address and examine to identify problems and take corrective actions. By identifying successes, positive budget variation can reinforce operational changes that have resulted in improved performance or growth.

Methods of Preparing Budgets

Budgeting methods include several processes that can be used to prepare budgets depending on the goals of the budget. A business will generally use the same method from year to year to be consistent. The important point to consider in choosing a method to prepare a budget is will it provide the necessary accuracy and detail to produce the expected financial results? Will it be a realistic budget given the market environment, competition, and condition of the hotel or restaurant?

Zero-based budgeting is a budgeting method that involves preparing each year's budget from actual needs and costs. No goals or historical information is used. It is a bottom up budgeting approach. It is very detailed and involves many specific formulas. For example, preparing a zero-based budget for guest supplies in the Rooms Department will involve calculating the historical cost per rooms sold for each item classified in the guest supply line account. Then a review of these costs and any expected changes will be considered. Shampoo cost per occupied room, soap cost per occupied room, and stationery cost per occupied room are all multiplied by the budgeted number of rooms sold by month and by year to establish the budgeted dollar amount by month and by year for the guest supply budget.

Historical budgeting is a budget that is based on previous year's actual expenses. Previous year's actual expenses establishes the base and the budget is adjusted up or down based on changes in volumes, material costs, inflation, or any changes in operations. For example, preparing a historical-based budget for guest supplies in the Rooms Department will involve identifying last year's actual costs per month and then increasing it by a certain percentage based on changes in any of the variables that are appropriate and that would apply to the next year's costs. For example, if inflation is expected to increase by 4% and rooms sold are expected to increase by 1%, then the budget for guest supplies will be last year's actual expense increased by 5%.

Goal-based budgeting is a budget that is based on an established goal determined by the corporate office, senior management, or owners. This is a top-down budgeting approach. The business is given a number or target from the owner or corporate office and the business fills in the budget details to meet the goals. If management wants revenues to increase by 5% and profits to increase by 6%, then the budget will be prepared based on last year's actual results and increased by 5% in revenues and 6% in profits. While this is an easy and quick way to prepare a budget, the danger is that it may or may not accurately reflect what is realistic and what is happening in the business and the current market.

Revenue Budgets

Revenue budgets are prepared by using the basic revenue formula of rate × volume for each market segment in the Rooms Department or each meal period in the Restaurant Department. Management will identify how increased revenues can be achieved by either increasing rooms sold or customer counts or increasing average room rates and guest checks if demand is strong. If demand is not strong, it will be difficult to increase rooms sold or average rates in the Rooms Department and also difficult to increase customer counts and average checks in the Restaurant Department. Management will make the decision when and how much any increases in rooms sold or average rate can be realistically achieved and put into the budget for next year.

The zero-based budgeting approach considers each day and determines the number of rooms expected to be sold for each market segment. These rooms sold are then multiplied by the average room rate budgeted for the market segment to calculate the budgeted room revenue. The sum of all the market segments is the total room revenue budget for the day. The days are totaled to get the weekly and monthly budgets. The same approach is used in the restaurant by adding the meal periods together to get total restaurant revenues for the day.

The historical budgeting approach will take historical daily averages of rooms sold and add the expected percentage increase to get the total rooms sold budget for a day. This can also be done for a week at a time. The weekly totals will then have to be broken down into the daily budgeted rooms sold. The budgeted average room rate is then multiplied by the budgeted rooms sold to get the total revenue budget for the day. A similar process is used in the restaurant.

The goal budgeting approach will involve the owner or corporate office establishing the amount of revenue increases expected for the next year's budget. The room revenue budget is then prepared by filling in the rooms sold and average room rates necessary to produce the daily room revenues to meet the established revenue budget. The restaurant revenue budget is likewise prepared using customer counts and average guest checks necessary to produce the meal period revenues to meet the established revenue budget.

Expense Budgets

Expense budgets are prepared differently for the four major expense categories (cost of sales, wages, benefits, and direct operating expenses) and involve historical averages and relationships between volume expressed as revenue dollars, units such as rooms sold or customer counts, or other formulas.

Cost of sales budgets can be prepared using any of the three budgeting methods. Zero-based food cost budgets are prepared by costing out each menu item and multiplying by the menu counts for that item to determine food cost dollars. All the menu items are added up to determine the food cost budget in dollars and percentage. Historical food cost budgets are based on the actual food costs and are changed by any expected price increases due to inflation or productivity gains to determine food cost in dollars and percentage. Goal-based food cost budgets are determined by the food cost percentage established by the owner or corporate office.

Wage budgets are the most complicated and detailed to prepare. The hourly employee wage cost budgets are generally prepared by a zero-based budgeting approach. Formulas such as man-hours per occupied room or man-hours per customer are applied to budgeted rooms sold or budgeted customer counts. These man-hours are then multiplied by expected average wage rates to determine the wage cost budget in dollars for each wage classification. Wage budgets can also be prepared more quickly using the historical budgeting method by taking the average man-hours or wage cost and changing them based on inflation or wage rate increases and any changes in volume levels. For example, if revenues increase by 5%, then the historical wage cost will increase by 5%.

Benefit budgets are relatively simple to prepare. The formula used is the historical benefit costs to wage cost percent calculated by dividing actual benefit expense by actual wage cost. The resulting historical benefit cost as a percent of wage cost is multiplied by the dollar amount in the wage budget to get the new dollar amount for the benefit budget.

Direct operating expense budgets are prepared by using many different formulas and choosing the one that best expresses the relationship between expense costs and volume levels. These budgeting formulas include the following:

1. *Historical average* involves taking the average cost of the previous year for a line account (linen, guest supplies, and china) over a specific time and then using that amount for the budget. For example, if the historical average linen cost per month was $7,000, then the linen budget amount for the new fiscal year will be $7,000 per month.

2. *Historical average plus inflation* or expected cost increases involves applying expected cost increases to historical average costs. If the linen vendor in our previous example is increasing linen cost by 5%, we would multiply $7,000 by 5%, then the budget amount for the new fiscal year will be $7,350 each month, which would plan for any cost increases.

3. *Percent of sales* involves using the relationship between expense costs in dollars and revenues in dollars. For example, cleaning supply expenses is 0.3% of room's sales for the previous year. This percentage is calculated by dividing actual cleaning supply dollar expense for last year by actual room sales of the previous year. The new cleaning supply budget would be calculated by multiplying the new budgeted room sales by 0.3%. For example, total budgeted room revenue of $8,000,000 times 0.3% would result in the cleaning supply budget of $24,000 for the year.

4. *Cost per occupied room or cost per customer served* involves using the relationship between expense costs and rooms sold. This is similar to cost percentage but uses the relationship of expense in dollars divided by total rooms sold. For example, guest supply total expense in dollars divided by total rooms sold results in actual guest supply cost per occupied room of $3.15. The guest supply budget for the upcoming year would be calculated by multiplying the budgeted rooms sold by the $3.15 cost per occupied room. If next year's budgeted rooms sold are 10,000 rooms, the guest supply budget would be $31,500.

5. *Specific formulas* are used to budget based on established costs. For example, the central reservation budget could be based on the formula $5 per reservation made through the central reservation office. The reservation cost budget would be calculated by multiplying the expected number of reservations received through the central reservations office by $5.

6. *Allocations* use formulas to spread the cost over several departments by established allocation percentages. For example, allocating Laundry Department costs back to the Rooms, Restaurant, and Banquet Departments based on the number of items washed or the amount of pounds of linen washed for each department. A typical Laundry Department allocation might be rooms 70%, restaurant 10%, and banquet 20%.

7. *Contract budgeting* involves taking the dollar amount of an annual contract and spreading the cost back to each month. For example, a $24,000 annual contract for cleaning outside windows would be budgeted at $2,000 per month.

Profit Budgets

The formula for profit is revenues minus expenses. The profit budgets are, therefore, determined by making this calculation. Budgeted department revenues minus all the budgeted department expenses equals budgeted Department Profit. Compared to budgeting revenues and expenses, this is a rather basic calculation. All the revenue department profits are added up to produce Total Department Profits. Then the total Expense Center department expenses are subtracted to produce House Profit. Finally, the total fixed costs department expenses are subtracted to get the Net House Profit.

Realistically, the Department Profit budget is the result of all the assumptions, calculations, formulas, and ratios used in budgeting revenues and expenses. Chemists would call profits residue, what is left over! The profits that are left over after using revenues to pay for all expenses are the lifeblood of any business. Therefore, it is the most examined, challenged, and documented number in an operating budget.

CAPITAL EXPENDITURE BUDGETS

The primary concern of hospitality managers is the department operating budget as it is the financial report that compares their actual monthly financial performance to the budget and previous year. We briefly discussed other budgets used in business that a manager should be aware of, specifically the preopening budget and the construction budget referred to earlier in the chapter. The Director of Finance at a hotel will generally have the responsibility for these budgets.

A hospitality manager needs to have a good understanding of capital expenditure projects (CEP) budget because this budget plans the financial needs for the purchase of long-term equipment, financing of projects such as rooms redo's or restaurant renovations, and other long-term operating needs. Managers need to plan for and obtain the necessary capital expenditure funds to provide for their long-term equipment and operational needs.

Definition

Capital Expenditure Budgets are the formal budgets that identify the need for replacing long-term assets of the business, for renovating the business, and for expanding the business. When a business is started, the capitalization determines the amount of investment necessary to start the business and identifies where the expenditures on property, plant, and equipment (PP&E) will be made. **Property, Plant, and Equipment (PP&E)** is the term used to identify the long-term investments in long-term assets that will serve the business for more than one year.

These expenditures are long term in nature and the PP&E will last for 1–30 years. Funds for capitalization come from paid-in capital (owners), the issuance of common stock (investors), or outside financing (long-term liabilities) such as bank loans or lines of credit.

Characteristics

Let's review the characteristics of a capital expenditure budget presented earlier in the chapter.

1. They identify purchases of specific pieces of equipment such as a laundry machine, airport van, kitchen oven, kitchen refrigeration units, mechanical motors, or housekeeping vacuums.
2. They identify projects that involve many pieces of equipment, construction costs, or activities such as rooms soft goods redo, restaurant renovation, or major equipment replacement.
3. Budget items must have a useful life of more than one year.
4. Budget items must have a minimum cost or value.
5. Projects must contain the details of all expenditures necessary to complete the project.
6. Projects or expenditures have different approval levels. For example, items costing under $5,000 might be approved by the General Manager while items costing over $5,000 might need corporate or owner approval.
7. Small expenditures (under $20,000, for example) can be included in one list, totaled and approved.
8. Large expenditures (projects over $20,000, for example) are itemized and approved one by one.

Because capital expenditure items and PP&E are quite different from the expenses budgeted in the annual operating budgets, the CEP budget is prepared and reviewed in a different way.

Preparing Capital Expenditure Budgets

Capital expenditure budgets are prepared based on the needs of the hotel or restaurant. Replacing major equipment and completing major renovations involves a great deal of operational and financial planning because the results of these budgets will affect many years of operations and generally involve larger amounts of money.

IDENTIFYING CAPITAL EXPENDITURE PROJECTS AND NEEDS   During the year, department heads will identify equipment that needs replacement or areas of the hotel that need to be upgraded or renovated. These capital needs will be divided between those with small costs that are easily replaced and those with large costs that are more expensive to replace or complete. Estimates are obtained and all projects are reviewed by the Executive Committee Member and then submitted to the Director of Finance.

The Director of Finance will accumulate all capital expenditure requests and categorize them according to size and type of expenditure. The main categories might be as follows:

1. Equipment costing under a set amount, for example under $2,500.
2. Equipment costing more than a set amount, for example over $2,500.
3. Projects costing under a set amount, in our example under $20,000.
4. Projects costing over a set amount, in our example over $20,000.

All equipment and projects under the $20,000 amount will be listed on one capital expenditure list as one project and approved all together. Then it will be the hotel's responsibility to complete each project within the dollar amount budgeted for each item contained on the approval list.

Equipment and projects over the $20,000 amount will be listed separately and contain all the necessary information describing the equipment or project and the dollar cost involved to complete the project. There can be many pieces of equipment, types of construction, and dollar costs in these project budgets. For example, a restaurant redo might include the cost to purchase several items such as new tables, chairs, point of sale equipment, and carpet. It will also include the cost to install the carpet, repaint the restaurant and, replace any wall coverings. A project with 15 items will include the cost of each item and the total for all items. The final project cost will include expenses such as materials and supplies, labor, permits and fees, and taxes.

Following are some examples of capital expenditure requests:

Projects Under $20,000

$3,000 Housekeeping vacuums—15 @ $200 each

$6,000 Front office brass bellman carts—4 @ $1,500 each

$10,000 Kitchen stainless steel prep tables—2 @ $5,000 each

$16,000 Kitchen convection oven—1 @ $16,000

$2,000 Sales and marketing computers—4 @ $500 each

$37,000 Total under $20,000 Projects

Projects Over $20,000

$85,000 Airport van

$48,000 Restaurant upgrade

   $10,000 Carpet—material and labor

   $8,000 Tables and chair replacement

   $20,000 Painting, vinyl materials, and labor

   $3,000 Artwork

   $4,000 Fees and permits

   $3,000 Contingency

$36,000 Laundry dryers—2 @ $18,000 each

$169,000 Total over $20,000 Projects

$206,000 Total Capital Expenditure Budget

Usually, CEP requests will be more than the amount available in CEP escrow or **reserve** accounts. The General Manager will review the CEP list prepared by the Director of Finance with his Executive Committee and together they will prioritize and determine which projects to keep on the list and which projects to cancel or defer to the next year. Once the CEP budget is approved, the hotel can proceed to purchase the equipment or start the projects but must remain within the established budget. If there are cost overruns, the hotel might have to cancel other projects and use the approved budget amount for these projects to pay for the cost overruns. The hotel must also be sure that the necessary funds are available in the cash account or escrow reserve account to pay the project costs as they are incurred.

FUNDING CAPITAL EXPENDITURE PROJECTS   Funding to pay for capital expenditure projects could be obtained from outside sources such as bank loans or owner contributions. However, the main source of finance for these projects is from the cash flow generated from business operations.

A company will determine what percent of sales it is willing to commit to set aside in capital expenditure reserve or escrow accounts. A new hotel will not require as much additional capital investment as an older hotel that has equipment and materials wearing out and need replacement. A new hotel might set aside 3% of total annual sales while an older hotel might set aside 5% of total annual sales in its CEP escrow account.

Let's use an older hotel as an example. If the total annual sales for the hotel are $20 million dollars, 5% of that amount or $1 million will be set aside in the CEP escrow or reserve account for that year. It means that the hotel will have $1 million to allocate and spend on CEP projects for the year. Each month, the Director of Finance will make an accounting entry and transfer funds from the operating cash account to the CEP escrow or reserve cash account. When equipment is purchased or projects are completed, a check will be drawn from the CEP cash account to make payments.

Operating managers do not generally get involved with CEP accounting as this is done by the Director of Finance. However, they are involved in choosing the equipment, preparing estimates to ensure that it meets requirements and stays within the budgeted costs, and overseeing projects to ensure that the work is completed as planned and also stays within the CEP budget. It can become very competitive between hotel departments to obtain approval and funding for equipment and projects that they need. In our example, if the owner approves only $175,000 for capital expenditures for the year, the General Manager will reduce the hotel's request by $31,000. This means deciding which capital expenditure projects to remove from the list. A hospitality manager's ability to clearly explain and justify any CEP projects will be an important factor in securing approval for those projects and ensuring that his or her department has what it needs to operate successfully.

Summary

Budgets play a critical role in the success of any business. Budgets connect actual operations with financial needs and results. They are the annual formal financial plan for the operations of the coming year. Management's actual performance will be evaluated against the budget to determine if expected results have been achieved.

Annual operating budgets are used to plan for the next year and to evaluate actual financial performance from month to month and for the year. Hospitality managers will be involved with the preparation of their department budgets and will use that budget in planning their department operations. Operating budgets include the detailed financial plans for revenues, expenses, and profits.

Several other budgets are used in business besides the annual operating budget. The capital expenditure budget plans for the long-term needs of the business and has an impact on many years of business operations. Hospitality managers will need to understand and be involved in the preparation of capital expenditure budgets to secure additional investments and capital expenditures. Other budgets include preopening and construction budgets administered by the Director of Finance. Generally, hospitality managers will not be involved with these budgets.

Hospitality Manager Takeaways

1. Operations managers must have a complete understanding of consolidated hotel budgets, their annual department operating budget, and to be able to use them in the daily operations of their departments. Department budgets are a key management tool.
2. Operations managers must have the ability to prepare their annual department operating budget and their capital expenditure budgets, and be actively involved in the budget approval process.
3. Hospitality managers must understand and be able to use appropriate budgeting formulas for revenues, wages, and other direct operating expenses.
4. Actual department financial results will be compared to the budget and last year to evaluate the success of operating results.
5. Capital expenditure budgets are very important and provide the long-term equipment needs and plan for renovation projects that are essential in maintaining department operations.

Key Terms

Budget: the formal business and financial plan for a business for one year.

Annual operating budget: the primary budget used by department managers. It contains the specific revenue goals, the specific expense amounts, and the profit objectives that each department is expected to meet for the year.

Consolidated hotel budget: the summary budget for the entire hotel including revenues, expenses, and profits.

Department budget: the specific and detailed budget for an individual department that provides all the financial specifics for revenues and expenses in line accounts.

Capital expenditure budget: the formal budget that identifies the need of replacing long-term assets of the business for renovation and expansion.

Construction budget: the budget that identifies all the costs to construct and build a hotel or restaurant.

Escrow: an account established to collect and reserve money to be used at a later date. Same as reserve account.

Preopening budget: the budget established to guide a new business as they prepare to open for business.

Property, Plant, and Equipment (PP&E): the term used to identify the long-term investments in long-term assets that will serve the business for more than one year.

Reserve: an account established to collect money to be used at a later date. Same as an escrow account.

Review Questions

1. Why is the annual department operating budget the most important financial report for a hospitality manager to know, understand, and use?
2. Name five characteristics of a department operating budget.
3. Why is a capital expenditure budget important and how is it used by hospitality managers in operating their departments?
4. Name five characteristics of a capital expenditure budget.

5. What is the difference between a consolidate hotel budget and a department operating budget?
6. What are the five ways of budgeting direct operating expenses.
7. Name and describe the three main ways of preparing an operating budget.
8. How is a budget used to evaluate actual financial performance?

Practice Exercises

There are two budget problems to complete. First, calculate amounts to use in budgeting based on actual information and formulas. Second, prepare an annual budget based on that information. Information for the Rooms Department of the Flagstaff Hotel for the first *six periods* of the year is as follows:

Room Revenue		$8,713,000
Transient Rooms Sold	83,730	
Group Rooms Sold	16,270	
Total Rooms Sold	100,000	
Operating Expenses		
Linen		$31,100
Cleaning Supplies		24,000
Guest Supplies		104,800
Outside Services		24,000
Laundry		80,500
Concierge Expense		60,000
Office Supplies		19,200
Reservation Expense		
Reservation Department	$150,000	
Fixed Reservation Center Cost	180,000	
Variable Reservation Center Cost	251,200	
Total Reservation Expense		581,200
All Other Expense		120,000
Total Operating Expenses		$1,044,800
Total Operating Expense Percentage		12.0%

Problem 1

Use the following formulas to calculate each one of the line items: They are used to prepare the annual budget for the coming year. Round off the average cost per period to whole dollars, cost per occupied room to whole cents, cost per occupied room to whole cents, and the percentage of sales to four decimals. Use the laundry and reservation information as supplied.

1. Linen: Calculate the average cost per period.
2. Cleaning supplies: Calculate the average cost per occupied room.
3. Guest supplies: Calculate the average cost per occupied room.
4. Outside services: Calculate the average cost per period.
5. Laundry: Calculate at 70% of total laundry department expense per period and laundry department expense at $115,000 for six periods.
6. Concierge level expense: Calculate as a percentage of total room sales.
7. Office supplies: Calculate as a percentage of total room sales.
8. Reservation cost
   A. Reservation Department cost at $25,000 per period.
   B. Fixed expense at $50 per total number of rooms in hotel per period.
   C. Variable expense at $6 per reservation. Calculate the reservations as 50% of transient rooms sold.
9. All other expense at $20,000 per period.

Problem 2

Prepare the annual operating expense budget for the next year using the formulas from Problem 1 and the following assumptions: Remember there are 13 accounting periods in a fiscal year, each with 4 weeks and 28 days.

Room Revenue		$19,184,000
Transient Rooms Sold	184,000	
Group Rooms Sold	34,000	
Total Rooms Sold	218,000	
Operating Expense Annual Budget		
Linen		
Cleaning Supplies		
Guest Supplies		
Laundry		
Concierge Expense		
Office Supplies		
Reservation Expense		
Reservation Department Cost		
Fixed Reservation Center Cost		
Variable Reservation Center Cost		
Total Reservation Expense		
All Other Expense		
Total Operating Expenses $		
Total Operating Expense %		

CHAPTER

10

Forecasting: A Very Important Management Tool

LEARNING OBJECTIVES

- To understand the fundamentals of business forecasting
- To understand the different uses of forecasts
- To understand the different types and time periods of forecasts
- To be able to prepare revenue forecasts
- To be able to prepare wage forecasts and wage schedules

CHAPTER OUTLINE

INTRODUCTION

Forecasts are used in business to assist management in the short-term operations of their businesses. More than any other financial document, forecasts are the key management tools used to plan the details of the daily operation of hotels and restaurants for the next week. Like the operating budget, forecasts look to the future and assist management in the detailed planning of operations for the next week or month. They involve the shortest time period (daily and weekly) and are the final financial document prepared in advance of the next week's daily operations. For example, weekly revenue forecasts are used to develop weekly wage schedules containing daily schedules as a business plan for the next week of operations.

The major inputs to a forecast are first, the historical daily averages provided by Revenue Management or other demand tracking programs, second, the established budget, and third, recent events that affect the current operating environment of the business. Revenue Management looks to the past and provides detailed information on historical daily room revenues, rooms sold, and average room rates by market segment. The operating budget is the formal annual financial plan for a business and is prepared once a year. The next year's budget is generally approved by December and is not changed during the budget year. *Forecasts are used to update the budget.* Recent events and trends in the marketplace affect the business environment and need to be considered as the year progresses. As the recession of 2009 unfolded, forecasts became an extremely important management tool in trying to identify new revenue levels and controlling operating expenses. The forecast is the management and financial tool that updates the budget to reflect these changes. It is then used to plan the details of each day's operations. Forecasts can either increase or decrease the original budget numbers based on historical information, recent market information, and current trends.

Weekly forecasts consider the original budget, current market conditions and trends, and combine them with ratios and formulas to forecast current revenues or labor costs that help plan daily operations in detail for the next week. Forecasts for the next month or accounting period will be more general in nature. **Ratios** identify the relationships between the two components of revenues (rate and volume), the two components of wages (rate and labor man-hours), and the important components of other operating expenses. *Ratios and formulas are used to calculate appropriate expense levels in relation to different revenue levels that reflect current market conditions.*

This chapter discusses revenue and wage forecasts—how they are prepared and used. This chapter builds on the information presented in the revenue management and budget chapters.

FORECASTING FUNDAMENTALS

Definition

Forecasts are the financial documents that update the operating budget. While the operating budget is a permanent financial plan for a year, the forecast is flexible and provides a way to make weekly or monthly changes to the budget to reflect current trends and economic/market conditions. Budgets are generally prepared in the fourth quarter of the current year for the next year. The budget for the first quarter is fairly current, being only a couple of months old. However, the budgets for the third and fourth quarters are over eight months old and many changes may have occurred in the marketplace that would affect the budget and the operations of a business. Forecasts are therefore valuable management tools used to update the budget so that it reflects current business levels and conditions.

Forecasting is not an exact science and forecasts generally are not expected to balance or tie into other financial numbers. Forecasting involves using current information and combining this information with established ratios and formulas to estimate or project future business levels and operations. These ratios are based on existing relationships between revenues and expenses. They can be applied aggressively or conservatively in forecasting depending on the current management operating philosophy and business strategy.

Last Year, Budgets, and Forecasts

There is a logical progression for the preparation of financial documents used as management tools in operating a business. Two aspects are involved. The first is historical in nature reflecting past actual results and the second is forward looking in nature reflecting the plans or expectations for future results.

All financial documents used in the planning of business operations start with a review of last year's actual financial performance. This is the historical aspect of financial planning. These numbers are facts and are the results of actual business operations for previous months or years. They become the foundation for preparing the operating and capital expenditure budgets for the next year. If last year's financial results are good, then a business will try to continue the strategies and operations that produced those successful financial results in next year's budget. If last year's financial results are not good, then a business will identify the problem areas and plan the necessary improvements that will produce the intended financial results. In both situations, the annual budget will lay out the details for the next year's operations including the expected financial results. It is the most important and the most formal financial document that plans for the future.

Once the annual operating budget is prepared, the next step is to update the budget by preparing forecasts that reflect any changes in current market conditions, the economy, or other current trends in business volumes and revenues. Forecasts plan for the future, are short-term in nature, and are intended to be flexible. They are the last financial and operating planning document and are prepared by using the current actual market trends and information. The weekly revenue forecasts and the weekly wage schedules are used to plan the specifics of daily operations for the next week. When the week is over, actual financial results are compared to the forecast, the budget, and last year's actual results. Major variations are analyzed and financial critiques are prepared to explain the causes and discuss solutions that will improve operations and meet financial objectives.

In review, the progression of financial documents used in planning business operations begins with last year's actual results that are used to prepare the annual operating budget. The budget is then updated during the year by preparing the forecasts, which update the budget and provide management with the most current information to plan the next week's daily operations.

TYPES AND USES OF FORECASTS

Forecasting Relationships with Last Year and the Budget

As already discussed, the main uses of numbers and financial reports are to measure financial performance and to provide a management tool for operating managers to use in operating their business. The Profit and Loss Statement (P&L) is the main financial report for measuring the operating performance. The Balance Sheet and Statement of Cash Flows also provide useful financial information for measuring other parts of financial performance such as company net worth and cash flows. Forecasting mainly involves financial activity that is reported in the P&L Statement. Therefore, the P&L will be the focus of forecasting in this chapter.

One exception is the importance given to owners and managers for forecasting the required cash flow to maintain daily operations. Owners are interested in how much cash they will receive and how much cash they have to provide and when. Managers are interested in how much cash is available to operate their departments. Cash flow forecasting is generally performed by the accounting office.

The forecasting relationship with last year's actual results and the current year budget can be illustrated with the following timeline:

1. Last year's actual results will be provided and reviewed week by week.
2. Management will determine the realistic improvements or achievable growth objectives for next year compared to last year.
3. Management and accounting will prepare the formal operating budget, a detailed financial plan by week, month, and year outlining the financial goals for the next year.
4. The final operating budget will be approved for the next year containing specific monthly or accounting period financial plans including dollar amounts, percentages, and statistics. This budget is approved by senior management and owners and distributed to all departments and will be used for the entire year.
5. Before the beginning of a month or accounting period, the accounting office will often provide a weekly breakout of the budget for each department.
6. Each department will then review the budget for the next week. If there are no meaningful changes, the department managers will use the weekly budget as their weekly forecast and will plan the next week—day by day— according to the budget numbers.
7. If there are meaningful changes—either increases or decreases—the department managers will update the budget in a new forecast by making changes that reflect more accurately the current business environment. These changes that update the budget become the weekly forecast.

This timeline demonstrates the process that takes actual financial performance (last year) and projects it into the future with a formal annual financial operating plan (the budget). The last step is to review the budget, make any changes or updates (the forecast), and use this information to plan the details for the next week's operations. A forecast column may be included in the monthly P&L. Forecasts are included on internal management reports that are generally reviewed daily and weekly. This includes reviewing actual revenues and labor costs and comparing them to the forecast, the budget, and last year. Any changes or differences are explained in variation reports called critiques.

The fact that weekly forecasts are not generally included in the monthly or accounting period P&L does not mean they are not important. It means that they are used primarily as an internal management tool to plan, operate, and analyze daily and weekly operations. In fact, operations managers will spend more time with the weekly financial information than with the P&L. This is because they use the forecasts daily in their operations, critique the variations daily and weekly, and make any necessary changes that will improve performance. Effectively using the weekly forecasts and other internal management reports will generally lead to better financial performance on the monthly or period P&L Statements.

Weekly, Monthly, Quarterly, and Long-Term Forecasts

The **weekly forecast** provides the plans and details of operations for each shift or department for each day of the week. As the week unfolds, daily revenue reports and daily labor productivity reports containing actual results are distributed. The financial results from these reports are compared to the weekly forecast and provide operations management with the detailed results of the previous day and also the week to date operating results. This includes efforts to maximize revenues and efforts to minimize expenses day by day. The shift or line managers have the direct responsibility to operate their departments according to the most recent forecasts. They, with their employees, operate their departments in providing products and services to customers that produce the financial results. Therefore, they spend a lot of time reviewing, analyzing, changing, and forecasting the numbers that measure their operations.

An essential part of the weekly forecast is the critique that analyzes last week's results. Companies have weekly forms that are useful for capturing the actual, forecast, budget, and last year's information. Recent technology developments provide a vast amount of detailed information almost instantaneously for managers to use. The strongest operations managers in any business will posses both operating skills and financial knowledge so they can make the best use of the daily and weekly operating information.

Weekly reports are primarily internal management reports. They provide information that measures financial performance; however, their main use is as a management tool.

Monthly forecasts or accounting period reports are used equally as a management tool and to project expected financial performance. These are formal reports that are distributed inside and outside the company to interested stakeholders. They provide the actual financial results of operations and compare them to the budget and to last year. Sometimes the forecast is included on a formal P&L. Critiques are also prepared for the formal P&L, and operations managers and accounting managers use the weekly critiques to explain the operating results for the month. Operations managers are expected to prepare these critiques and review them with their direct manager or in the hospitality industry, with their Executive Committee Member. Then the critiques are presented to and discussed with the General Manager. The final step usually involves providing this information to the regional or corporate office and to the appropriate owners.

Quarterly forecasts are primarily used to plan and project the financial performance for the next one or two quarters. Senior management and the owners are interested to see and review what level of business can be expected in the near future. While operations managers, along with the accounting department managers, can prepare these longer term forecasts, they will not spend as much time on quarterly forecasts as they will on daily and weekly forecasts.

The final forecasts are the long-term forecasts, which are not as detailed as weekly and quarterly forecasts, but are intended to give the general direction of expected business operations in the future. These long-term forecasts are more general in nature and will probably be prepared by the accounting office. They will include sales, profit, cash flow projections, average room rate, occupancy, and RevPAR projections. Companies can include different time periods in their long-term forecasts. Marriott looks at the next six accounting periods. Four Seasons includes an end-of-year forecast that combines the current year-to-date actual performance with a forecast to the end of the year so that management will always have an idea of how the end-of-year actual/forecast performance compares to last year's actual results and the current year's budget. This is important to the owner in planning for cash inflow or outflow.

Revenue, Wages, and Operating Expense Forecasts

Weekly forecasts focus on the most important financial elements of operating performance. In the hospitality industry, this means focusing primarily on revenues and labor costs.

Maximizing revenues, as discussed in previous chapters, involves analyzing past performance and forecasting expected levels of performance in the future. Revenue forecasts are critical to the success of any business because in addition to forecasting expected revenues, they are also used to plan and schedule appropriate expense levels. Operations managers need to plan changes in operating expenses to handle the forecasted business levels. If a business does not forecast revenues for the next week or month, it is managing out of the rearview mirror and can get caught in some difficult situations by not seeing and adjusting to changes in the market and their business levels.

The key component of revenue forecasting is volume. Specifically, this is rooms sold for room revenues, customers served for restaurant revenues, and man-hours for wage schedules. How many customers are projected to stay at the hotel or eat in the restaurant? Operations managers need to schedule appropriate labor costs and order appropriate materials and supplies to properly service the expected rooms sold or customer counts. This involves volume levels and not average rates. For example, if a hotel is forecasting $50,000 more revenue for the week and it is all the result of higher average room rates, the hotel will not have any more guests in the hotel than the budget. Generally, no changes need to be made to wages or operating expenses. However, if the additional $50,000 is the result of selling more rooms (volume), then operations managers will need to schedule more employees, particularly housekeepers, and purchase more supplies and materials to be able to provide expected products and services to their additional guests. If they do not make these changes, they might run out of supplies or not have enough employees working to provide the expected levels of service to these additional customers.

The same example can be used in forecasting restaurant revenues. If revenue increases are the result of higher average checks, probably no incremental expenses will be incurred. However, if the increases are the result of higher customer counts (volume), then incremental expenses will probably be incurred in wage costs, food costs, and other operating expenses. Forecasting is the management tool that assists operations managers in planning and controlling expenses, given the changing levels of customers and revenues.

Controlling labor costs is the next most important responsibility of operations managers in all departments. In the hospitality industry, total hotel wage costs are generally 20%–25% of sales and will also produce another 5%–10% in benefit costs. Because most of the labor costs are in hourly wages, which are a variable expense, managers are expected to schedule more or less wage cost based on the forecasted volume levels. **Variable expenses** are expenses that fluctuate or change directly with the change in business levels and volumes. Housekeepers, bellmen, and servers are examples of variable wage positions that require more or less employees based on higher or lower forecasted business volumes.

Managers must control their hourly wage costs to maintain productivities and profit margins. This means sending employees home early on slow days and calling them in to work on busier days in response to short-term changes in business volumes (the current revenue forecast). It also means changing work schedules for the next few days if business has slowed down or picked up since the most recent weekly forecast was made.

Wage costs are all about controlling variable hourly wages. Changing man-hours to reflect business levels is essential in managing and minimizing wage and benefit expenses. This also includes controlling overtime, which is a very expensive use of labor because of the time and a half overtime premium generally paid for working overtime hours. Management costs are generally fixed and, therefore, are not subject to changes in business levels like hourly wages. **Fixed expenses** are expenses that are relatively constant and do not change with different business levels and volumes. Secretaries in Sales Departments and accounting clerks in Accounting Departments along with management wages are examples of typical fixed wage positions.

The last expense to control according to business levels is direct operating costs. This primarily includes managing the food costs in the Restaurant and Banquet Departments. Along with wages, these are the largest expenses in the Food and Beverage Departments and are also subject to the changing business levels. It is very important to manage food inventories because a high percentage of food is subject to time restrictions and perishability. Other operating expenses such as cleaning supplies, guest supplies, china, glass, silver, and linen cannot be controlled as quickly or directly as controlling wage and food costs. However, they are not perishable and can be used over many months and sometimes over many years. To control these expenses, managers must pay close attention to purchasing and receiving, invoicing, par levels and physical inventories, and interdepartmental transfers. They will primarily use the amounts budgeted in the monthly or accounting period budget in controlling these expenses.

Marco Island Marriott Resort and Spa Marco Island, Florida

This 727-room resort property in Florida on the Gulf of Mexico offers a vast range of resort activities for pleasure travelers and group meetings. This includes beach activities and water sports on a three mile stretch of white sand, three swimming pools in a tropical atmosphere, golf with an everglades feel, and a new spa with Balinese-influenced treatments. Guests can dine at any of the eight restaurants ranging from casual to fine dining to sunset on the beach. There are 27 meeting rooms, including a 19,000-square-foot ballroom with 225,000 square feet of total meeting space indoors and outdoors that provide guests with many opportunities to enjoy the South Florida climate. Visit their Web site at www.marcoislandmarriott.com.

Consider the importance and complexity of the weekly forecasts at this major beach resort. The Director of Revenue Management is responsible for forecasting both transient and group rooms sold for the resort that will be the basis for all department

Photo Courtesy of Marco Island Marriott Beach Resort, Golf Club & Spa.

weekly revenue forecasts. The Food and Beverage Director alone is responsible for the preparation of over a dozen revenue departments. Consider the difference between a weekly forecast of major group business and a weekly forecast of mainly transient business. Think about the number of weekly wage schedules that are prepared each week!

Answer the following questions:

1. Refer to the hotel organization chart in Chapter 3. Prepare an organization chart for the Marco Island Marriott Beach Resort including all the different revenue departments. (*Hint*: There are more than a dozen.)
2. Give three items that you would discuss in preparing the weekly forecast if you were meeting with the Director of Restaurants and the Director of Catering.
3. Discuss the importance the weekly rooms sold forecast would have in the golf, spa, and restaurant revenue forecasts.

REVENUE FORECASTING

The Importance of Room Revenue Forecasts

Room revenue forecasting is the starting point for maximizing all hotel revenues and controlling all hotel expenses—the two most important financial goals in maximizing profits and cash flows for any operations manager. Identifying the causes of increases or decreases in actual business levels, understanding financial ratios and formulas used in revenue forecasting, and preparing accurate and useful forecasts are essential to the success of any department or business.

Room revenue forecasts are also used to prepare restaurant and banquet revenue forecasts. To forecast restaurant revenues, the Restaurant Manager will consider the following details included in the room revenue forecast:

1. Total rooms sold or occupied for each day
2. Number of guest per room
3. Number of group rooms and number of transient rooms occupied

They will then look at the banquet weekly forecast to determine what percentage or amount of guests will be attending meal functions provided by banquets. This will affect the number of guests available to dine in the hotel's restaurants.

To forecast banquet revenues, the Banquet Manager uses guaranteed customer counts in Banquet Event Orders (BEOs) as well as the number of group rooms blocked for a specific piece of business. The revenue forecast will include the actual number of rooms picked up by a group and will tell the Banquet Manager if the meal function is expected to meet the customer counts guaranteed in the contract.

Most of the other revenue departments, including Beverage, Gift Shop, Telephone, and Recreation, will forecast their revenues based on rooms sold or room sales. These departments can use sales per occupied room to forecast their department sales. For example, the Gift Shop will have an historical average sales per occupied room. Managers will use this amount and multiply it by the number of occupied rooms for the day or week to develop their weekly and monthly forecasts.

Volume: The Key to Forecasting

We will emphasize one more time that all forecasting is based on the volume of business activity. **Volume** is the part of the revenue equation that provides the quantity of products or services consumed by the guest. Each revenue department applies a formula based on rooms sold or hotel guests (volume) to calculate and forecast its department revenues. Examples of formulas used include the following:

1. Rooms Occupied × Average Sales per Room = Department Sales
2. Rooms Occupied × Average Guests per Room = Total Hotel Guests
3. Total Hotel Guests × Average Check per Guest = Department Sales

Any of these formulas can be used to calculate and forecast the revenue for a specific department. Notice that these formulas require a forecasted volume level stated as total rooms occupied or total guests. This volume number is then applied to an average room rate, average guest check, average expenditure per room, or other formula to calculate a department sales forecast in dollars. **Rate** is the part of the revenue equation that provides the dollar price that guests or customers are willing to pay to secure a room or meal. The next section provides more details and examples of how rooms occupied and number of guests are used to prepare wage schedules and other cost control plans and schedules.

The formula for room revenue is

Rate × Volume, specifically

Average Room Rate × Number of Rooms Occupied

Room revenue forecasting applies this formula with current actual information to determine the next week's revenue forecast. Steps in the process of preparing weekly room revenue forecasts begin with forecasting volume levels and then applying an average room rate to calculate or forecast the total room revenue dollars.

1. Historical averages are used to provide a starting point for forecasting. This can be average rooms sold for each day of the week for room revenues and average customers per day and meal period for restaurants.
2. Current trends and market conditions are then applied to these averages. If a hotel has been busier than usual during the last several weeks, the revenue forecast prepared will probably be higher than the historical averages. If a hotel has been slower during the previous weeks, the revenue forecast will

be adjusted downward from the historical averages when weekly forecasts are prepared. In each of these examples, the operations managers will add or reduce 5, 10, 20, or any other number of rooms from the historical averages to reflect current demand and market conditions.

3. Often forecasts are prepared for each market segment and then added together to get the total room revenue forecast. For example, transient rooms sold are forecasted based on information from a Revenue Management program, while group rooms sold are forecasted based on group room blocks—both definite and tentative—and the actual pickup of rooms held in the room block. The two market segments are added together to get the total room revenue forecast.

4. The last step is determining an appropriate room rate to apply to each room sold or an appropriate average check to apply to each customer in the restaurant. Historical room rates and restaurant average checks are the starting point and then adjustments are made based on any room rate increases or menu price increases to get the current room rate or average check. This process can also be done by market segment (transient, group, or contract) or meal period (breakfast, lunch, or dinner). The more detailed the forecasting of rooms sold and customer counts, the more accurate the forecast. Only forecasting total rooms sold for the week and using one average room rate for the week will give a very general forecast. Forecasting volumes and average rates by market segment and meal period will result in more detail and accuracy.

To help understand forecasting and the elements that an operations manager can use in developing forecasts, refer to Exhibits 10.1 and 10.2. They contain the individual elements and steps used to generate weekly forecasts.

EXHIBIT 10.1
ROOM REVENUE FORECASTING TWOSOMES

MARKET SEGMENT	Transient Group
DAY OF WEEK	Weekdays–Monday–Thursday Weekends–Friday–Sunday
RESERVATION STATUS	Reservations Made Reservations to be Made (Pickup)
GROUP STATUS	Confirmed/Definite Tentative
ROOM REVENUE	Rooms Sold $\times$ Average Room Rate

EXHIBIT 10.2
ROOM SERVICE AND RESTAURANT FORECASTING THREESOMES

ROOM SERVICE **BREAKFAST, LUNCH, and DINNER**

Guests per Occupied Room

Capture Rates

Customers × Average Check

RESTAURANT **BREAKFAST, LUNCH, and DINNER**

Hotel Guests + or − Adjustments

Outside Guests + or − Adjustments

Customers × Average Check

These elements or steps in preparing forecasts will be used in the forecasting problem sets where weekly forecasts will be prepared for room revenues, room service revenues, and restaurant revenues. They represent an orderly way to consider all of the variables that can affect a weekly revenue forecast. To illustrate, let's discuss the process for developing a weekly room revenue forecast and see how this process flows through the room revenue forecasting twosomes.

First, we will break our rooms sold forecast into the major rooms' market segments—transient (business and pleasure) and group. Next we will consider two different time frames, weekday rooms sold and weekend rooms sold for transient and group. Focusing on the transient market segment, we will look at the actual reservations already made and then forecast how many more reservations will be made between today and the day of the week that we are forecasting—rooms pickup. Adding these two together gives the transient rooms sold forecast.

In the group market segment, we will look at the number of group rooms with confirmed contracts or definites and then forecast how many of the tentative group contacts will sign contracts and become definites. Adding these two together gives the group rooms sold forecast.

The next step is to convert rooms sold to room revenue. This twosome involves multiplying the transient rooms sold each day by the transient average room rate for each day to get transient daily revenue. Adding the daily revenues up for all seven days gives the total transient room revenue forecast for the week. We do this step again in multiplying the group rooms sold each day by the group average room rate for each day. Adding the daily revenues up for each day gives the total group room revenue forecast for the week.

The final step is to add the transient numbers to the group numbers to get our weekly rooms sold forecast and weekly room's revenue forecast.

The process is the same for forecasting room service and restaurant revenues with the only difference being customer counts replacing the rooms sold and average checks replacing the average room rates.

WAGE FORECASTING AND SCHEDULING

Wage Forecasting Fundamentals

Managing and controlling wage cost is a major responsibility of hospitality managers in maintaining department productivities and profit margins. **Profit margin** is the percentage of a revenue dollar that remains as profit after all expenses have been paid. The reasons for this are as follows:

1. Wages are generally the largest expense of each revenue department in hospitality operations. The only exception is retail where cost of goods sold is generally higher. Total wage costs in a full-service hotel will be in 20%–30% range.
2. Hourly wages are variable and therefore hourly wage schedules can be prepared and adjusted up or down based on the volume levels of current revenue forecasts.
3. Each wage dollar produces an associated benefit cost, generally in the range of 25%–40% of total wage costs. For example, each dollar of wage cost will generate 25–30 cents in benefit costs. Controlling wage expenses will therefore result in controlling benefit expenses. If a department has a wage cost problem, they will generally also have a benefit-cost problem.

Managers in revenue departments spend a great deal of time reviewing revenue forecasts and then preparing wage schedules that appropriately support volume levels. This is the primary way that department labor productivities are controlled and profit margins are maintained.

Labor Standards, Forecasting, and Ratios

Many ratios and formulas can be used in preparing wage schedules that maintain budgeted and expected productivities. The primary forecasting formulas used in a hotel are used in the Rooms Department and Food and Beverage Departments.

ROOMS DEPARTMENT FORMULAS

Productivity Formulas

$$\text{Total Man-Hours per Occupied Room} = \frac{\text{Total Department Man-Hours}}{\text{Total Occupied Rooms}}$$

Housekeeper Man-Hours Based on Rooms Cleaned per Eight-Hour Shift
Front Desk Clerk Man-Hours Based on Check-Ins per Eight-Hour Shift
Front Desk Cashier Man-Hours Based on Check-Outs per Eight-Hour Shift

Cost Percent Formulas

$$\text{Wage Cost per Occupied Room} = \frac{\text{Total Department Wage Cost in Dollars}}{\text{Total Occupied Rooms}}$$

$$\text{Wage Cost Percentage} = \frac{\text{Total Department Wage Cost in Dollars}}{\text{Total Department Revenues in Dollars}}$$

RESTAURANT DEPARTMENT FORMULAS

Productivity Formulas

$$\text{Total Man-Hours per Customer Count} = \frac{\text{Total Department Man-Hours}}{\text{Total Covers}/\text{Customer Counts}}$$

Server Man-Hours Based on Number of Tables per Shift or
Number of Covers/Customers per Shift

Cost Percentage Formulas

$$\text{Wage Cost per Customer Count} = \frac{\text{Total Department Wage Cost in Dollars}}{\text{Total Customers}}$$

$$\text{Wage Cost Percentage} = \frac{\text{Total Department Wage Cost in Dollars}}{\text{Total Department Revenue Dollars}}$$

These ratios are applied to the forecasted volumes that produce weekly revenue forecasts for both the Rooms Department and all Food and Beverage Departments. They are important in ensuring that scheduled wage costs and direct operating costs are in line with the current revenue forecasts.

Summary

Forecasting is an important management tool for any business. It is the process of reviewing past financial information and combining it with present trends and market conditions to project business volume for the next week or month. It is important for a business to be aware of the economic conditions in its market and the actions and performance of its primary competitors so that they can prepare accurate weekly forecasts.

Forecasting includes projecting future revenues and scheduling future expenses to maintain budgeted productivities and profit margins. This all starts with volumes as expressed in rooms sold or customer counts. The amount of business activity in a hotel or restaurant will require an established level of wages and other operating expenses to deliver the expected products and services to customers and also maintain expected profit margins and productivities. As business volumes increase, additional wages and operating expenditures become necessary to properly deliver these expected levels of service. Likewise, when business levels decrease, these wage and operating expenses will also need to be reduced to maintain productivities and avoid unproductive waste in wage and operating costs.

It is important for operations managers in any business to possess adequate forecasting skills to enable them to adjust operating expenses with expected levels of business in their weekly forecasts.

Hospitality Manager Takeaways

1. Weekly forecasting of revenues and wage costs for the next week is a critical factor in maximizing revenues, controlling expenses, and maintaining department productivities and profits.
2. Volume—rooms sold and customer counts—is the starting point of all forecasts.
3. There is a direct relationship between revenue volume and variable expenses.
4. Forecasting is primarily a management tool that has a major impact on maximizing financial performance.

Key Terms

Fixed expenses: expenses that are relatively constant do not change with different business levels and volumes. Secretaries in Sales Departments and accounting clerks in Accounting Departments are examples of fixed wage positions.

Forecast: a type of report that updates the budget.

Monthly forecast: a forecast of revenues for the next month, including average rates and volumes for specific market segments, departments, or meal periods.

Profit margin: the percentage of a revenue dollar that remains as profit after all expenses have been paid.

Quarterly forecast: a forecast that projects revenues over a longer time period and is completed by adding together the forecasts for each month of the quarter.

Rate: the part of the revenue equation that provides the dollar price that guests or customers are willing to pay to secure a room or meal. Typically, average room rates and average guest checks are used to calculate total room or restaurant revenues. It also provides the hourly rate of pay for wage forecasting and scheduling.

Ratios: formulas that are used to calculate appropriate expense levels in relation to different revenue levels.

Variable expenses: expenses that fluctuate or change directly with the change in business levels and volumes. Housekeepers, bellmen, and servers are examples of variable wage positions.

Volume: the part of the revenue equation that provides the quantity of products or services consumed by the guest. Typically, rooms sold or occupied and customer counts are used to calculate total room or restaurant revenues. It also provides man-hours required for wage forecasting and scheduling.

Weekly forecast: the forecast for the next week that includes *revenues and expenses, with a focus on wage forecasts,* and provides the details by day and by shift for the costs of providing the actual products and services expected by guests.

Review Questions

1. Name two ways in which weekly forecasts are different from monthly or quarterly forecasts.
2. Why is volume so important in forecasting?
3. Define fixed and variable wage expenses and give two examples of wage positions in each category.
4. Name the seven steps in the forecasting timeline.
5. What are the formulas for room revenue forecasts and restaurant revenue forecasts?
6. What is the formula for forecasting hourly wage expense?
7. List three important wage ratios.
8. Why are weekly forecasts so important to managing a business profitability?

Practice Exercises

Revenue Forecasting Problem Sets

This section involves the revenue forecasting process for the Rooms, Room Service, and Restaurant Departments. The process will be to first present the forecast for the first week to explain and demonstrate how a weekly forecast is prepared and how it is used. Information will then be given to prepare the second week forecast that will include changes from the first week that increase or decrease the volume and revenue. Students will prepare the second week forecast for practice. It will be discussed in class and the answers are provided in the book. Students can do this work individually or in groups.

The third week forecast will include changes from the first week forecast either increasing or decreasing rooms sold compared to the first week forecast. Students will prepare the third week forecast as a problem set and turn it in. It will be graded and is worth 25 points. Students can do the third week forecast individually or as a group. The fourth week forecast will be an in-class 25-point quiz where students are expected to prepare the fourth week forecast by themselves.

This process will be followed for room revenue forecasts, restaurant and room service revenue forecasts, and front desk and housekeeping wages forecasts.

Room Revenue Forecasts

Developing the Rooms Department revenue forecast involves two steps. The first is to forecast rooms sold and the second is to forecast room revenue. The rooms sold forecast involves several variables as demonstrated in the following matrix:

	Transient Rooms	Group Rooms	Total Rooms
Rooms Forecasting Matrix			
Confirmed transient reservations			
Forecasted "pickup" reservations			
Total transient rooms sold forecast			
Definite group rooms			
Tentative group rooms			
Total group rooms sold forecast			
TOTAL ROOMS SOLD FORECAST			

The important elements of forecasting room revenues can be combined into pairs of information. Each one of these pairs or "twosomes" is important in preparing room revenue forecasts. Let's review them again.

Room Revenue Forecasting Twosomes

Forecasting Element	Forecasting Twosome
Market Segment	Transient rooms and Group rooms
Day of Week	Weekdays Monday–Thursday Weekends Friday–Sunday
Reservation Status	Confirmed reservations made Reservations to be made (pickup)
Group Status	Definite, groups with a signed contract Tentative, groups still to be booked
Room Revenue Calculations	Rooms sold by market segment Times average room rate per segment

The forecast for each of these segments is prepared in different ways. The transient room reservations confirmed or guaranteed are generated from the Revenue Management or demand tracking system of the hotel for each day. The Hotel Director of Revenue Management or Hotel Reservations Manager then projects or forecasts the number of additional reservations expected to be made between the current date and the day of arrival, including the same day walk-ins. These pickup reservations are added to the confirmed reservations to forecast the total rooms sold for the day.

The group rooms forecast is generated by the group booking report that provides the number of definite group rooms booked per day according to the group room blocks. The Director of Sales and Marketing will then determine the amount of tentative or prospective group rooms that are in negotiations having a high probability of becoming definites. Tentative group rooms that are expected to become definites are then added to existing definites to get the forecasted group rooms sold for the week.

When the total rooms sold forecast for the week is completed, average room rates are projected for each segment for each day. Total room revenues are then calculated by multiplying rooms sold times the average room rate for each market segment and then adding them together to get the total rooms revenue forecast for each day for the next week. The weekly forecast will include rooms sold, occupancy percent, average room rate, and total room revenue for each day of the week and for the total week. The hotel selling strategy team then reviews, approves, and distributes the weekly revenue forecast.

The steps to prepare a room revenue forecast are as follows:

1. Collect confirmed transient reservations and definite group reservations for each day of the week (DOA) from the Revenue Management report and group rooms report.
2. Project the number of expected additional transient reservations pickup and tentative group reservations for each day.
3. Determine the daily average room rate for transient and group rooms sold.
4. Calculate the daily room revenue for transient and group rooms by multiplying the daily number of rooms sold times the daily average room rate to get the daily room revenue.
5. Add the total daily rooms sold for each day of the week to get the total rooms sold for the week.
6. Add the total daily revenue for each day of the week to get the total room revenue for the week.
7. Calculate the average weekly room rate by dividing total room revenue for the week by total rooms sold for the week.
8. Calculate the daily and weekly occupancy percent by dividing daily rooms sold by total hotel rooms per day and per week.
9. Double check the weekly amounts by adding the daily rooms sold and room revenues across for the seven days and comparing it by adding the transient and group market segment down to get the same total rooms sold for the week and the same total room revenue for the week.

Apply this process to the weekly practice exercises to calculate the total weekly room revenues. Following are the worksheets and weekly forecasts to use in preparing weekly room revenue forecasts. Week 1 will be provided as an example and explain how the weekly room revenue forecast was prepared. Week 2 will have changes in rooms sold compared to the first week and be a practice week with the answers provided in the book. Students should use Week 2 to learn the forecasting process and be prepared to do the Week 3 forecast. Week 3 will again have changes from Week 1 forecast and be a 25-point practice exercise that will require students to calculate and prepare the 3rd week room revenue forecast that will be turned in and graded. Week 4 will also have changes from Week 1 in rooms sold for transient and group and will be a 25-point in-class quiz.

ROOMS SOLD FORECASTING WORKSHEET

WEEK _____ PERIOD _____

MARKET SEGMENT	Offset Friday/ Friday	Saturday	Sunday	Monday	Tuesday	Wednesday	Thursday	Friday	Total
TRANSIENT ROOMS									
Reservations Booked									
Reservations Pickup									
Total Transient Reservations									
GROUP ROOMS									
Definite Groups									
Tentative/Prospective Groups									
Total Group Reservations									
TOTAL ROOM RESERVATIONS									
OCCUPANCY PERCENTAGE									
Arrivals/Check-ins									
Departures/Check-outs									

ROOM REVENUE FORECASTING WORKSHEET

WEEK _____ PERIOD _____

MARKET SEGMENT	Friday/	Saturday	Sunday	Monday	Tuesday	Wednesday	Thursday	Friday	Total
TRANSIENT REVENUE									
Rooms Sold									
Average Rate									
Total Transient Revenue									
GROUP REVENUE									
Rooms Sold									
Average Rate									
Total Group Revenue									
TOTAL REVENUE									
Total Rooms Sold									
Occupancy Percentage									
Average Rate									
Total Room Revenue									

ROOMS SOLD FORECASTING WORKSHEET–600 ROOMS

1 WEEK 1 PERIOD

MARKET SEGMENT	Offset Friday/	Saturday	Sunday	Monday	Tuesday	Wednesday	Thursday	Friday	Total
TRANSIENT ROOMS									
Reservations Booked		150	120	300	400	400	350	180	1,900
Reservations Pick Up		10	10	30	50	40	40	20	200
Total Transient Reservations		160	130	330	450	440	390	200	2,100
GROUP ROOMS									
Group #1		30	20	20	10				80
Group #2				70	80	80	80	10	320
Group #3					40	40	20	20	120
Group #4					20	20	20	20	80
Total Group Reservations		30	20	90	150	140	120	50	600
TOTAL ROOM RESERVATIONS	300 /	190	150	420	600	580	510	250	2,700
OCCUPANCY PERCENTAGE		31.7%	25.0%	70.0%	100%	96.7%	85.0%	41.7%	64.3%

ROOM REVENUE FORECASTING WORKSHEET
__1__ WEEK __1__ PERIOD

MARKET SEGMENT	Friday/ Saturday	Sunday	Monday	Tuesday	Wednesday	Thursday	Friday	Total
TRANSIENT REVENUE								
Rooms Sold	160	130	330	450	440	390	200	2,100
Average Rate	$ 110	$ 110	$ 130	$ 145	$ 145	$ 140	$ 110	$ 133.55
Total Transient Revenue	$17,600	$14,300	$42,900	$65,250	$63,800	$54,600	$22,000	$280,450
GROUP REVENUE								
Rooms Sold	30	20	90	150	140	120	50	600
Average Rate	$ 100	$100	$ 120	$ 125	$ 125	$ 125	$ 100	$ 120.08
Total Group Revenue	$ 3,000	$ 2,000	$10,800	$18,750	$17,500	$15,000	$ 5,000	$ 72,050
TOTAL REVENUE								
Total Rooms Sold	190	150	420	600	580	510	250	2,700
Occupancy Percentage	31.7%	25.0%	70.0%	100%	96.7%	85.0%	41.7%	64.3%
Average Rate	$108.42	$108.67	$127.86	$140.00	$140.17	$136.47	$108.00	$ 130.56
Total Room Revenue	$20,600	$16,300	$53,700	$84,000	$81,300	$69,600	$27,000	$352,500

Practice Exercise 1

Week 2 of Period 1
A Busier Week

For the second week, the hotel is forecasting a busier week and more rooms sold than in the first week's forecast. To prepare the second week rooms sold forecast, use the following steps:

1. Begin with the first weeks *rooms sold forecast*. All changes will be made to the transient rooms sold numbers from the first week.
2. Increase the second weeks rooms sold forecast as follows: Weekdays are Monday through Thursday, weekends are Friday through Sunday:
   A. Increase transient weekday and weekend rooms reservations by 15 per day.
   B. Increase the transient reservations pickup per day by 10 on weekdays and 5 on weekends.
   C. Total the transient rooms sold by day and add up the seven days to get the total rooms sold for the week. Check this weekly total rooms sold number by adding down the weekly reservations made plus weekly reservations picked up.
   D. Total the group rooms sold by day for all of the group room blocks to get the daily group rooms forecast.
   E. Add up the daily group room totals for the seven days to get the weekly group room totals.
   F. Add the daily transient and group rooms sold for each day to get total the daily rooms sold forecast.
   G. Add the seven days of total rooms sold to get the total weekly rooms sold. Check that by adding total transient rooms sold for the week to total group rooms sold for the week.
3. Calculate the daily and weekly occupancy percent by dividing total rooms sold by total hotel rooms, 600 for each day and 4,200 for the week.
4. Disregard the arrivals and departure lines. They will be used to forecast and schedule front office wages.
5. Use the following 2nd Week Forecast Form for your calculations:
   Check your forecast with the answers on the 2nd week forecast that follows the blank forecast page. Be sure and prepare your forecast first before checking it to the correct forecast.

   To forecast the total room revenue for the second week, use the same daily room rates for the transient and group as in the first week and make the calculations on the rooms revenue forecasting worksheet. Take the daily rooms sold from the rooms sold forecasting worksheet and enter them on the room revenue forecasting worksheet. You will find this worksheet after the rooms sold forecasting worksheet. Remember that you will have to calculate new daily average room rates on the bottom of the worksheet and new weekly average room rates on the right side of the worksheets for each week forecasted.

ROOMS SOLD FORECASTING WORKSHEET

_2_ WEEK _1_ PERIOD
A BUSIER WEEK

MARKET SEGMENT	Offset Friday/ Saturday	Sunday	Monday	Tuesday	Wednesday	Thursday	Friday	Total
TRANSIENT ROOMS								
Reservations Booked +15 per day w/d and w/e								
Reservations Pickup +10 per day w/d and +5 per day w/e								
Total Transient Reservations								
GROUP ROOM								
Definite Groups #1		20	30	30	30			110
#2		30	30	30				90
#3				40	40	40	20	140
Tentative/Prospective Groups #1					50	50		100
Total Group Reservations								
TOTAL ROOM RESERVATIONS								
OCCUPANCY PERCENTAGE								
Arrivals/Check-ins								
Departures/Check-outs								

ROOMS SOLD FORECASTING WORKSHEET
ANSWERS
2 WEEK 1 PERIOD
A BUSIER WEEK

MARKET SEGMENT	Offset Friday/	Saturday	Sunday	Monday	Tuesday	Wednesday	Thursday	Friday	Total
TRANSIENT ROOMS									
Reservations Booked +15 per day w/d and w/e		165	135	315	415	415	365	195	2,005
Reservations Pickup +10 per day w/e, +5 per day w/e		15	15	40	60	50	50	25	255
Total Transient Reservations		180	150	355	475	465	415	220	2,260
GROUP ROOMS									
Definite Groups #1			20	30	30	30			110
#2			30	30	30				90
#3					40	40	40	20	140
Tentative/Prospective Groups #1						50	50		100
Total Group Reservations		-0-	50	60	100	120	90	20	440
TOTAL ROOM RESERVATIONS		180	200	415	575	585	505	240	2,700
OCCUPANCY PERCENTAGE		30.0%	33.3%	69.2%	95.8%	97.5%	84.2%	40.0%	64.3%
Arrivals/Check-ins									
Departures/Check-outs									

ROOM REVENUE FORECASTING WORKSHEET
SAME AVERAGE DAILY RATES AS WEEK #1
__2__ WEEK __1__ PERIOD

MARKET SEGMENT	Friday/	Saturday	Sunday	Monday	Tuesday	Wednesday	Thursday	Friday	Total
TRANSIENT REVENUE									
Rooms Sold									
Average Rate									
Total Transient Revenue									
GROUP REVENUE									
Rooms Sold									
Average Rate									
Total Group Revenue									
TOTAL REVENUE									
Total Rooms Sold									
Occupancy Percentage									
Average Rate									
Total Room Revenue									

ROOM REVENUE FORECASTING WORKSHEET
ANSWERS
2 WEEK 1 PERIOD

MARKET SEGMENT	Friday/ Saturday	Sunday	Monday	Tuesday	Wednesday	Thursday	Friday	Total
TRANSIENT REVENUE								
Rooms Sold	180	150	355	475	465	415	220	2,260
Average Rate	$ 110	$ 110	$ 130	$ 145	$ 145	$ 140	$ 110	$ 133.21
Total Transient Revenue	$19,800	$16,500	$46,150	$68,875	$67,425	$58,100	$24,200	$301,050
GROUP REVENUE								
Rooms Sold	-0-	50	60	100	120	90	20	440
Average Rate	-	$ 100	$ 120	$ 125	$ 125	$ 125	$ 100	$ 120.34
Total Group Revenue	$ -0-	$ 5,000	$ 7,200	$12,500	$15,000	$11,250	$ 2,000	$ 52,950
TOTAL REVENUE								
Total Rooms Sold	180	200	415	575	585	505	240	2,700
Occupancy Percentage	30.0%	33.3%	69.2%	95.8%	97.5%	84.2%	40.0%	64.3%
Average Rate	$110.00	$107.50	$128.55	$141.52	$140.90	$137.33	$109.17	$ 131.11
Total Room Revenue	$19,800	$21,500	$53,350	$81,375	$82,425	$69,350	$26,200	$354,000

Problem Set 2

25 Points
Week 3 of Period 1
Another Busy Week

This problem set is worth 25 points and can be done individually or in a group. Follow the same steps as in forecasting the second week. Following are the changes to be used in forecasting the third week:

1. Begin with the *first week rooms sold forecast*. All changes will be made to those numbers.
2. Increase the third weeks rooms sold forecast as follows:
   A. Increase weekday transient room reservations 30 per day.
   B. Increase weekday transient pickup reservations 15 per day.
   C. Increase weekend transient room reservations 20 per day.
   D. Increase weekend transient pickup reservations 10 per day.
3. Third week group room blocks are as follows:

		Sat	Sun	Mon	Tue	Wed	Thurs	Fri	Total
Definite group	#1	20	40	40	40				140
	#2		30	30	20				80
Tentative group	#1				40	40	40	20	140
	#2					70	70	40	180

4. Complete the total rooms sold forecasting worksheet.
5. Enter the Week 3 rooms sold from the rooms sold worksheet onto the Week 3 room revenue forecasting worksheet.
6. Use the same daily average rates as Week 1 for both the transient and group rooms sold.
7. Calculate the total room revenue by day for Week 3 and complete the Week 3 room revenue forecasting worksheet.

The 25 points will be graded on the daily and weekly totals from the room revenue forecasting worksheet. Turn both forecasting worksheets in for credit.

ROOMS SOLD FORECASTING WORKSHEET
25-POINT PROBLEM SET
__3__ WEEK __1__ PERIOD

MARKET SEGMENT	Offset Friday/ Friday	Saturday	Sunday	Monday	Tuesday	Wednesday	Thursday	Friday	Total
TRANSIENT ROOMS									
Reservations Booked									
Reservations Pickup									
Total Transient Reservations									
GROUP ROOMS									
Definite Group #1									
Definite Group #2									
Tentative Group #1									
Tentative Group #2									
Total Group Reservations									
TOTAL ROOM RESERVATIONS									
OCCUPANCY PERCENTAGE									
Check-Ins									
Check-Outs									

ROOM REVENUE FORECASTING WORKSHEET
25-POINT PROBLEM SET
__3__ WEEK __1__ PERIOD

MARKET SEGMENT	Friday/ Saturday	Sunday	Monday	Tuesday	Wednesday	Thursday	Friday	Total
TRANSIENT REVENUE								
Rooms Sold								
Average Rate								
Total Transient Revenue								
GROUP REVENUE								
Rooms Sold								
Average Rate								
Total Group Revenue								
TOTAL REVENUE								
Total Rooms Sold								
Occupancy Percentage								
Average Rate								
Total Room Revenue								

The final part of the room revenue forecasting section is to prepare the fourth week forecast. This will be given as a 25-point quiz and students are expected to do their own work on this quiz.

Restaurant and Room Service Forecasts

This section will involve the revenue forecasting process for the Restaurant and Room Service Departments. The rooms sold forecast for the hotel is used by all the departments in the hotel to forecast because it is the best indicator of business activity in the hotel. We will use the same rooms sold forecasts for Period 1 that was prepared in the previous section to prepare the restaurant and room service revenue forecasts. Many of the steps in forecasting food and beverage revenues are the same as those used in forecasting room revenues.

We will follow the same format as that used in the room revenue forecasts by starting with a discussion of how the first week room service and restaurant forecast was prepared and then prepare and discuss the second week forecast. The third week forecast again is a 25-point practice exercise. The fourth week forecast will be a 25-point in-class quiz.

Note how similar the restaurant and room service forecasting process is to the rooms forecasting process. This includes the format of the forecasting worksheets. The forecasting process will include forecasting customers and average checks to calculate restaurant and room service revenues. The weekly forecast will be prepared day by day and added up for the total weekly customers, average check, and revenues. The breakfast, lunch, and dinner meal periods of a restaurant will replace the transient and group market segments used in the room forecast.

Refer to the following restaurant and room service forecasting worksheets as we go over the steps to prepare each of these forecasts. We will start with the room service forecast and then move on to the restaurant forecast.

Room Service Customer Count Forecast

1. Enter the transient, group, and total rooms sold by day for the week from the appropriate weekly rooms sold forecast that were used in the previous rooms forecasting section.
2. Convert the rooms sold by day to hotel guest count by day by using the hotel's historical average of number of guest per occupied room. In our forecasting examples, we will use a historical average of 1.2 guests per room.
3. Identify the percentage capture rates calculated from the room service history for each meal period. A capture rate is the historical percentage of hotel guests that use room service for each meal period. In our forecasting examples, we will use guest capture rates of 25% of hotel guest counts for room service breakfast, 8% for room service lunch, and 15% for room service dinner. This step converts hotel guests into meal period customers.
4. Calculate room service customers by day by meal period by multiplying the meal period capture rate by the daily guest counts.
5. Add up the seven days of room service daily customer counts to get the weekly total customer counts. Check by adding across the seven daily totals for the week and comparing them by adding down the three meal period totals for the week. They should be the same.
6. Transfer room service customer counts for each meal period and day and the total to the room service revenue worksheet.

Restaurant Customer Count Forecast

1. Enter the historical average daily customer count for each day for each meal period on the restaurant forecasting worksheet. Total the week down and across.
2. Based on the forecasted hotel house counts and on the outside activities, enter the appropriate house count adjustment that will reflect the changes from the historical daily customer counts in expected business levels for the week for the restaurant.
3. Total the new forecasted daily customer counts for each day by adding or subtracting the house count adjustment number to the historical daily customer count. The adjustment can be zero if there is no need to adjust the historical average. This gives you total customers for the day. Add the seven days across to get the weekly totals and check by adding the three meal period totals down.
4. Transfer restaurant customer counts to the restaurant revenue worksheet.

Room Service and Restaurant Revenue Forecasts

1. Double check the customer counts for each outlet by comparing the customer counts calculated on the customer count forecasting worksheet to the customer counts forecasts entered on the revenue forecasting worksheets. They should be the same.
2. Enter daily average checks by meal period for each day. These are obtained from historical daily average checks for each meal period in the restaurant and in room service.
3. Calculate the meal period revenue for each day and each meal period by multiplying meal period customer counts by meal period average checks.
4. Add up the revenues for the seven days to get the total revenue for each meal period for the week. Check by adding down the total weekly revenues for the three meal periods. The total weekly revenues should be the same.
5. Calculate the weekly average check for each meal period and the total week by dividing total weekly sales by total weekly customer counts.
6. Check your weekly totals by adding the seven days of daily customer counts and revenues across and comparing that by adding down the three weekly meal period totals for customers and revenues. They should be the same.
7. You will have one restaurant and room service customer count forecast worksheet and two separate revenue forecasting worksheets—one for room service revenues and the other for restaurant revenues.

CUSTOMER COUNT FORECASTING WORKSHEET
ROOM SERVICE AND RESTAURANT
_____ WEEK _____ PERIOD

	Saturday	Sunday	Monday	Tuesday	Wednesday	Thursday	Friday	Total
Total Rooms Sold								
Guest Count @ 1.2 guests per room								
Room Service Capture Rates								
Breakfast @ 25%								
Lunch @ 8%								
Dinner @ 15%								
Total Room Service Customers								
Restaurant Customer Counts								
Breakfast daily average								
Breakfast customer adjustment								
Total Breakfast Customers								
Lunch daily average								
Lunch customer adjustment								
Total Lunch Customers								
Dinner daily average								
Dinner customer adjustment								
Total Dinner Customers								
Total Restaurant Customers								

ROOM SERVICE REVENUE FORECASTING WORKSHEET

_____ WEEK _____ PERIOD

	Saturday	Sunday	Monday	Tuesday	Wednesday	Thursday	Friday	Total
Breakfast								
Customer Counts								
Average Check								
Revenue								
Lunch								
Customer Counts								
Average Check								
Revenue								
Dinner								
Customer Counts								
Average Check								
Revenue								
Total Room Service								
Customer Counts								
Average Check								
Total Room Service Revenue								

RESTAURANT REVENUE FORECASTING WORKSHEET
WEEK _____ PERIOD _____

	Saturday	Sunday	Monday	Tuesday	Wednesday	Thursday	Friday	Total
Breakfast								
Customer Counts								
Average Check								
Revenue								
Lunch								
Customer Counts								
Average Check								
Revenue								
Dinner								
Customer Counts								
Average Check								
Revenue								
Total Restaurant								
Customer Counts								
Average Check								
Total Restaurant Revenue								

CUSTOMER COUNT FORECASTING WORKSHEET
ROOM SERVICE AND RESTAURANT
1 WEEK 1 PERIOD

	Saturday	Sunday	Monday	Tuesday	Wednesday	Thursday	Friday	Total
Total Rooms Sold	190	150	420	600	580	510	250	2,700
Guest Count @ 1.2 per room	228	180	504	720	696	612	300	3,240
Room Service Capture Rates								
Breakfast @ 25%	57	45	126	180	174	153	75	810
Lunch @ 8%	19	15	41	58	56	49	24	262
Dinner @ 15%	35	27	76	108	105	92	45	488
Total Room Service Customers	111	87	243	346	335	294	144	1,560
Restaurant Customer Counts								
Breakfast daily average	100	100	75	125	150	150	125	825
Breakfast customer adjustment								
Total Breakfast Customers								
Lunch daily average	40	30	30	60	80	80	50	370
Lunch customer adjustment								
Total Lunch Customers								
Dinner daily average	60	50	100	120	140	120	80	670
Dinner customer adjustment								
Total Dinner Customers								
Total Restaurant Customers	200	180	205	305	370	350	255	1,865

231

ROOM SERVICE REVENUE FORECASTING WORKSHEET
__1__ WEEK __1__ PERIOD

	Saturday	Sunday	Monday	Tuesday	Wednesday	Thursday	Friday	Total
Breakfast								
Customer Counts	57	45	126	180	174	153	75	810
Average Check	$ 10	$ 10	$ 12	$ 12	$ 12	$ 12	$ 10	$ 11.56
Revenue	$ 570	$ 450	$1,512	$2,160	$2,088	$1,836	$ 750	$ 9,366
Lunch								
Customer Counts	19	15	41	58	56	49	24	262
Average Check	$ 12	$ 12	$ 14	$ 15	$ 15	$ 15	$ 12	$ 14.18
Revenue	$ 228	$ 180	$ 574	$ 870	$ 840	$ 735	$ 288	$ 3,715
Dinner								
Customer Counts	35	27	76	108	105	92	45	488
Average Check	$ 14	$ 14	$ 16	$ 18	$ 18	$ 16	$ 14	$ 16.43
Revenue	$ 490	$ 378	$1,216	$1,944	$1,890	$1,472	$ 630	$ 8,020
Total Room Service								
Customer Counts	111	87	243	346	335	294	144	1,560
Average Check	$11.60	$11.59	$13.59	$14.38	$14.38	$13.75	$11.58	$ 13.53
Total Revenue	$1,288	$1,008	$3,302	$4,974	$4,818	$4,043	$1,668	$21,101

RESTAURANT REVENUE FORECASTING WORKSHEET

1   WEEK   1   PERIOD

	Saturday	Sunday	Monday	Tuesday	Wednesday	Thursday	Friday	Total
Breakfast								
Customer Counts	100	100	75	125	150	150	125	825
Average Check	$ 9	$ 9	$ 10	$ 11	$ 11	$ 10	$ 9	$ 9.94
Revenue	$ 900	$ 900	$ 750	$1,375	$1,650	$1,500	$1,125	$ 8,200
Lunch								
Customer Counts	40	30	30	60	80	80	50	370
Average Check	$ 11	$ 11	$ 12	$ 13	$ 13	$ 13	$ 11	$ 12.27
Revenue	$ 440	$ 330	$ 360	$ 780	$1,040	$1,040	$ 550	$ 4,540
Dinner								
Customer Counts	60	50	100	120	140	120	80	670
Average Check	$ 13	$ 13	$ 15	$ 16	$ 16	$ 15	$ 13	$ 14.82
Revenue	$ 780	$ 650	$1,500	$1,920	$2,240	$1,800	$1,040	$ 9,930
Total Restaurant								
Customer Counts	200	180	205	305	370	350	255	1,865
Average Check	$10.60	$10.44	$12.73	$13.36	$13.32	$12.40	$10.65	$ 12.16
Total Revenue	$2,120	$1,880	$2,610	$4,075	$4,930	$4,340	$2,715	$22,670

CUSTOMER COUNT FORECASTING WORKSHEET
ROOM SERVICE AND RESTAURANT PRACTICE WEEK
__2__ WEEK __1__ PERIOD

	Saturday	Sunday	Monday	Tuesday	Wednesday	Thursday	Friday	Total
Total Rooms Sold	180	200	415	575	585	505	260	2,720
Guest Count @ 1.2 per room								
Room Service Capture Rates								
Breakfast @ 25%								
Lunch @ 8%								
Dinner @ 15%								
Total Room Service Customers								
Restaurant Customer Counts								
Breakfast daily average								
Breakfast customer adj +10 w/d								
Total Breakfast Customers								
Lunch daily average								
Lunch customer adj +5 all days								
Total Lunch Customers								
Dinner daily average								
Dinner customer adj +15 all days								
Total Dinner Customers								
Total Restaurant Customers								

ROOM SERVICE REVENUE FORECASTING WORKSHEET
__2__ WEEK __1__ PERIOD
PRACTICE WEEK

	Saturday	Sunday	Monday	Tuesday	Wednesday	Thursday	Friday	Total
Breakfast								
Customer Counts								
Average Check *same*								
Revenue								
Lunch								
Customer Counts								
Average Check *same*								
Revenue								
Dinner								
Customer Counts								
Average Check								
+50 cents All days								
Revenue								
Total Room Service								
Customer Counts								
Average Check								
Total Revenue								

RESTAURANT REVENUE FORECASTING WORKSHEET

_2_ WEEK _1_ PERIOD
PRACTICE WEEK

	Saturday	Sunday	Monday	Tuesday	Wednesday	Thursday	Friday	Total
Breakfast								
Customer Counts								
Average Check +50 cents *All Days*								
Revenue								
Lunch								
Customer Counts								
Average Check *same*								
Revenue								
Dinner								
Customer Counts								
Average Check *same*								
Revenue								
Total Restaurant								
Customer Counts								
Average Check								
Total Revenue								

CUSTOMER COUNT FORECASTING WORKSHEET
ROOM SERVICE AND RESTAURANT
PRACTICE WEEK ANSWERS
2 WEEK 1 PERIOD

	Saturday	Sunday	Monday	Tuesday	Wednesday	Thursday	Friday	Total
Total Rooms Sold	180	200	415	575	585	505	260	2,720
Guest Count @ 1.2 per room	216	240	498	690	702	606	312	3,264
Room Service Capture Rates								
Breakfast @ 25%	54	60	125	173	176	152	78	818
Lunch @ 8%	17	19	40	55	56	48	25	260
Dinner @ 15%	32	36	75	104	105	91	47	490
Total Room Service Customers	103	115	240	332	337	291	150	1,568
Restaurant Customer Counts								
Breakfast daily average	100	100	75	125	150	150	125	825
Breakfast customer adj +10 w/d			10	10	10	10		40
Total Breakfast Customers	100	100	85	135	160	160	125	865
Lunch daily average	40	30	30	60	80	80	50	370
Lunch customer adj +5 all days	5	5	5	5	5	5	5	35
Total Lunch Customers	45	35	35	65	85	85	55	405
Dinner daily average	60	50	100	120	140	120	80	670
Dinner customer adj +15 all days	15	15	15	15	15	15	15	105
Total Dinner Customers	75	65	115	135	155	135	95	775
Total Restaurant Customers	220	200	235	335	400	380	275	2,045

ROOM SERVICE REVENUE FORECASTING WORKSHEET
2   WEEK   1   PERIOD
PRACTICE WEEK ANSWERS

	Saturday	Sunday	Monday	Tuesday	Wednesday	Thursday	Friday	Total
Breakfast								
Customer Counts	54	60	125	173	176	152	78	818
Average Check—Same as first week	$ 10	$ 10	$ 12	$ 12	$ 12	$ 12	$ 10	$ 11.53
Revenue	$ 540	$ 600	$1,500	$2,076	$2,112	$1,824	$ 780	$ 9,432
Lunch								
Customer Counts	17	19	40	55	56	48	25	260
Average Check—Same as first week	$ 12	$ 12	$ 14	$ 15	$ 15	$ 15	$ 12	$ 14.14
Revenue	$ 204	$ 228	$ 560	$ 825	$ 840	$ 720	$ 300	$ 3,677
Dinner								
Customer Counts	32	36	75	104	105	91	47	490
Average Check +50 cent	$14.50	$14.50	$16.50	$18.50	$18.50	$16.50	$14.50	$ 16.89
Revenue	$ 464	$ 522	$1,238	$1,924	$1,943	$1,502	$ 682	$ 8,275
Total Room Service								
Customer Counts	103	115	240	332	337	291	150	1,568
Average Check	$11.73	$11.74	$13.74	$14.53	$14.53	$13.90	$11.75	$ 13.64
Total Revenue	$1,208	$1,350	$3,298	$4,824	$4,895	$4,046	$1,762	$21,383

RESTAURANT REVENUE FORECASTING WORKSHEET
2 WEEK 1 PERIOD
PRACTICE WEEK ANSWERS

	Saturday	Sunday	Monday	Tuesday	Wednesday	Thursday	Friday	Total
Breakfast								
Customer Counts	100	100	85	135	160	160	125	865
Average Check +50 cents *All days*	$ 9.50	$ 9.50	$10.50	$11.50	$11.50	$10.50	$ 9.50	$ 10.47
Revenue	$ 950	$ 950	$ 893	$1,553	$1,840	$1,680	$1,188	$ 9,054
Lunch								
Customer Counts	45	35	35	65	85	85	55	405
Average Check—Same as first week	$ 11	$ 11	$ 12	$ 13	$ 13	$ 13	$ 11	$ 12.25
Revenue	$ 495	$ 385	$ 420	$ 845	$1,105	$1,105	$ 605	$ 4,960
Dinner								
Customer Counts	75	65	115	135	155	135	95	775
Average Check—Same as first week	$ 13	$ 13	$ 15	$ 16	$ 16	$ 15	$ 13	$ 14.77
Revenue	$ 975	$ 845	$1,725	$2,160	$2,480	$2,025	$1,235	$11,445
Total Restaurant								
Customer Counts	220	200	235	335	400	380	275	2,045
Average Check	$11.00	$10.90	$12.93	$13.61	$13.56	$12.66	$11.01	$ 12.45
Total Revenue	$2,420	$2,180	$3,038	$4,558	$5,425	$4,810	$3,028	$25,459

CUSTOMER COUNT FORECASTING WORKSHEET
ROOM SERVICE AND RESTAURANT
PROBLEM SET—25 POINTS
_3_ WEEK _1_ PERIOD

	Saturday	Sunday	Monday	Tuesday	Wednesday	Thursday	Friday	Total
Total Rooms Sold—from								
3rd week Rooms forecast	210	230	445	595	595	545	290	2,910
Guest Count @ 1.2 per room								
Room Service Capture Rates								
Breakfast @ 25%								
Lunch @ 8%								
Dinner @ 15%								
Total Room Service Customers								
Restaurant Customer Counts								
Breakfast daily average								
Breakfast customer adj +20 w/e								
Total Breakfast Customers								
Lunch daily average								
Lunch customer adj +10 w/e								
Total Lunch Customers								
Dinner daily average								
Dinner customer adj +15 w/e								
Total Dinner Customers								
Total Restaurant Customers								

ROOM SERVICE REVENUE FORECASTING WORKSHEET
__3__ WEEK __1__ PERIOD
PROBLEM SET

	Saturday	Sunday	Monday	Tuesday	Wednesday	Thursday	Friday	Total
Breakfast								
Customer Counts								
Average Check—Same as week 1								
Revenue								
Lunch								
Customer Counts								
Average Check—Same as week 1								
Revenue								
Dinner								
Customer Counts								
Average Check +50 cents								
Revenue								
Total Room Service								
Customer Counts								
Average Check								
Total Revenue								

241

RESTAURANT REVENUE FORECASTING WORKSHEET
__3__ WEEK __1__ PERIOD
PROBLEM SET

	Saturday	Sunday	Monday	Tuesday	Wednesday	Thursday	Friday	Total
Breakfast								
Customer Counts								
Average Check—Same as week 1								
Revenue								
Lunch								
Customer Counts								
Average Check—Same as week 1								
Revenue								
Dinner								
Customer Counts								
Average Check—Same as week 1								
Revenue								
Total Restaurant								
Customer Counts								
Average Check								
Total Revenue								

CUSTOMER COUNT FORECASTING WORKSHEET
ROOM SERVICE AND RESTAURANT
WEEK _____ PERIOD _____

	Saturday	Sunday	Monday	Tuesday	Wednesday	Thursday	Friday	Total
Total Rooms Sold								
Guest Count @ 1.2 per room								
Room Service Capture Rates								
Breakfast @ 25%								
Lunch @ 8%								
Dinner @ 15%								
Total Room Service Customers								
Restaurant Customer Counts								
Breakfast daily average								
Breakfast customer adjustment								
Total Breakfast Customers								
Lunch daily average								
Lunch customer adjustment								
Total Lunch Customers								
Dinner daily average								
Dinner customer adjustment								
Total Dinner Customers								
Total Restaurant Customers								

ROOM SERVICE REVENUE FORECASTING WORKSHEET

_____ WEEK _____ PERIOD

	Saturday	Sunday	Monday	Tuesday	Wednesday	Thursday	Friday	Total
Breakfast								
Customer Counts								
Average Check								
Revenue								
Lunch								
Customer Counts								
Average Check								
Revenue								
Dinner								
Customer Counts								
Average Check								
Revenue								
Total Room Service								
Customer Counts								
Average Check								
Total Revenue								

RESTAURANT REVENUE FORECASTING WORKSHEET

WEEK _____ PERIOD _____

	Saturday	Sunday	Monday	Tuesday	Wednesday	Thursday	Friday	Total
Breakfast								
Customer Counts								
Average Check								
Revenue								
Lunch								
Customer Counts								
Average Check								
Revenue								
Dinner								
Customer Counts								
Average Check								
Revenue								
Total Restaurant								
Customer Counts								
Average Check								
Total Revenue								

Wage Forecasting Problem Sets

This section involves the wage forecasting process for the Front Office and Housekeeping Departments. The weekly wage forecasts are probably the most valuable tool for management in controlling wage costs and ensuring that wages scheduled are in relation to the business volume expected for the week. The weekly wage schedule identifies the number of man-hours needed for the week based on changing weekly revenue forecasts.

We will use the same process to prepare weekly wage schedules as we used in preparing weekly revenue forecasts. The first week of the period will be presented and shown how the wage forecasts are prepared including ratios and formulas. The second week will be given as an in-class exercise. The third week will be a 25-point homework practice exercise and the fourth week will be a 25-point in-class quiz. We will use the weekly room's forecasts that were prepared earlier in this section to complete the wage schedules.

Front Desk Clerks are scheduled based on the number of expected arrivals or check-ins on the p.m. shift. Employees can be scheduled for full eight-hour shifts or part-time shifts of four to six hours or any other appropriate number of hours. The weekly wage schedule will include number of guest arrivals, number of employees necessary to check in that amount of arrivals, number of man-hours needed per shift, and the total wage cost in dollars. The steps to prepare the front desk clerk weekly wage schedule are as follows: (round employees and man-hours to one decimal point)

1. Identify the number of daily check-ins from the weekly revenue forecast.
2. Divide by the number of check-ins per shift that an employee can handle. We will use 50 check-ins per shift in our example. This will give the number of employees needed per day.
3. Multiply by eight-hour shifts to get the number of man-hours needed by day and week.
4. Multiply by the hourly rate of pay to get wage cost in dollars. We will use $9 in our example.
5. Calculate for each day to get the daily wage cost and add up for the seven days of the week to get weekly number of employees, weekly man-hours, and total weekly wage cost.

Front desk cashiers are scheduled based on the number of expected departures or check-outs on the a.m. shift. The steps are the same as in scheduling front desk clerks. However, there are some differences. We will use 75 check-outs per shift because many guest use express check-out or in-room check out and don't have to come down to the front desk to check out. Therefore, a morning cashier can check out more guests per shift than check in arriving guests per shift. We will have a higher hourly rate of pay of $10 because cashiers generally have more responsibility with cash banks and are often more experienced employees. The rest of the process is the same as the front desk clerks.

Housekeepers are scheduled based on the number of rooms cleaned per shift per day. A key difference is that housekeepers clean the rooms from the previous day. Therefore, housekeeper daily schedules are based on the occupied rooms from the previous night. We will refer to these as offset rooms. For example, on Saturday, the housekeepers will be cleaning the rooms that were occupied on Friday night.

1. Identify the number of occupied rooms from the previous night.
2. Divide the number of occupied rooms from the previous night by the number of rooms cleaned per day per housekeeper, 16 in our example, to get the number of employees to be scheduled.
3. Multiply the number of employees by eight-hour shifts to get man-hours per day.
4. Multiply by the average hourly rate ($8 per hour in our example) to get total daily wage cost.
5. Calculate for each day the total daily man-hours and wage costs and add up the seven days to get weekly number of employees, weekly man-hours, and weekly wage cost.

The entire process of wage scheduling begins with the weekly forecasted number of rooms sold by day. This identifies how busy the hotel is and what level of employee staffing will be required to take care of the expected hotel guests for each day. Each department head is responsible for preparing the weekly wage schedules. The Front Office Manager will prepare two wage schedules, one for the a.m. shift and one for the p.m. shift. The Director of Housekeeping will prepare one schedule since housekeepers generally work an 8:00–4:30 shift with half an hour lunch time.

We will now prepare the weekly forecasts for the first period. Remember that front desk clerks are scheduled based on the daily guest arrivals or check-ins, that the front desk cashiers are scheduled based on the daily guests departures or check-outs, and that housekeepers are scheduled based on the offset rooms sold, or in other words, the rooms occupied the previous night. In all examples, the typical week runs from Saturday through Friday. For housekeepers, the schedule is also from Saturday through Friday, but it is based on the rooms sold from Friday through Thursday—the offset rooms.

WAGE FORECASTING WORKSHEET
__1__ WEEK __1__ PERIOD

Category	Offset Friday/	Saturday	Sunday	Monday	Tuesday	Wednesday	Thursday	Friday	Total
Departures		160	140	50	100	140	200	350	1,140
Arrivals		50	100	320	280	120	130	90	1,090
Rooms Sold	300 /	190	150	420	600	580	510	250	2,700/2,750*
Occupancy %		31.7%	25.0%	70.0%	100%	96.7%	85.0%	41.7%	64.3%
Desk Clerks—Arrivals									
Number of employees @ 50 per shift		1.0	2.0	6.4	5.6	2.4	2.6	1.8	21.8
× 8 hour shift		8.0	16.0	51.2	44.8	19.2	20.8	14.4	174.4
× hourly rate $9		$ 72	$144	$461	$ 403	$ 173	$ 187	$ 130	$ 1,570
Cashiers—Departures									
Number of employees @ 75 per shift		2.1	1.9	.7	1.3	1.9	2.7	4.7	15.3
× 8 hour shift		17.1	14.9	5.3	10.7	14.9	21.3	37.3	121.5
× hourly rate $10		$ 171	$149	$ 53	$ 107	$ 149	$ 213	$ 373	$ 1,213
Housekeepers @ 16 rooms per day									
Number of employees		18.8	11.9	9.4	26.3	37.5	36.3	31.9	172.1
× 8 hour shift		150	95	75	210	300	290	255	1,375
× hourly rate $8		$1,200	$760	$600	$1,680	$2,400	$2,320	$2,040	$11,000

*equals offset rooms sold for Friday through Thursday

Note: Round employees and labor hours to one decimal, wage cost to whole dollars

WAGE FORECASTING WORKSHEET
2 WEEK 1 PERIOD
PRACTICE WEEK

Category	Offset Friday/	Saturday	Sunday	Monday	Tuesday	Wednesday	Thursday	Friday	Total
Departures		140	105	60	150	135	190	405	1,185
Arrivals		60	125	275	310	145	110	140	1,165
Rooms Sold	260 /	180	200	415	575	585	505	240	2,700/2,720*
Occupancy %		30.0%	33.3%	69.2%	95.8%	97.5%	84.2%	40.0%	64.3%

Desk Clerks—Arrivals

Number of employees
@ 50 per shift

× 8-hour shift

× hourly rate $9

Cashiers—Departures

Number of employees
@ 75 per shift

× 8-hour shift

× hourly rate $10

Housekeepers @ 16 rooms
per day

Number of employees

× 8-hour shift

× hourly rate $8

*equals offset rooms sold for Friday through Thursday

Note: Round employees and labor hours to one decimal, wage cost to whole dollars

WAGE FORECASTING WORKSHEET
2 WEEK 1 PERIOD
PRACTICE WEEK ANSWERS

Category	Offset Friday/ Saturday	Sunday	Monday	Tuesday	Wednesday	Thursday	Friday	Total
Departures	140	105	60	150	135	190	405	1,185
Arrivals	60	125	275	310	145	110	140	1,165
Rooms Sold	260/ 180	200	415	575	585	505	240	2,700/2,720*
Occupancy %	30.0%	33.3%	69.2%	95.8%	97.5%	84.2%	40.0%	64.3%
Desk Clerks—Arrivals								
Number of employees @ 50 per shift	1.2	2.5	5.5	6.2	2.9	2.2	2.8	23.3
× 8-hour shift	9.6	20.0	44.0	49.6	23.2	17.6	22.4	186.4
× hourly rate $9	$ 86	$180	$396	$ 446	$ 209	$ 158	$ 202	$ 1,677
Cashiers—Departures								
Number of employees @ 75 per shift	1.9	1.4	0.8	2.0	1.8	2.5	5.4	15.8
× 8-hour shift	15.2	11.2	6.4	16.0	14.4	20.0	43.2	126.4
× hourly rate $10	$ 152	$112	$ 64	$ 160	$ 144	$ 200	$ 432	$ 1,264
Housekeepers @ 16 rooms per day								
Number of employees	16.3	11.3	12.5	25.9	35.9	36.6	31.6	170.1
× 8-hour shift	130.4	90.4	100.0	207.2	287.2	292.8	252.8	1,360.8
× hourly rate $8	$1,043	$723	$800	$1,658	$2,298	$2,342	$2,022	$10,886

*equals offset rooms sold Thursday through Friday

Note: Round employees and labor hours to one decimal, wage cost to whole dollars

WAGE FORECASTING WORKSHEET
3 WEEK 1 PERIOD
25-POINT PRACTICE EXERCISE

Category	Offset Friday/	Saturday	Sunday	Monday	Tuesday	Wednesday	Thursday	Friday	Total
Departures		125	200	75	70	250	225	275	1,220
Arrivals		100	100	200	225	300	200	100	1,225
Rooms Sold	360/	335	235	360	515	565	540	365	2,915/2,910*
Occupancy %		55.8%	39.2%	60.0%	85.8%	94.2%	90.0%	60.8%	69.4%

Desk Clerks—Arrivals

Number of employees
@ 50 per shift

× 8-hour shift

× hourly rate ___

Cashiers—Departures

Number of employees
@ 75 per shift

× 8-hour shift

× hourly rate ___

Housekeepers
@ 16 rooms per day

Number of employees

× 8-hour shift

× hourly rate ___

*equals offset rooms sold for Friday through Thursday

Note: Round employees and labor hours to one decimal, wage cost to whole dollars

WAGE FORECASTING WORKSHEET

__4__ WEEK __1__ PERIOD
25-POINT QUIZ

Category	Offset Friday/ Friday	Saturday	Sunday	Monday	Tuesday	Wednesday	Thursday	Friday	Total
Departures									
Arrivals									
Rooms Sold									
Occupancy %									
Desk Clerks—Arrivals									
Number of employees @ 50 per shift									
× 8-hour shift									
× hourly rate ___									
Cashiers—Departures									
Number of employees @ 75 per shift									
× 8-hour shift									
× hourly rate ___									
Housekeepers @ 16 rooms per day									
Number of employees									
× 8-hour shift									
× hourly rate ___									

CHAPTER 11

Corporate Annual Reports

INTRODUCTION

A Corporate Annual Report is the formal documentation of a company's operating and financial performance for a fiscal year. It contains a range of information that individual and institutional investors can read to understand the company's performance for the recent year. Although annual reports record historical operating and financial results, they are also used to discuss operating strategies and the direction of future operations. These "forward-looking statements" always mention the uncertainties in the marketplace and in global economies and that there are no guarantees of future financial performance.

One of the reasons that the Corporate Annual Report is so valuable to investors is that the financial information that it presents is governed by strict accounting reporting requirements and compliance standards. Each company must have the financial information in their annual report audited for compliance to required accounting rules, principles, and procedures by an independent accounting company. These **Certified Public Accounting** companies (CPAs) are independent companies that audit and examine all the financial information contained in a company annual report and attest that the information is correct and accurate. **Attest** means confirming or verifying the accuracy and completeness of information. The required independent auditor's opinion is intended to give investors confidence that the financial information presented in a Corporate Annual Report is accurate, consistent, and conforms to Generally Accepted Accounting Principles (GAAP).

Originally, Corporate Annual Reports contained primarily financial information about the corporations operating performance. Over the years, annual reports have grown to include additional information about the different operating divisions, as well as of the entire corporation's financial performance. It also includes the vision, culture, and core values of the corporation, the strategies for growth in the future, and a good amount of public relations that highlight the strengths and successes of the corporation.

Corporate Annual Reports are also available on company Web sites. The company home page will generally have a link for "company information" and a link on that page for financial information and for the Corporate Annual Report. A note of caution: Do not download the annual report on your computer as most hotel and restaurant companies include many color pictures and it will take a long time to download or print. If you have a fast computer, the download will be faster. Following are some Web sites for major hotel and restaurant companies. Visit at least two of them and scroll through to see what annual reports look like and see what information they contain. Reading and browsing the annual reports on your computer is much easier than downloading or printing them out because of their length.

www.marriott.com

www.starwood.com

www.whitelodging.com

www.fairmont.com

www.hosthotels.com

www.brinker.com

www.darden.com

While the majority of hotel and restaurant companies are **publicly traded companies**, there are many major hospitality companies that are privately owned and therefore do not have to publicly report or disclose their financial information. They do have Web sites that contain other relevant information about their corporations. For example:

www.fourseasons.com

www.hyatt.com

www.pappas.com

THE PURPOSE OF CORPORATE ANNUAL REPORTS

Definition

A company's **Corporate Annual Report** is the formal company document that reports the company's operating and financial results for the most recent fiscal year. A company's **fiscal year** is one year of business operations. Fiscal years generally end December 31, the same time as the calendar year, but they can also end at other times, specifically the end of any quarter. Smaller more concise quarterly operating reports can be issued covering operations for the 1st quarter—March 31; the 2nd quarter—June 30; the 3rd quarter—September 30; and the 4th quarter—December 31. A company can choose when its fiscal year will end but for convenience and consistency, most fiscal years end at the same time as the calendar year, December 31. Regardless of the fiscal year ending date, the annual reports will generally cover business operations for 365 days.

Shareholders elect a Board of Directors generally ranging from 6 to 15 members. A **Board of Directors** is a group of people that is responsible to oversee all operational aspects of a company. A Chairman of the Board is elected to lead the board. This is generally the most powerful position in a company's organization. The Board of Directors is also responsible for selecting the President or **Chief Executive Officer (CEO)** of the company. This position will have the direct responsibility for the day-to-day operations of the company.

Regulations and Independent Auditors

To ensure that all the financial information contained in a Corporate Annual Report is accurate and reliable, and prepared according to accepted accounting practices, several key regulations and requirements have been imposed on all publicly traded companies and the Corporate Annual Reports that they publish.

First, any company that is publicly traded on a stock exchange must meet the requirements established by the **Securities and Exchange Commission (SEC)**. The SEC is the government agency responsible for regulating the operations of companies publicly traded on major stock exchanges like the New York Stock Exchange or the NASDAQ Exchange. These regulations require consistency, conformity, and reliability in the preparation and distribution of financial statements and reports and in the accuracy and reliability of the numbers or financial information contained in Corporate Annual Reports.

If a company is privately owned and has not issued any form of company stock, there is no need to issue an annual report. This is because there are no outside investors, therefore, no financial information is required to be made available to the public. Privately held companies are not subject to regulations of the SEC because they have no company stock available to the public and are not traded on any stock exchange.

Second, standards for the accurate and consistent collecting and reporting of company financial information must meet the standards, procedures, and requirement established by the Accounting Standards Board. They have issued what is called GAAP (Generally Accepted Accounting Principles). These are policies and guidelines that companies use in performing accounting responsibilities and preparing financial statements. This review insures that the company's financial information was properly prepared, is consistent, and conforms to established and approved accounting policies and regulations.

Third, the **Independent Audit Report** provides an "audit opinion" of an outside, independent accounting firm. This opinion verifies that the financial information is correct and accurate and that any reader can rely on the accuracy of financial information presented to make an investment decision regarding the company. Most opinions are favorable but an audit opinion can also be "qualified," meaning that there are a few issues that have been discovered that need to be addressed and that some of the financial information might be questionable. The qualified opinion alerts the reader to those questionable issues. On some occasions, the audit opinion will be unfavorable and they will not endorse or support the financial information contained in the annual report. This is a warning to readers that the financial information is not reliable, may not be accurate, and its preparation and reporting do not conform to GAAP or SEC standards.

Following is an example of an audit opinion contained in a recent Marriott International Corporate Annual Report given by Ernst & Young, the independent audit company for Marriott International, in the section Report of Independent Registered Public Accounting Firm on Internal Control over Financial Reporting:

> In our opinion, management's assessment that Marriott International, Inc. maintained effective internal control over financial reporting as of December 29, 2006, is fairly stated, in all material respects, based on the COSO (Committee of Sponsoring Organizations of the Treadway Commission) criteria. Also, in our opinion, Marriott International, Inc. maintained, in all material respects, effective internal control over financial reporting as of December 29, 2006, based on the COSO criteria.

The formal audit opinion is stated in the Marriott International, Inc. Corporate Annual Report section on Report of Independent Registered Public Accounting Firm:

> In our opinion, the financial statements referred to above present fairly, in all material respects, the consolidated financial position of Marriott International, Inc. as of December 29, 2006 and December 30, 2005, and the consolidated results of its operations and its cash flows for each of the three fiscal years in the period ended December 29, 2006, in conformity with U.S. generally accepted accounting principles.

Public Relations

The Corporate Annual Report offers a great opportunity for a company to highlight achievements and results of the previous years. There are many pictures of "trophy" or new hotels or restaurants, smiling employees with new products and happy customers, and lists of company achievements and recognition.

The report also provides an opportunity for the company to highlight significant achievements and results. Important operating results might be the acquisition of a company, the development of a new product or process, or exceeding an important company goal. Important financial results might include the highest revenue or profit levels that the company has ever achieved, the largest percentage increase in revenues or profits, or a large increase in the stock price or earnings per share.

Public relations is information and news releases prepared by the company and focuses on the positive achievements of a company and makes sure that these achievements and results are made known to potential investors and others interested in the company through press releases, the news media, or the Internet. The Corporate Annual Report is often the public relations highlight of the year and it features an opportunity to present this positive information about the company to interested readers and investors.

Uses of Corporate Annual Reports

The primary use of a company's Corporate Annual Report is to present the actual and audited financial results and other financial information for the most recent year. The financial information will also include three- or five-year financial summaries so that readers can see the historical trends that the company hopes shows improvements and growth in financial performance. It enables the readers to compare results from different time periods. The focus is on the three main financial statements: the P&L Statement, the Balance Sheet, and the Statement of Cash Flows. The 10th revised edition of the *Uniform System of Accounts for the Lodging Industry* also includes the Consolidated Statement of Changes in Stockholders Equity. This statement highlights the financial changes in the various types of company stock, retained earnings, and any other changes that affect the stockholders equity accounts of the company.

There is also a great deal of accompanying documentation that provides more details and explanation to the key financial numbers. These are called Notes to Consolidated Financial Statements and can include financial charts and graphs and narratives explaining in more detail the accounts, the changes in the account balances, and other important financial information.

Since 2002, there has been a greater emphasis on the senior officers of the company verifying or attesting to the accuracy and reliability of the financial results. In addition to the independent auditors' "audit opinion," the Security and Exchange Commission now requires that the CEO and the Chief Financial Officer of the company also endorse or "sign off" on the financial information contained in the annual report. This means that they know and understand the financial information contained in the annual reports and that they attest or confirm that the financial information has been prepared correctly and that the results accurately and fairly represent the operations of the company to the best of their knowledge for the last fiscal year.

Many companies have chosen to focus on the culture and core values of their company in their annual reports in addition to reporting the financial performance for the recent year. They take time to discuss the vision, priorities, and core values that their company wants to instill in all their employees. They want the readers to be aware of how the company operates, where their priorities are centered, and how it expects to meet operating and financial goals.

General Electric is one company that highlights its company culture first and then its financial performance in its annual reports. Visit their Web site www.ge.com and see how their annual report is arranged and what the company's management would like the reader to learn about the GE vision.

The third use of annual reports is to provide detailed operating information about the different divisions, brands, or components of their company. Hotel companies now include revenue information by brand that includes comparisons of the recent year's average room rate, occupancy percentage, and RevPAR to the previous year. This is also where new acquisitions or new product development is detailed and operating highlights of each division are presented. It is a brief review of the opportunities; challenges; and operating results for the year of the division, brand, or concept.

THE MESSAGE TO SHAREHOLDERS

Performance for the Year

The Message to Shareholders is an opportunity for the senior management of a company to present a message covering all the important aspects and achievements of the company for the year. Typically, the letter is written by the Chairman of the Board of Directors, the President of the company, or the CEO of the company. Generally there will be one manger in each one of these positions but sometimes one person holds all three titles and positions. Often a picture of them will be included to personalize the message. It is nice to see a picture of who is in charge of the company that you have invested your money in.

The Message to Shareholders will include comments on corporate operations, financial results, and goals and strategies for the future. Although most of these comments will be positive and offer a bright future, they should also address any company disappointments and negative results. Shareholders want to know the disappointments and bad information as well as the good information. Although the operating and financial information highlights company performance in the past, the strategy of a company and established goals set the path that the company expects to take in the future to overcome obstacles, meet new challenges, grow and expand, and achieve established operating and financial goals.

It is important to address how a company plans to grow and improve operating and financial performance. The two main areas to examine are comparable (comp unit) financial performance and the financial performance that results from the growth and addition of new units or stores. **Comp unit** growth compares the performance of existing hotels, restaurants, or stores. This means comparing the operating and financial performance of existing hotels, restaurants, or stores from year to year. It is important to know if these existing units are increasing sales and profits. The second area of growth is new unit growth. **New unit growth** is the result of opening new units. If a company is successful and customers are buying its products and services, there will be opportunities to open new units and continue to grow. A strong company will show growth in revenues and profits in both comp units and the addition of revenues and profits from new units. It is very important for investors to understand where and how a company is increasing revenues and profits in both the short term and long term.

Company Culture

As previously mentioned, many companies now choose to focus equal attention on their corporate vision, culture, and core values as well as on their financial results. These companies want to emphasize the positive impact that the strength of their company culture and core values, strong processes and favorable work environments, and all that is positive about the company has on operating and financial performance. Companies value and recognize their employees in achieving superior operating and financial results. They show that good operating and financial results are achieved because of their outstanding and dedicated employees.

Visit the Web sites for Marriott International www.marriott.com and Darden Restaurants www.darden.com and read the Message to Shareholders. You will come to know how important both of these companies feel that their employees (associates at Marriott and crew members at Darden) are the most valuable part of their company and also the main reason for the success of the company.

Strategies for the Future

The final important element of the Message to Shareholders is to comment on the future of the company. All interested stakeholders, including bankers, individual and institutional investors, employees, and customers, want to know the plans and directions that the company is planning for in the future. This will include discussing expectations of the company, comments on the status of the industry, addressing major positive and negative issues on the horizon, and discussing any new opportunities that the company is exploring.

Let's outline the main themes and strategies of the Message to Shareholders in a recent Marriott International Corporate Annual Report. The main sections are the introduction, revenue generation, reinvention and innovation, social responsibility, and optimism for the future. Following are quotes from two of the sections:

Social Responsibility: "We've always believed that in addition to operating our company profitably, we must do it responsibly. We are focused on five signature issues that leverage our expertise and resources to sustain communities where we do business: shelter and food, the environment, readiness for hotel careers, vitality of children and embracing diversity and inclusion."

Optimism for the Future: "Although the near-term business outlook remains uncertain, we are confident in the future of our industry and our company. With more than 80 years in business, 50 of those focused on the hotel industry, we have been through many difficult economic cycles. Each time, we have emerged a stronger and better company. With the best people, great places worldwide and a strong sense of purpose, we are excited to continue building economic prosperity in the communities we call home."

Darden Restaurants is the largest casual dining restaurant company in the world. The Darden Restaurants Letter to Shareholders starts off with their "passion" to create a great company, which they define as "a winning organization financially—translating sales and earnings growth which is competitively superior within our industry into top quartile total shareholder return within the S&P 500 and a special place—one that everyone wants to be part of because they have an opportunity to fulfill their professional and personal dreams." The rest of the Letter to Shareholders is divided into sections on goals and strategy, fiscal 2008 highlights, financial highlights, fiscal 2009 outlook, and conclusion.

Other themes include the need to change, innovation and continuous improvement, and transform and build strong, relevant brands. Darden seeks "to build a multi-brand growth company—bound together by a unifying culture, shared expertise and a common approach to the business—that operates existing brands at a consistently high level and successfully adds new brands."

Host Hotels and Resorts is the owner of 127 premium branded hotels and resorts in 10 countries and over 50 markets. "We will be the premier hospitality real estate company. We will own the highest-quality assets in prime urban, airport and resort/convention locations. Creating value through aggressive asset management and disciplined capital allocation to generate superior performance, we will maximize stockholders' returns through a combination of dividends, growth in funds from operations and increases to net asset value per share."

The Message to Stockholders follows the mission statement and after an introduction is divided into the following sections: managing for tomorrow, investing for the future, building a strong foundation, and a brighter tomorrow. While acknowledging the turbulent economic environments and credit market turmoil, Host management focuses on the strength and positioning of their hotel portfolio and the aggressive revenue enhancement and cost-cutting programs that were initiated in the last half of the year to protect profit margins and optimize cash flow.

The Message to Shareholders is a valuable part of the annual report and provides a framework and foundation to better understand the operating and financial results of the company. By examining excerpts from the three annual reports of Marriott International, Darden Restaurants, and Host Hotels and Resorts, we can see how important the core values, mission statement, and corporate culture are to producing outstanding products and services that result in successful operating and financial results.

THE CONTENT OF THE CORPORATE ANNUAL REPORT

Operating and Financial Results by Brand, Concept, or Division

The next section of the Corporate Annual Report provides a mixture of operating results and financial results. This will include describing in more detail successes, growth, new product or service development, and any other significant operating achievements. Pictures of happy, productive employees serving happy, satisfied customers in bright and friendly settings are generally featured. There will also be financial highlights for that particular hotel brand, restaurant concept, or industrial division. A **brand** is the lodging term that identifies different types of hospitality properties that serve specific hospitality market segments. A **concept** is the restaurant term that identifies different types of restaurant operations that provide specific dining experiences and serve specific market segments. A **division** is the manufacturing term that identifies the industry and different types of products produced by a company, including the markets that they serve.

We will again look at the organization of this section in the Marriott, Darden, and Host annual reports.

MARRIOTT   After the Message to Shareholders is a short section on risk factors and forward-looking statements and then management's discussion and analysis of financial condition and results of operations. This section presents both operating and financial information in different formats to help the reader understand the results of the current year compared to the previous year. Marriott also presents the lodging products by segment in the following matrix:

	Lodging Properties U.S. Non U.S. Total	Total Rooms U.S. Non U.S. Total
North American Full-Service		
North American Limited-Service		
International		
Luxury		
Timeshare		
Total		

This is followed by a chart that shows the revenues, income, and equity earnings for the last three years for each lodging segment.

The next section is very informative and presents detailed information for each lodging segment, including occupancy percentage, average room rate, and RevPAR for the last two years. This is further separated into North American operations and World Wide or System Wide operations. By studying this section, readers can evaluate the operating performance of each brand to identify trends and operating strengths and weaknesses.

The pages that follow get into more detailed and complicated explanations of nonoperating activities that generally interest only accountants, financial advisors, bankers, and institutional investors. If you take the time to read and understand these pages, you will have a good understanding of Marriott's financing activities in addition to Marriott's financial performance. There is a difference between financing and financial performance. Financing activities refer to capitalization or how Marriott raises or obtains money or capital to grow the company (investments and loans). Financial performance refers to the revenues, income/profits, and cash flows generated by all the operating activities of Marriott.

At this point in time, if you can understand the operating and financial results presented in a Corporate Annual Report, you are doing fine. Focus on this information because that is what the content of this book is about and it is also what you should be able to understand and use. Hospitality managers will use these financial concepts in the daily operations of their hotel or restaurant. Consider all other information as above and beyond—good to know but probably hard to understand.

DARDEN   The next section in the Darden annual report gives brief introduction about each restaurant concept.

Red Lobster—A Refreshing Seaside Dining Experience

Olive Garden—An Idealized Italian Family Meal

Longhorn Steakhouse—A Friendly Western-Style Dining Experience

The Capital Grill—A Personalized Experience

Bahama Breeze—A Caribbean Escape

Seasons 52—Seasonally Inspired

It is followed by a section that describes the value and strength of the Darden Company and how it is able to operate successfully and grow consistently. It is framed by the introduction "What Else We Bring to the Table."

Expertise	Scale
Direction	Confidence
Responsibility	

The next sections follow the required format and address management's discussion and analysis of financial condition and results of operations in great detail. This is where the reader can find out about sales and profit trends, accounting policies, taxes, and capital and financing activities.

Darden Restaurants Corporate Office

The corporate headquarters for Darden Restaurants is in Orlando, Florida. The company was founded after World War II by Bill Darden. Today, Darden is the largest casual dining company in the world with six distinct restaurant concepts and over 1,700 restaurants. The support of the many "crew members" that work in these restaurants flows from the corporate office where support functions such as new menu development, test kitchens, restaurant design and development, staffing, marketing, and sales. The corporate culture of Darden focuses on how the corporate staff can assist all restaurants in delivering on the core mission "to nourish and delight everyone we serve."

In the fall of 2009, Darden opened their new corporate headquarters building that was designed and equipped for peak sustainability. "Darden's new home will be a place of pride and performance that honors our heritage as industry pioneers. We are committed to achieving Leadership in Energy and Environmental Design (LEED) certification."

1. Name three support services that the Darden Corporate Research and Design Department would provide for existing restaurants.
2. What is the difference between the Research and Design Department and the Menu Design and Development Department?
3. Name three activities that the Corporate Accounting and Finance Department provides for the Darden restaurants.

Logos Courtesy of Darden Restaurants, Inc., Orlando, Florida

HOST   Host operates as a real estate investment trust, all of its holdings are hotel and resort properties. It owns the hotels and then hires Marriott, Hyatt, Four Seasons, and other full-service hotel brands to manage them. Therefore, its annual report discusses many of the same operating trends, economic challenges, and growth opportunities that are discussed in the Marriott annual report. To this is added information on credit markets, access to capital, Balance Sheet strength, and other financial information that will describe Host's ability to assist hotel management companies in achieving the best possible operating and financial results for their properties. They reinforce their commitment to the long term, their mission statement, and the strength of their hotel portfolio as ways to navigate in a difficult economy and a challenging hospitality industry.

These three companies provide a good range of examples of how companies report and discuss their operations and achievements. Each has its own culture, vision, and focus that are a result of their corporate culture and core values. The pictures and information provide an opportunity for readers to see and learn about company operations, including the employees that produce the products and services and the customers that purchase or enjoy those products and services.

Other Corporate Themes and Information

This section of an annual report provides the opportunity for the company to present and highlight other company priorities and activities. It can be located at the beginning, middle, or end of the narrative part of the annual report and highlight company culture, core values, initiatives, recognitions, and progress. This information is intended to provide readers with a feel of the company—where it places its priorities, the atmosphere and work environment that it seeks to create, the expectations for performance and growth, and examples of projects and activities the company participates in to give back to the community and its members.

FINANCIAL RESULTS FOR THE YEAR

This final section of the annual report contains all the financial numbers or results, including specific financial activities or results and the explanations of these activities.

Independent Auditors Report and Management Responsibilities Report

This is perhaps the most important part of any Corporate Annual Report. The fact that an independent public accounting firm has examined all the financial reports and the procedures used to prepare the reports of the company and then confirms that they conform to GAAP and SEC guidelines is intended to give credibility to the numbers and confidence that the numbers can be used to accurately describe and analyze company operations.

Recently, senior management has been required to "attest" or verify the correctness of the numbers and the procedures and processes that produced those numbers. The **Management Responsibility Report** is the section of the Corporate Annual Report that contains the senior management opinion that the operating and financial information contained in the annual report is accurate and correctly portrays the financial condition of the company.

The CEO or Chairman of the Board now must also sign off that they concur that all the operating activities and the financial position of the company as reported in the financial results are accurate and correctly represent both the capitalization of the company and the operating results and financial results of the company for the year.

The Three Main Financial Statements

The section presenting the financial results of a company contains the official and audited Profit and Loss Statement, the Statement of Cash Flows for the year, and the Balance Sheet as of the last day of the fiscal year. Recently added to this list of formal financial statements is the Consolidated Statements of Changes in Stockholders Equity and Accumulated other Comprehensive Income or Loss. This shows the changes from year to year in company stock activities, retained earnings, unearned compensation, and accumulated other comprehensive income or loss.

The P&L Statement includes the current year's financial results compared to last year's financial results. Companies may also include three- or five-year comparisons so that the reader can see the trends and changes in financial performance from year to year. The P&L is a summary of the company's financial results from operations that includes the totals of the main revenues and expense accounts and the different profit accounts. The P&L section can also include supporting documentation that breaks out some of the P&L results into more detail or by division, brand, or concepts.

The Balance Sheet includes the current year's balances and those of the previous year for assets, liabilities, and owner equity accounts. This enables the reader to identify and compare the changes in asserts, liabilities, and owner equity. The changes in the current accounts—assets and liabilities—represent how working capital was used during the year in the companies operations to produce products and services. The changes in the long-term accounts—assets, liabilities, and owner equity—represent how the company used debt via bank loans or obtained capital by raising equity and how it was used in the purchase of long-term assets. The Balance Sheet provides many numbers that are used in calculating important ratios used in financial analysis.

The Statement of Cash Flows shows how cash was generated and used in company operations for the year. It starts with cash flow generated from the operations for the year and that amount is adjusted by operating activities that increase or decrease the operating cash flow. The result is net operating cash flow for the year. The next two sections are cash flows that resulted from investing and cash flows that resulted from financing activities. The final section compares cash at the beginning of the year and cash at the end of the year. All these changes are identified and show how cash is generated and used in company operations during the year.

Notes to Consolidated Financial Statements

Notes to Consolidated Financial Statements is the section of annual reports that presents the detailed financial explanation of accounting and financial information contained in the annual report. There are many complicated transactions and activities and the notes are expected to clearly explain the details of these complicated transactions. The idea is to explain each of the transactions and to ensure that they are legitimate and conform to required and accepted accounting policies and procedures. Because of the details included in the notes, they can be difficult to understand and will require specific knowledge and experience to be able to analyze and evaluate.

Summary

The Corporate Annual Report is the most important report or publication that a company makes available to all individual or institutional investors. It is published each year and includes detailed operating and financial information for the past year. This includes the three main financial statements—Profit and Loss Statement, Balance Sheet, and Statement of Cash Flow. The annual report also includes many other supporting financial documents, schedules, and notes explaining the financial transactions or account balances.

One of the most important parts of an annual report is the audit opinion issued by an independent accounting firm that attests or verifies that the financial information contained in the annual report was prepared according to GAAP, that the financial information is correct, and that it accurately portrays the financial condition of the company. Now a company's Chairman of the Board or CEO as well as the Chief Financial Officer have to confirm that the financial information is accurate and correct by signing off on the financial information contained in the annual report.

The annual report also contains the Message to Shareholders where the Chairman of the Board, CEO, and President report on the activities and achievements of the company for the year. Another important section describes each operating division, brand, or concept and provides a brief discussion of the operations and achievements of the past year.

Companies take advantage of the annual report to make it an important public relations document. It is an opportunity to feature and recognize dedicated employees, satisfied customers, new products or services, and any awards and achievements that the company has received. The Corporate Annual Report is a very thorough document and companies make a great effort to make it complete and detailed.

Hospitality Manager Takeaways

1. A Corporate Annual Report is the formal yearly report of a companies operating and financial results for the most recent fiscal year. This includes Profit and Loss Statements, Balance Sheets, and the Statement of Cash Flows.

2. The financial results include the consolidated results of all the divisions, brands, and concepts of the company.

3. The Corporate Annual Report must include an audit opinion of the correctness and accuracy of

the financial information presented by an independent Certified Public Accounting firm.

4. The Message to Shareholders is a key component of the annual report that provides the Chairman of the Board or CEO of the company an opportunity to present and discuss the company's performance and plans for the future.

Key Terms

Attest: to confirm or verify the accuracy of operating and financial information.

Board of Directors: the group that is responsible to oversee all operational aspects of a company. The chief executive officer of a company reports to the Board of Directors and is also a member of the Board of Directors.

Brand: the lodging term that identifies different types of hospitality properties that serve specific hospitality market segments.

Certified Public Accountant: an independent accounting firm that has the responsibility to examine and verify the correctness and accuracy of a company's financial information. It issues an audit opinion in an annual report stating that the company meets or does not meet established reporting and accounting guidelines.

Chief Executive Officer (CEO): this position will have the direct responsibility for the day-to-day operations of the company and reports to the Board of Directors.

Comp unit: stores, units, hotels, or restaurants in a company that have been operating for more than two years.

Concept: the restaurant term that identifies different types of restaurant operations that provide specific dining experiences and serve specific market segments.

Corporate Annual Report: the formal company document that reports the company's operating and financial results for the most recent fiscal year.

Division: the manufacturing term that identifies the different types of products produced by a company, including the industry that it is in and the markets that they serve.

Fiscal year: the financial year for reporting a company's financial results. It can be the same as or different from the calendar year ending December 31.

Independent Audit Report: a section of the Corporate Annual Report that contains the audit opinion presented by an independent and certified public accounting company.

Management Responsibility Report: a section of the Corporate Annual Report that contains the senior management opinion that the operating and financial information contained in the annual report is accurate and correctly portrays the financial condition of the company.

New unit growth: the growth resulting from the opening of new units.

Notes to Consolidated Financial Statements: a section of an annual report that presents the detailed financial explanation of accounting and financial information contained in the annual report.

Public relations: information and news releases prepared by the company.

Publicly traded company: any company that offers to the public the opportunity to invest in the company by purchasing stock in the company that is bought and sold on publicly traded stock exchanges.

Securities and Exchange Commission (SEC): the government agency that has the responsibility of regulating the public stock exchanges (New York Stock Exchange, NASDAQ, and several other exchanges).

Review Questions

1. Name two types of government agencies or organizations that monitor the financial information contained in Corporate Annual Reports.
2. The company financial information is verified by an internal body and an external body. Name them.
3. Define division, brand, and concept and explain why they are important in discussing company operations.
4. Why is a company's vision, core values, and culture important to mention in its annual report?
5. What is the current P&L information for the year compared to?
6. What is the Balance Sheet information for the year compared to?
7. What is the Statement of Cash Flow information compared to?
8. Why are Notes to the Consolidated Financial Statements important?

Practice Exercises

1. Visit the Web sites of at least two hospitality industry companies and do the following:
   A. Print the message to shareholders
   B. Print the three main financial statements
   C. Print at least one other financial document such as the three-year or five-year revenue and profit summary or key financial information summary.
2. Choose the company that you would recommend to buy stock in or go to work for and explain why. Use the financial statements and include at least three statistics or categories that show financial growth or stability.
3. Which company do you think has the strongest strategy, culture, and vision that will help it be successful in the future? Explain why.

12

Personal Financial Literacy

LEARNING OBJECTIVES

- To understand important concepts of personal finance
- To be able to apply business accounting concepts to personal finance
- To learn about the different ways to use assets to produce income
- and create personal equity and net worth
- To understand the importance of planning for retirement when you are young
- To be able to develop a personal financial plan

CHAPTER OUTLINE

INTRODUCTION

Many of the accounting concepts and methods of financial analysis discussed in this book involving a business can be used in managing an individual's personal finances. This chapter will discuss how these concepts can help individuals in understanding and managing their personal finances. It is often the case that parents don't have an understanding of money and finance and either cannot or do not teach their children about managing money effectively. Also, schools do not teach students about the fundamentals of understanding, earning, and managing money. The result is that often young adults start their careers with little or no knowledge of effectively earning and managing their money. All too often, recent college graduates incur large amounts of debt (including low-interest student loans and high-interest credit card debt) that create major financial hardships and take years to pay off.

Financial literacy is the ability to understand money—how you get it, how you use it, and how you grow it. Unfortunately, most people don't take the time or have the opportunity to learn about managing their own money. Managing money requires financial knowledge, discipline, strategy and goals, and a financial plan to achieve those goals. Anyone can improve their financial position if they obtain the necessary knowledge and skills and have the discipline to use them. It is important to start when young to develop and apply fundamental money management principles to enable individuals to manage their ongoing financial needs and create **equity** and **net worth** over the long run and for retirement. The young have time as an advantage in growing their personal net worth.

This chapter includes information from prominent authors and corporate programs on money management and investing. This will include learning about the fundamental concepts of managing and investing money and how to develop your own personal financial plan. Two important goals are, first, to generate enough monthly income or cash flow to live as you would like (current time) and, second, to develop the knowledge and establish goals to increase your own equity or net worth (the long-term). An excellent source for this information is the book *Rich Dad Poor Dad—What the Rich Teach Their Kids about Money that the Poor and Middle Class Do Not* by Robert Kiyosaki (1997, Warner Business Books).

PERSONAL FINANCIAL LITERACY

Definition

Personal *financial literacy* is the ability to know and understand the management of money to achieve personal financial and investment goals. Financial literacy is not just for the rich, the old, or people who are able to make large investments but also for the young and the average person who may only be able to invest in small amounts. The knowledge and principles are the same in each situation and can lead to very beneficial financial results for anyone willing to learn and apply these basic financial principles.

Kiyosaki offers one rule regarding financial literacy. "You must know the difference between an asset and a liability, and buy assets. If you want to be rich, this is all you need to know. It is rule #1. It is the only rule" (p. 58). This may sound rather simple, but most people have no idea of how profound this rule is. Most people struggle financially because they do not know the difference between an asset and a liability. Kiyosaki's definitions are again simple: an asset puts money in your pocket and a liability takes money out of your pocket.

Most adults work to receive a paycheck. This paycheck generally comes every two weeks on Fridays. Retired people and some other workers get their paycheck once a month on the first day of the month. What they do with that paycheck is directly related to their understanding of fundamental money management principles.

What a person does with his or her paycheck demonstrates another valuable financial concept, which is understanding the relationship of being cash flow rich and Balance Sheet poor or cash flow poor and Balance Sheet rich. To demonstrate this concept, consider a weekly paycheck and how it is used. If it is spent paying existing expenses and paying off credit cards, then the person is *cash flow poor.* No money is left for investing, saving, or doing new or important things. If it is spent on necessary expenses and a portion invested and a portion saved, this person can also be considered *cash flow poor.*

Let's next consider the effect on the Balance Sheet of each of these people. In the first example, the person is controlled by his or her expenses, only paying bills and possibly overspending their weekly pay by purchasing on credit cards. This leads to more debt on the Balance Sheet and now we have a person who is *cash flow poor and Balance Sheet poor.* They are incurring liabilities rather than assets.

In the second example, the person is still spending or using all of their weekly paycheck, but they are choosing to purchase assets as well as paying expenses. They are investing. For example, The person is contributing 6% to his or her company retirement plan and investing 5% in savings account. While such a person might still be considered *cash flow poor*, the person is on his or her way to becoming *Balance Sheet rich* because of investing in assets in addition to necessary liabilities.

Personal Income Statement

We have already discussed company Profit & Loss Statements for separate departments in a hotel and Consolidated P&L Statements for the entire hotel, and corporate annual reports containing a Consolidated P&L Statement for an entire company. The P&L measures the ability of a company to maximize revenues and minimize expenses resulting in maximum profits.

These same accounting concepts apply to an individual's personal finance and money management. Maximizing revenues in a company is the same as maximizing income for an individual. Unfortunately, most individuals relate their income only to the company paycheck, which they generally receive weekly or every other Friday. These individuals completely miss an important point of understanding and managing money by relying on their paycheck as their only source of income. Financially literate individuals find ways to have *additional* sources of income and do not rely only on a company paycheck. They increase or grow their income by developing additional sources of income other than their paycheck by investing in assets. Specifically, this means saving some of their income and investing in savings accounts or other investments where his or her money will work for them earning interest, dividends, or appreciation in value.

Minimizing or managing expenses is just as important to an individual as it is to a company in order to maximize profitability. For an individual it is building equity or net worth instead of maximizing profits. This means managing income and expenses so that you have money left over after paying expenses. This money can be saved or invested. In today's society, it is far too easy for an individual to spend money that they do not have, especially with the use of credit cards, with the intent of paying it off later. Often individuals spend all of their paychecks on expenses or liabilities but never in investing in assets. Then it gets worse. He or she charges more expenses on credit cards that they will have a very difficult time paying off. This is very bad financial management of their money. Consider the following points: First, these individuals are spending all of their income and not saving or investing any of it. Second, they are spending more than they are earning with the paycheck they receive every other Friday. Third, they are charging additional expenses on credit cards that will include interest charges, minimum payments, and late fees. Remember our profit formula for a business: *Revenue minus expenses equal profits.* For individuals, the profit formula is income (generally from monthly paychecks) minus expenses equals money available to increase personal equity or net worth by saving or investing. If individuals spend more than they earn, they will have no savings. Personal equity and net worth will decrease and eventually become negative, which is similar to a company having an operating loss instead of a profit.

Fourth, today's individuals are not only spending more than they are making *but are also charging excess expenditures on credit cards!* This provides them a way to live with a loss by just putting it on plastic. The result is debt that grows rather than declines. Often the minimum monthly payments that these individuals make on their credit cards only pay the interest expense and do not reduce the outstanding balance at all. Finally, the fifth bad thing that many individuals are doing is paying high interest rates on their credit cards. His or her finances are out of control! Individuals spend more than they make and put excessive expenditures on credit cards with high interest rates that will be difficult to pay off. This often leads to two people having to work or one person doing multiple jobs just to meet their monthly expenses and make the minimum monthly credit card payments. *Note, we didn't say that individuals are paying off their credit cards. We said most individuals just make the minimum monthly payments that generally pay only the interest charge. They are never able to reduce the principal and pay off their credit cards.* This leads to what Kiyosaki calls *the rat race.*

Personal Cash Flow

Cash flow is the ability to maintain enough cash in your bank account or to increase the cash in your bank account so that you can cover all incurred living expenses. This primarily refers to an individual's checking account but will also include a savings account if there is one.

A *positive cash flow* means that an individual maintains enough money in his or her checking account to pay all the monthly expenses without taking money out of savings or investment accounts. This means they are earning more income than they are spending on expenses. Their cash account is increasing or growing, giving them flexibility and options on what to do with the cash accumulating in their checking and savings accounts.

A *negative cash flow* means that an individual does not maintain enough money in his or her checking account to pay one's monthly expenses. These individuals have to take money out of their savings or investment account or else they put the excess expenses on a credit card just to take care of their monthly expenses. This means they are spending more money on expenses than they are earning with their paycheck. Again, note that we did not say the excess money pays off the credit card balances. Generally, the monthly minimum payment will pay the interest expense first and any remaining amounts will make a partial payment on the total credit card outstanding balance. And additional expenses are often incurred for late payments or balances above the authorized amounts.

Generally, there are three main reasons that individuals cannot maintain a positive monthly cash flow. First, they have only one source of income—their paycheck every other Friday. Second, they do not understand the difference between spending money on expenses and liabilities and investing in income-producing assets. Third, they do not have the financial knowledge and discipline to keep their monthly expenses lower than their monthly income and save.

Personal Balance Sheet

An individual has assets, liabilities, and owner equity just like a business does. These might look different from a business, but they cover the same concepts of financial literacy and money management. This includes both current and long-term assets and liabilities. Often, individuals do not consider their money and finances as a business but are only concerned with how much money they make with each paycheck and how they are going to spend it or try to make ends meet.

Kiyosaki has very basic descriptions of assets and liabilities. Remember them!

> *Assets put money into your pocket*
> *Liabilities take money out of your pocket* (Kiyosaki, 1997, p. 61).

We all make choices of what we are going to do with the money we earn. Unfortunately, many individuals get caught up in the *rat race* and end up trying to spread their income around to pay the monthly rent, utilities, groceries and gas, and minimum monthly credit card payments. They really don't have any financial choices because they owe everyone. They have to pay for their expenses first and have no money left to save or invest. This is living from paycheck to paycheck and being caught in the rat race. Therefore, our definition of the **rat race**: not having financial literacy, spending more than earning, abusing credit cards, and living from paycheck to paycheck.

Kiyosaki's Rule #1 is knowing the difference between assets and liabilities and to invest in assets. This means that an individual must understand the importance of savings and investing and allocate some of his or her monthly income to savings and investments (assets). This requires financial knowledge and financial discipline. Assets earn income. For example, savings accounts pay interest daily, monthly, or annually. Investment accounts including stocks and mutual funds pay dividends and hopefully appreciate in value. Real estate generates positive cash flow and also hopefully appreciates in value.

Certificates of Deposit (CDs) also pay interest according to specific time periods. CDs are generally in three month, six month, annual, or longer time periods. Investments in the stock market generally pay dividends quarterly or annually and have the potential to have the stock price go up (appreciation). However, there is also the risk that the stock price can go down. The point is that individuals who have financial literacy discipline themselves to investing some portion of their income, even if it is only 5% or 10% of their monthly income, into assets. These assets work for them by generating income in the form of interest and dividends. This gives them the opportunity to start building equity or net worth and controlling their expenses. This means they will eventually own more than they owe.

The return on any savings account or investment is related to the risk incurred by making that investment. The lower the risk, the lower the return. The higher the risk of appreciation or depreciation, the higher the potential gain or loss. Table 12.1 illustrates a typical range of returns for savings and investments:

Exhibits 12.1 and 12.2 illustrate a college student's Balance Sheet during his or her senior year. We will use March 31 as our Balance Sheet date.

Since Total Assets must equal Total Liabilities and Equity, the difference between the Total Assets of $11,100 and the Total Liabilities and Equity of $26,000 is a negative $14,900. This individual owes $14,900 more than he or she owns and, therefore, has a *negative net worth or no net equity.*

Because total assets must equal total liabilities plus equity, the difference between the total assets of $23,500 and total liabilities and equity of $16,700 is a positive $6,800. This individual owns more than he or she owes and, therefore, has a *positive net worth or net equity.*

Let's look at the similarities and differences in these two examples. Both the students have $10,000 in student loans, $2,000 in furniture, and have four different liabilities. The difference is that the financially literate student has a smaller car loan, smaller credit card balance, and smaller store credit card debt. This student evidently bought a lower price car and made a larger down payment, resulting in a smaller car loan and monthly payment. He or she has been smarter and more disciplined and, therefore, has a larger balance in his or her checking and savings account. And, he or she has been able to develop $3,000 in investments and has a positive net worth of $6,800. *This student is investing in assets!*

TABLE 12.1   Risk and Returns

Savings Accounts	Lowest risk	1%–2% Interest
Certificates of Deposit	Lower risk, fixed time period	2%–5% Interest
Bonds	Some risk, debt obligation	3%–7% Interest
Mutual Funds	Moderate risk, price increase or decrease potential	0%–6% Dividends
Individual Stocks	Highest risk, price increase or decrease potential	0%–6% Dividends

EXHIBIT 12.1
NO FINANCIAL LITERACY

Assets			Liabilities	
Cash—Checking account	$	100	Car loan @ 9%	$ 6,000
Cash—Savings account		-0-	Student loan @ 4%	$10,000
Investments		-0-	Credit card debt @ 16%	$ 5,000
Total Current Assets	$	100	Store credit cards @ 9%	$ 2,000
			Total Liabilities	$23,000
Car	$ 8,000			
Furniture	2,000		**Equity**	
Insurance policies	-0-		Car	$ 2,000
Savings Bonds	1,000		Grandparents Gifts	1,000
Total Long Term Assets	$11,100		(savings bonds)	
			Total Equity	$ 3,000
			TOTAL LIABILITIES	
TOTAL ASSETS	$11,100		AND EQUITY	$26,000
		BOOK NEGATIVE NET WORTH		$14,900

EXHIBIT 12.2
BASIC FINANCIAL LITERACY

Assets			Liabilities	
Cash—Checking account	$	500	Car Loan @ 9%	$ 1,000
Cash—Savings account		2,000	Student loan @ 4%	10,000
Investments		3,000	Credit card debt @ 12%	500
Total Current Assets	$	5,500	Store credit cards @ 9%	200
			Total Liabilities	$11,700
Car	$ 5,000			
Furniture	2,000		**Equity**	
Insurance Policies	10,000		Car	$ 4,000
Savings Bonds	1,000		Grandparents gifts	1,000
Total Long Term Assets	$18,000		(savings bonds)	
			Total Equity	$ 5,000
			TOTAL LIABILITIES	
TOTAL ASSETS	$23,500		AND EQUITY	$16,700
		BOOK POSITIVE NET WORTH		$ 6,800

The other student has spent more than he or she has saved using credit cards and probably purchased items that he or she cannot afford or could do without. As a result, this student has more liabilities than assets resulting in little, if any, money in savings and checking accounts, a great deal of debt, and a negative net worth of $14,900. *This student is spending on liabilities!*

These examples include both large and small differences, but they add up to a big difference. The student in Exhibit 12.1 has a negative net worth of $14,900 and the student in Exhibit 12.2 has a positive net worth of $6,800. The difference is $21,700! The student in Exhibit 12.2 has incurred many of the same liabilities but because of financial literacy has managed to save and invest, spend wisely, and minimize liabilities and expenses. This student has put to use Rule #1: Invest in assets. Although these investments start small, they are a beginning and have resulted in the student having a positive rather than a negative net worth. This student's asset column is growing.

Another valuable concept in the management of assets is the importance of building principal. **Principal** is the dollar amount that is in an account, which is earning interest or dividends and has the potential to increase or decrease. It is the amount of money invested in income-producing assets. It is money that is earning money in the form of interest, dividends, or value appreciation. **Interest** is the return on the principal in a savings account. **Dividend** is the return on the principal invested in a company stock or mutual fund. It is assets working for you. For example, $1,000 invested in a savings account is $1,000 of principal that can earn interest or dividends. If the interest rate is 3% per year, this principal of $1,000 will earn $30 of interest per year. At the end of the year, the interest earned will be added to the principal. Therefore, the principal for the second year will be $1,030 earning interest at 3%. Interest earned for the second year will be $30.90. This shows the value of reinvesting interest earned and dividends paid to increase the principal.

There are three primary ways in which the principal can grow. First, an individual can contribute his or her own money to the principal from their paycheck or other sources of income by making monthly contributions. This demonstrates Rule #1 investing in assets. Second, a company or employer can make matching contributions to retirement or 401K accounts for their employees and, therefore, increase the principal. *This is the most important concept to understand in creating individual wealth and net worth—take advantage of company contributions in addition to individual contributions to increase the principal.* Third, the principal can grow by reinvesting the interest and *dividend* that the principal earns. The larger the principal or higher the interest or dividend rate, the faster the principal will grow because larger amounts of money is working for you.

MANAGING PERSONAL FINANCES

The Rat Race

The *rat race* is when individuals spend more money than they earn. They are not able to control or save their money because they have continually overspent their income resulting in monthly expenses higher than their monthly income. They will then probably take on a second job to pay off their debts. But often, they will use the additional income to continue spending rather than paying off their credit cards, which was their original intent. Thus, the rat race—not having control of their money, continuing to over spend, not making progress in paying off debt, and not being able to invest in assets.

These individuals either do not know about Kiyosaki's Rule #1 or they are not disciplined enough to follow it. The first step that they must take to get out of the rat race is to realize that they are in it and are spending more money than they are earning. They must change their financial habits and how they use and manage their money. Otherwise, they will stay in the at race and probably get in deeper and deeper.

Evaluating Your Personal Financial Position

Every individual establishes a pattern for earning and spending money. Unless a person starts learning about managing money and developing financial literacy and discipline, he or she will continue to earn and spend, totally unaware of the value of saving and investing in assets. Financial literacy starts with changing this pattern to a pattern of understanding, earning, investing, and then spending. The investment part comes before the spending part. Because they have financial literacy and financial discipline, they reduce their expenditures and learn to live on the amount remaining after they have saved or invested.

Take a look at your own pattern of managing your money. Do you spend more than you earn each month? Are you unable to save or invest? Are your debts getting larger each month instead of getting smaller? Do you continually use your credit card to buy things that you really do not need or cannot afford? If your answers are yes to some or all of these, then you are caught up in the rat race!

The most important point to understand at this time is that it is never too late to learn and to start managing your money. It doesn't matter what your age is, the amount of money you make, or the amount of debt that you have. You can always learn about managing money, the need to change your spending habits, and the importance of starting to manage your money in ways that will enable you to invest, build a principal, and to be able pay all your expenses. It starts with an individual taking responsibility of his or her own financial actions, and making commitment to control expenses, start saving and investing, and improve his or her financial condition.

Developing Financial Literacy

It is important that individuals make the effort to analyze their current financial position and then to learn and apply smart money management principles. It will require discipline and a change in an individual's habits and lifestyle. But it will be worth the change as an individual regains control of his or her financial situation and has the freedom to choose how one can invest and spend rather than be controlled by his or her expenses and debt obligations. The important thing is to change, even if it is in small steps.

In *Rich Dad, Poor Dad*, Kiyosaki offers six steps or lessons that will lead to financial independence and the ability to manage and control money and finances (Table 12.2):

TABLE 12.2   Six Lessons for Financial Independence

1. The rich don't work for money—the poor and middle class work for money, the rich have money work for them.

2. Teach financial literacy, the ability to read numbers. The rich buy assets. The poor only have expenses. The middle class buys liabilities they think are assets.

3. Mind your own business. Invest your income in assets that will earn additional income for you.

4. The history of taxes and the power of the corporation.

5. The rich invent money. They understand numbers, develop investment strategies, understand markets, and understand the law.

6. Work to learn—Don't work for money. Always increase your knowledge. Be able to manage cash flow, things and processes including time, yourself and your family, and people.

These steps are an effective guideline for getting out of the rat race and controlling your income. Begin by choosing the lesson that will be most meaningful to you. Then, commit to consistently using that lesson in managing your monthly financial resources. Then, add a second lesson and build on your financial literacy. The more of these lessons or financial concepts the individual understands and practices, the stronger the financial condition of an individual will become.

EVALUATING ASSETS AND SOURCES OF INCOME

Company Programs

Many companies offer retirement plans (401K accounts) for their employees that include matching financial company contributions to an employee's individual retirement account. A **401K account** is a company sponsored long-term retirement account that includes both employee and company contributions. **Company contributions** are the dollar amount that a company contributes to an employee's company retirement account. These programs are based on the amount of money an employee contributes to his or her personal 401K account offered through the company. For example, Marriott International will contribute one dollar for every dollar the employee contributes up to 3% of the employee's salary. For the next 3% of employee contributions, Marriott International will contribute 50 cents for every dollar the employee contributes. This represents a return to the employee of 100% on the employee's contributions up to 3% of his or her salary and a return of 50% on the employee's contributions for the next 3% of his or her salary. If a Marriott International employee contributes 6% of his or her salary to the company 401K account, the company contribution amount will be 75% of the employee's contribution.

Hyatt Hotels and Resorts 401K plan is very similar to that of Marriott International. Hyatt will match 100% of an employee's first 3% and 50% on an employee's next 2% up to a maximum of 5% of employee contributions. Four

TABLE 12.3 Four Ways Company 401K Accounts Can Grow
1. Employee contributions from paychecks
2. Matching company contributions
3. The **earnings** (interest, dividends, and appreciation) on the total 401K principal
4. Any forfeitures or unvested amounts of other employees leaving the 401K plan

Seasons will contribute 3% of an employee's salary to the employee's 401K account regardless if the employee contributes to the plan or not.

The reason that company retirement programs should be the number one priority for an employee in investing in assets, increasing principal, and creating equity and net worth is because where else can an individual get someone else to contribute significant amounts to his or her retirement fund? While returns from interest and dividends are in the 1% to 3% range, the company contribution range is generally 25% to 100% of what the employee contributes. Table 12.3 summarizes the ways an employee's 401K plan can grow.

Companies make these contributions to 401K plans as an important benefit that will keep employees working and happy. By making these contributions, companies are sharing in the responsibility to provide long-term savings plans for retirement for their employees. It is a very attractive benefit to employees and one that becomes more valuable each year.

Companies can also provide stock purchase programs where employees can purchase company stock with no commission and often at a discounted price. Contributions to these plans can be made conveniently with payroll deductions that avoid commissions and other fees. This is another way for individuals to build wealth at nominal expense.

An equally important benefit that most companies provide is employee health benefits. **Benefits** are company programs offered to employees by a company that provides savings programs to invest in and health and insurance programs to participate in at reduced costs. Companies will pay all or a portion of the insurance premiums for their employees including health, dental, and vision insurance at group rates which are generally lower than individual rates. By paying a small or large part of this cost, the company reduces the amount that employees have to pay for insurance premiums. This in effect, increases an employees take-home pay. Companies might also offer at lower costs life insurance, disability insurance, and salary continuation to help employees when they have emergencies or accidents that require expensive medical care. It is important to take advantage of these programs because they enable employees to participate and receive these benefits at a lower cost than they could obtain on their own.

Understanding and enrolling in these savings and benefit programs can be a significant step in the process of building wealth and staying out of the rat race. They not only offer significant returns or cost savings but also provide a convenient and disciplined way to consistently save and invest for the future. Most large companies offer these programs, so it is up to the employee to learn about them and demonstrate that they have the financial literacy to participate in them and receive the benefit of insurance coverage at the lowest possible cost.

Individual Investment Accounts

In addition to company investment accounts, it is important for individuals to have their own investment or savings accounts. This is because company retirement programs are controlled by the company and intended for the long term. They are good in that they provide both employee and company contributions. But they also have restrictions that are intended to ensure that the money is available for retirement. Therefore, access to company retirement accounts is restricted including penalties and fees for early withdrawal of money from these accounts. For example, if contributions are made before tax, no withdrawals can be made without substantial penalties until the individual reaches the age of $59\frac{1}{2}$. These company retirement or investment accounts offer a valuable long-term component for investing.

An individual's personal savings or investment account is controlled by that person and the balance or principal is available to use or not to use as appropriate. It offers the flexibility of saving and investing with having access to those funds as needed. The access to and control of these individual accounts should be an important part of the investment strategy for any individual. The individual has control to make the principal increase with contributions, decrease with withdrawals, and hopefully appreciate in value with wise investment decisions. These individual investment accounts offer a short-term component for investment. They can include the following types of investments:

Cash savings accounts

Certificates of deposits

Money market funds

Individual stocks and bonds

Mutual funds

Annuities

Commodities and currencies

Retirement Planning

Another very valuable part of financial literacy is understanding the importance of planning for retirement at the beginning of an individual's career and not at the end. It is a fact that the sooner the individuals start making contributions to retirement, IRAs, or 401K accounts, the more the money they will have working for them for a longer time period to build up their retirement accounts. Time is in the favor of those who invest early in their careers. That is because these contributions steadily increase the principal and therefore the interest or dividends that the principal earns. Equally important is the time span that the principal is earning interest, dividends, and appreciation. It is a common sense that money contributed by individuals and the company over a 25-year period will be larger than over a 15-year period than over a 5-year period. More money working longer!

Let's talk about stock price appreciation and depreciation. **Appreciation** means that the value of an investment or an asset is going up over time. **Depreciation** means that the value of an investment or asset is going down over time. The rate at which an asset appreciates is closely associated with the amount of risk involved in investing in a particular asset. Generally, the higher the risk (**risk** being the probability of an investment increasing or decreasing in value and at what rate it increases or decreases), the higher the potential returns or appreciation. The lower the risk, the lower the potential returns. Let's add some sample average annual returns for some investments to the risk and return information presented earlier in the chapter.

1%–2% return	Bank savings accounts that are insured by the government
2%–6% return	Certificates of deposits (CDs) for specific time periods
4%–6% return	Long-term government bonds*
10%–13% return	Large and small company stocks*
3% cost	Inflation*

*Compound annual returns from 1926 to 2006 according to Morningstar Research.

When understanding risk and return, it is important to realize that diversifying investments is a good way to spread the risk of any investment portfolio. For example, if an individual placed his or her entire $100,000 portfolio only in one stock, his or her investment appreciation would rely on the performance of only one stock—a very risky strategy. However, if the same individual places one third in CDs, a low-risk investment, one third in long-term government bonds, a moderate-risk investment, and one third in large and small company stocks, a high-risk investment, he or she would have the opportunity to have his or her investment appreciate in three different ways with three different risk levels. Equally important is the fact that if the value of one investment goes down, it might be offset by increases in the other two investment choices.

Retirement should be a key part of any individual's investment strategy. Today there are so many savings and investment options available to assist in achieving retirement goals. An important part of financial literacy is understanding the retirement options and programs available and choosing the best ones that match an individual's retirement strategy. A small amount of money invested over a long period of time will result in a much larger retirement account than larger amounts of money invested over a short period of time. Knowledge and discipline are the starting points for an investment strategy that will provide a comfortable and satisfying retirement.

TABLE 12.4   Examples of Retirement Planning

Give Yourself a Financial Check-Up

TIAA—CREF

1. Create a budget
2. Pay down debt
3. Build an emergency fund
4. Review your insurance needs
5. Start saving for retirement

The 15-Minute Retirement Plan

CNN Money (from the editors of *CNN* and *Money Magazine*)

1. Ignore the big number
2. Get in the game
3. Put yourself on automatic
4. Don't obsess over portfolio building
5. Stick with a few funds
6. Update your plan annually

The Last 401K Guide You'll Ever Need

Money Magazine

1. Save early and often
2. Spread your money around
3. Limit company stock
4. Check in just once a year
5. Keep your hands off

Above are some examples of investment concepts and strategies that will help the beginning and seasoned investor alike. Note the similarity in some of these concepts highlighting their importance. So start building your financial literacy by reading, understanding, developing, and implementing your investment strategy (Table 12.4).

This chapter has provided information that will help an individual learn about the basics of managing money and help them start developing his or her financial literacy. There are many different ways to start managing our personal finances, but the important thing is to recognize where you are in your personal money management, where you want to be, what you need to do differently, and then change spending and saving habits to get you moving in that direction. Only then will you have control over your finances and be on the way to growing your financial resources and achieving financial flexibility.

Following is an example of a plan to develop financial literacy and to start managing money:

EXHIBIT 12.3
SIX STEPS TO MANAGING PERSONAL FINANCES

1. Develop financial literacy
   A. Actively seek to learn about investments
   B. Understand your personal financial statements
      1. Your Income Statement
      2. Your Balance Sheet
      3. Your Cash Flow
   C. Learn how money works
   D. Learn to live on 90% of your pay, invest the other 10%

2. Develop specific financial goals and strategies
   A. Short term of a year or less
   B. Long term from three to five to ten years
   C. Establish specific goals and time frames to get there
   D. Invest in assets, not liabilities and expenses

3. Discipline yourself to meet your financial objectives
   A. Start early, time is in your favor
   B. Be consistent, even if small amounts
   C. Control your credit cards and their interest rates

4. The first step is to develop and grow your principle
   A. Your principle is the amount you have to invest
   B. Small amounts do not earn significant returns
   C. Consistent savings will increase your principle

5. The second step is to invest in assets that will work for you
   A. Earnings from investments are your second income
   B. Diversify to spread and minimize risk
   C. Invest to meet your goals and to be consistent with your strategy

6. Stay out of the "rat race."

We-ko-pa Golf Club

The We-ko-pa Golf Club is outside of Phoenix, Arizona, on the Fort McDowell Yavapai Indian Reservation. It offers 36 holes of golf and is one of the three top-rated golf courses in Arizona according to the most recent Zagat ratings. Visit the We-ko-pa Web site at www.wekopa.com and take a tour of this magnificent golf facility. Because it is on tribal reservation land, there will never be roads, homes, or noise to detract from the beauty of the Arizona desert. However, be prepared to pay over $200 for a round of golf during the high season of January through April.

What kind of financial planning will you need to be able to afford to play the We-ko-pa golf course with your family or friends? If golf is not your game, refer

Photo Courtesy of the Fort McDowell Yavapai Nation, Fort McDowell, Arizona.

back to the hotels and resorts featured in each chapter of this book. Which one would you like to spend a week with your family or friends? To help you get there, consider the following:

1. What financial strategy will you need to develop and follow to grow your net worth so that you can afford vacations like these?
2. What are your strengths that will help you follow your financial strategies and reach your goals? What new strengths do you need to develop?
3. What are your weaknesses that you will need to overcome to achieve your financial goals? How will you overcome them?

Summary

Individuals can utilize many of the same financial concepts used by business to manage their own personal finances. Financial literacy is the ability to understand and use numbers effectively in financial management and planning. It is important because it gives an individual control over his or her finances and the freedom to be able to afford to do what they want to do.

There are many books on managing personal finances. *Rich Dad, Poor Dad* by Robert Kiyosaki is one book that clearly presents the fundamentals of personal financial management. It is important that individuals take the time to learn these money management fundamentals at an early age so that they can have their money work for them rather than having them work for their money.

A key point of financial literacy is understanding the importance of investing in assets. Assets put money in your pocket. Investing in assets involves building a principal amount (savings or investments) in dollars that earns interest or dividends and contributes these earning back to increasing the principal.

Liabilities and expenses take money out of your pocket and are typically what most individuals do with the money they earn from their paycheck. These individuals lack the financial knowledge and personal discipline to invest some amount of their income in assets before paying off liabilities and expenses.

Individuals can invest in both company savings accounts and their own savings or investment accounts. Company investment accounts such as 401K and retirement accounts offer the advantage of having a company contribute money to these accounts. However, they are for the long term and contain restrictions and penalties for early withdrawal. Individual investment accounts offer the advantage of ownership, flexibility, and control. They are more short term in nature and the money in these accounts is available for withdrawal without penalties to use when needed. A financial literate individual will take advantage of investing in both of these types of investment accounts.

Hospitality Manager Takeaways

1. It is important for hospitality managers to understand the management of money so that they can take advantage of company programs and individual accounts that can help them create equity and build individual net worth.

2. Assets put money in your pocket; liabilities take money out of your pocket.

3. Equity is the amount of assets, primarily investments and real estate that an individual accumulates and that is not encumbered by liabilities or debt.

4. Financial literacy is the knowledge about working with money that provides an individual with control over their money and the freedom to do what they would like to do because they have the financial resources necessary to pay for those activities.

5. Time and discipline are two key components of a strong investment strategy.

6. Retirement should be a part of an individual's investment strategy at the beginning of one's career and not at the end.

Key Terms

Appreciation: the value of an investment or an asset is going up over time.

Asset (Kiyosaki): puts money in your pocket.

Benefits: programs offered to employees by a company that provide savings programs to invest in and health and insurance programs to participate in at reduced costs.

Cash flow: the ability to maintain enough cash in your bank account or to increase the cash in your bank account so that you can cover all incurred living expenses.

Company contribution: the dollar amount that a company contributes to an employee's retirement account.

Depreciation: the value of an investment or asset is going down over time.

Dividend: the return on the principal invested in a company stock or mutual fund.

Earnings: money that is produced from an asset in the form of dividends or interest.

Equity: the difference between an individual's assets and liabilities.

401K accounts: company's long-term retirement accounts that include both employee and company contributions.

Financial literacy: the ability to understand numbers.

Interest: the return on the principal in a savings account.

Liability (Kiyosaki): takes money out of your pocket.

Net worth: what an individual has in investments that are unencumbered with corresponding liabilities or debt. Similar to equity.

Principal: the dollar amount in an account that is earning interest or dividends and that has the potential to appreciate or increase as well as decrease.

Rat race: not having financial literacy, spending more money than earning, abusing credit cards, and living from paycheck to paycheck.

Risk: the probability of an investment increasing or decreasing in value and at what rate it increases or decreases.

Review Questions

1. Describe the rat race, including how you get in it and get out of it.
2. Why are company 401K programs so important to employees?
3. Why are company benefit programs so important to employees?
4. Why is planning for retirement at the start of a career so important?
5. What is the difference between principal and interest?
6. What will be your biggest obstacle to investing?
7. Choose three activities that are important to you in getting started.
8. Which of the investing examples at the end of the chapter do you think is best for you? List the concepts and explain why?

Practice Exercises

1. Develop a 5-, 10-, and 25-year financial plan. Include the dollar amounts that you would like to have in your investment accounts and the strategies that you will use to achieve those goals.
2. From the three retirement plans presented in Table 12.4, make a list of at least five of the steps that you think will be important to you in developing a strong retirement program. Explain why you chose each of your retirement steps or concepts.
3. Prepare your current Balance Sheet. Think about current and long-term assets or liabilities. What is your current "Net Worth"?

GLOSSARY

Accounting Concepts—the bookkeeping methods and financial transactions used in daily business operations. (*Chapter 1*)

Accounting Department—a staff department that supports all other staff and operating departments in a hotel with regard to accounting procedures and hotel operations. (*Chapter 3*)

Accounting Period—a 28-day time period that can be used instead of calendar months to prepare management reports and financial statements covering hotel or restaurant operations. (*Chapter 3*)

Accounts Payable—products or services received by a company, but not paid for that are due within one year. Also, the process of approving invoices and issuing checks in payment for products and goods received by a hotel or restaurant. (*Chapters 3 and 5*)

Accounts Receivable—what the company is owed for providing products and services to customers. Revenues recorded but uncollected. The process of billing and collecting accounts settled after the guest or company has checked out of the hotel. (*Chapters 3 and 5*)

Allocations—the portion of an expense charged to a specific hotel for services received in connection with expenses incurred at the corporate level on behalf of all the hotels or restaurants in the company. (*Chapter 4*)

Annual Operating Budget—the primary budget used by department managers. It contains the specific revenue goals, the specific expense amounts, and the profit objectives that each department is expected to meet for the year. (*Chapters 2 and 9*)

    Consolidated Hotel Budget—the summary budget for the entire hotel, including revenues, expenses, and profits. (*Chapter 9*)

    Department Budget—the specific and detailed budget for an individual department that provides all the financial specifics for revenues, expenses, and profits. (*Chapter 9*)

Appreciation—the value of an investment or asset is going up over time. (*Chapter 12*)

Assets—the resources owned by a company that are used in the production of products and services by that company. (*Chapter 5*)

    Current—assets that are used or consumed during a one year time period.

Long Term—assets with a useful life of over one year.

Asset—puts money in your pocket. (*Chapter 12*)

Assistant Controller—a manager in the accounting office who reports to the Director of Finance and oversees specific functions in the accounting office, either Income Operations or Accounts Receivable. (*Chapter 3*)

Attest—to confirm or verify the accuracy of operating and financial information. (*Chapter 11*)

Balance Sheet—the financial statement that measures the value or net worth of a business as of a specific date. Also called the asset and liability statement (A&L). (*Chapters 1 and 5*)

Bench Rate—the base room rate that a hotel wants to achieve and sell to the public. (*Chapter 7*)

Benefits—programs offered to employees by a company that provide savings programs to invest in or health and insurance programs to participate in at reduced costs. (*Chapter 12*)

Board of Directors—the group that is responsible to oversee all operational aspects of a company. The chief executive officer of a company reports to the board of directors and is also a member of the board. (*Chapter 11*)

Booking Pace—the current rate at which reservations are being received for a specific DOA. The booking pace is compared to historical averages to determine if demand is stronger or weaker than historical averages. (*Chapter 7*)

Brand—the lodging term that identifies different types of hospitality properties that serve specific hospitality market segments. (*Chapter 11*)

Budget—the formal business and financial plan for a business for one year. (*Chapter 9*)

Capital Expenditure Budget—the formal budget that identifies the need for replacing long-term assets of the business for renovating and expanding the business. (*Chapter 9*)

Capitalization—identifies the way that a business obtains and uses money to start or expand a business by purchasing long-term assets. (*Chapters 1 and 5*)

Cash—funds that are in the cash account and are available for use in daily business operations. (*Chapter 5*)

Cash Flow—the ability to maintain enough cash in your bank account or to increase the cash in your bank account so that you can cover all incurred expenses. (*Chapter 12*)

Certified Public Accountant—independent accounting firms that have the responsibility of examining and verifying the correctness and accuracy of a company's financial information. They issue an audit opinion stating that the company meets or does not meet established reporting and accounting guidelines. (*Chapter 11*)

Change—the difference between two numbers. (*Chapter 2*)

Chief Executive Officer—this position will have the direct responsibility for the day-to-day operation of the company and reports to the board of directors. (*Chapter 11*)

Classification of Cash Flow—Operating activities, financial activities, and investment activities. (*Chapter 5*)

Comp Unit—stores, units, hotels, or restaurants in a company that have been operating for more than two years. (*Chapter 11*)

Company Contribution—the dollar amount that a company contributes to an employee's retirement account. (*Chapter 12*)

Comparison—to examine, to note the likeness or difference. (*Chapter 2*)

Competitive Set—a group of five or more properties selected by individual hotel management. A competitive set enables hotel managers to compare property performance with direct competition. (*Chapter 8*)

Concept—the restaurant term that identifies different types of restaurant operations that provide specific dining experiences and serve specific market segments. (*Chapter 11*)

Construction Budget—the budget that identifies all the costs involved to construct and build a hotel or restaurant. (*Chapter 9*)

Corporate Accounting Office—a central location that provides accounting support and services for individual hotels or restaurants operated by the company. (*Chapter 3*)

Corporate Annual Report—the formal company document that reports the company's operating and financial results for the most recent fiscal year. (*Chapter 11*)

Daily Revenue Report—a report that is prepared during the night audit shift and collects and reports actual revenue information for the previous day. (*Chapter 6*)

Day of Arrival (DOA)—the focus point of yield management systems. All historical reservation information and trends for a specific arrival day in the future. (*Chapter 7*)

Deductions from Income—the same as expense centers. The direct expenses of staff departments that support the operating departments of a hotel in providing products and services to customers. (*Chapter 4*)

Demand—a reflection of the customer's preferences and willingness to pay a specific price or rate for a product or service. (*Chapter 7*)

Demand Tracking—the part of revenue management utilizing computer programs to provide historical information of reservation booking patterns that provide historical averages and trends for a hotel. Also called yield systems. (*Chapter 7*)

Department Head—a manager that has direct responsibility for a specific hotel department. Department heads report to an executive committee member and have line managers and supervisors reporting to them. (*Chapters 3 and 4*)

Department Manager—the shift managers of a specific operating department who are responsible for the daily delivery of products and services to guests and for the financial performance of their department. (*Chapter 4*)

Department P&L—P&L statement for one specific department that includes all revenues and expenses in detail that are involved in operating that department. (*Chapter 4*)

Department Profits—the dollar amounts remaining in revenue centers/profit centers after the department recognizes all revenues and pays all expenses associated with operating that department for a specific time period. (*Chapter 4*)

Depreciation—the value of an investment or asset is going down over time. (*Chapter 12*)

Director of Finance—the executive committee member directly responsible for all accounting operations in a hotel. (*Chapter 3*)

Direct Report—the managers and positions that report directly to a senior manager. (*Chapter 3*)

Dividend—the return on the principal invested in a company stock or mutual fund. (*Chapter 12*)

Division—the manufacturing term that identifies the different types of products produced by a company, including the industry that is in the markets that they serve. (*Chapter 11*)

Earnings—money that is produced from an asset in the form of dividends or interest. (*Chapter 12*)

Equity—the difference between an individual's assets and liabilities. (*Chapter 12*)

Escrow—an account established to collect money to be used at a later date. Same as reserve account. (*Chapter 9*)

Executive Committee—the members of senior management who report directly to the General Manager and have responsibility for specific hotel departments. Department heads report to an executive committee member. (*Chapter 3*)

Expense Categories—the four major categories for collecting and reporting department expenses—cost of sales, wages, benefits, and direct operating expenses. (*Chapter 4*)

Expense Center—a staff department that supports the hotel operating departments—Sales and Marketing, Engineering, Human Resources, and Accounting. It has no revenues or cost of sales, just wages, benefits, and direct operating expenses. (*Chapter 4*)

External Customer—paying customers that stay in hotels and eat in restaurants and pay money for receiving those products and services. (*Chapter 3*)

401K Account—company long-term retirement accounts that include both employee and company contributions. (*Chapter 12*)

Financial Analysis—the separation of a business's management of monetary affairs into parts for individual study. (*Chapter 1*)

Financial Literacy—the ability to understand numbers. (*Chapter 12*)

Financial Management Cycle—the process of producing, preparing, analyzing, and applying numbers to business operations. (*Chapter 2*)

Fiscal Year—the financial year for reporting a company's financial results. It can be the same as or different from the calendar year ending December 31. (*Chapter 11*)

Fixed Expenses—direct expenses of a hotel that are constant and do not change regardless of the volume and level of business. Secretaries in the sales department and accounting clerks in the accounting department are examples of fixed positions. (*Chapters 4, 6, and 9*)

Flow Through—measures how much profit goes up or down as a percent of the change in revenue. Also referred to as retention. (*Chapters 1, 6, and 8*)

Forecast—a financial and operational report that updates the budget. (*Chapters 2 and 10*)

Weekly Forecast—the forecast for the next week that includes revenues and expenses, with a focus on wage costs, and provides the details by day and shift for providing the actual products and services expected by guests.

Monthly Forecast—a forecast of revenues for the next month, including average rates and volumes for specific market segments, departments, or meal periods.

Quarterly Forecast—a forecast that projects revenues over a longer time period and is completed by adding together the forecasts for each month of the quarter.

Full-Service Hotels—hotels with generally more than 200 rooms that operate food & beverage outlets, catering functions and meeting room rentals, gift shops, valet laundry, health workout facilities, and bellmen as well as other services and amenities. (*Chapter 3*)

Fundamental Accounting Equation—Assets = Liabilities + Owner Equity. (*Chapter 5*)

General Cashier—the position in the accounting department that collects, balances, and consolidates all the operating department deposits into one deposit for the hotel that goes to the bank each day. (*Chapter 3*)

General Manager—the senior manager in the hotel who is responsible for all hotel operations. All positions and activities are the responsibility of this person. (*Chapter 3*)

Group Room Block—a signed contract that identifies the number and pattern of group rooms for each night and the total group rooms for that event. It also includes the room rate, VIPs, people authorized to sign for charges, and other detailed information about the group. (*Chapter 7*)

Historical Average—average reservation information based on four or five years of hotel operations. (*Chapter 7*)

Horizontal Headings—the headings across the top of a P&L that identify the type, time, and amount of financial information. (*Chapter 4*)

House Profit or Gross Operating Profit—the profit amount that includes all revenues and expenses controlled by hotel management and measures management's ability to operate the hotel profitably. It is calculated by subtracting total expense center costs from total department profits. (*Chapter 4*)

Income—a term interchangeable with profits and earnings. (*Chapter 1*)

Income Accounting—the section of the accounting office that is involved with recording income, paying expenses, and assisting other hotel managers. (*Chapter 3*)

Income Journal—the section of the accounting office that is involved with recording the specific income by amount and account. (*Chapter 3*)

Income Statement—measures the operating success and profitability of a business over a specific period of time. See P&L Statement. (*Chapter 1*)

Incremental—an increase, something gained or added. In financial analysis it describes additional revenues, expenses, or profits beyond what was expected. (*Chapter 6*)

Independent Audit Report—the section of the Corporate Annual Report that contains the audit opinion presented by an independent and certified public accounting company. (*Chapter 11*)

Interest—the return on the principal in a savings account. (*Chapter 12*)

Internal Customers—employees that receive the support of other company employees in performing their job responsibilities. (*Chapter 3*)

Internal Management Report—a report that contains detailed operating information covering a specific time for a specific product, customer, department, or for the entire hotel or restaurant. (*Chapter 6*)

Inventory—assets in the form of materials and supplies that the company has purchased, but not yet used in the production of products and services. (*Chapter 5*)

Other Deductions—another term for hotel fixed expenses that are constant regardless of the volume levels of the hotel and include expenses like bank loans, lease payments, certificates and licenses, depreciation, and insurance expenses. (*Chapter 4*)

Last Year—the official financial performance of the previous year. (*Chapter 2*)

Liabilities—obligations owed by a company. (*Chapter 5*)

   Current—obligations that are due within one year.

   Long Term—obligations that are due longer than one year.

Liability—takes money out of your pocket. (*Chapter 12*)

Line Item or Line Account—a specific accounting code that collects and records all revenues or expenses classified within the description of the line account. (*Chapter 4*)

Line Manager—the entry-level management position that has face-to-face interaction with the customers and is responsible for operating the different shifts of a hotel department. (*Chapter 3*)

Liquidity—the amount of cash or cash equivalents that a business has to cover its daily operating expenses. (*Chapter 1*)

Management Responsibility Report—the section of the Corporate Annual Report that contains the senior management opinion that the operating and financial information contained in the annual report is accurate and correctly portrays the financial condition of the company. (*Chapter 11*)

Man-Hour or Labor Hour—the number of hours one employee works in performing his or her job responsibilities. Typically, full-time employees are scheduled for an 8-hour day and a 40-hour work week. (*Chapter 6*)

Market Capitalization—a measure of the value of a company that includes the number of shares outstanding held by individual and institutional investors times the current stock price of the company. (*Chapter 1*)

Market Segment—customer groups defined by expectations, preferences, buying patterns, and behavior patterns. (*Chapter 1*)

Market Share—the percentage of total room supply, room demand, or room revenue that a hotel has as a percent of some larger group. (*Chapter 8*)

Monthly Forecast—*see* Forecast.

Net House Profit, Adjusted Gross Operating Profit, or Net Operating Profit—identifies the amount of profit remaining after all hotel revenues are recorded and all direct hotel expenses are paid. It is equal to house profit minus fixed expenses. (*Chapter 4*)

Net Worth—what an individual has in investments that are unencumbered with corresponding liabilities or debt. Similar to equity. (*Chapter 12*)

New Unit Growth—the growth resulting from the opening of new units—hotels, restaurants, etc. (*Chapter 11*)

Notes to Consolidated Financial Statements—the section of an annual report that presents detailed financial explanations of accounting and financial information contained in the annual report. (*Chapter 11*)

Operating Department—a hotel department that records revenues and produces a profit by providing products and services to paying customers or guests. (*Chapter 3*)

Organization Chart—describes the reporting relationships, responsibilities, and operating activities for a department or business unit. (*Chapter 3*)

Owner Equity—the amount invested in a company by owners or investors, including Paid-in capital, common stock, and retained earnings. (*Chapter 5*)

Par—the specified amount of product that should be maintained in inventory to provide the necessary products and services to guests without interruption of services. This includes an order par that specifies when orders should be placed with suppliers to replenish inventories. (*Chapter 5*)

Peak Night—the night or nights in a group room block that has the largest number of occupied rooms. (*Chapter 7*)

Percentages—a share or proportion in relation to the whole or part. (*Chapter 2*)

> **Change**—measures the difference in percent between two numbers.
>
> **Cost**—measures the dollar cost or expense as a part of total applicable revenue.
>
> **Mix**—measures dollars or units as a part of a whole.
>
> **Profit**—measures the dollar profit as a part of total applicable revenues.

Pickup—the number of actual room reservations made by day for a group room block compared to the number of group rooms blocked for that night. It also includes the pace at which actual reservations are being made for a specific day and the percentage of actual room reservations made compared to the group room block for the day. (*Chapter 7*)

Point-of-Sale System (POS)—the equipment that records the customer transaction, including identifying the method of payment and reporting the type of transaction. (*Chapter 1*)

Preopening Budget—the budget established to guide a new business as they prepare to open for business. (*Chapter 9*)

Principal—the dollar amount that is in an account that is earning interest or dividends and that has the

potential to appreciate or increase as well as decrease. (*Chapter 12*)

Primary Competition—a group of similar hotels that compete for the same customer. Hotels that you often lose business to are primary competition. (*Chapter 8*)

Profit—the amount of revenues left over after all expenses have been paid. (*Chapters 1 and 2*)

Profit and Loss Statement—measures the operating success and profitability of a company over a specific time period. (*Chapter 1*)

Profit After Taxes—the amount of profit remaining after corporate taxes are paid that is divided among owners, management companies, and any other entities having an interest in the hotel. (*Chapter 4*)

Profit Before Taxes—the same as net operating profit. The profit amount remaining after all hotel operating expenses have been paid. (*Chapter 4*)

Profit Center—an operating department that produces revenues that result in profit by providing products and services to customers. It includes revenues, expenses, and profits and is a term that is interchangeable with revenue center. (*Chapter 4*)

Profit Margin—the percentage of a revenue dollar that remains as profit after all expenses have been paid. A profit percent calculated by dividing profit dollars by revenue dollars. It is an important measure of productivity. (*Chapters 8 and 9*)

Pro forma—the projected first year of operations prepared before actual operations begin. (*Chapter 2*)

Property—the term for the physical hotel or restaurant. (*Chapter 1*)

Property, Plant, and Equipment (PP&E)—the term used to identify the long-term investments in fixed assets that will serve the business for more than one year. (*Chapters 5 and 9*)

Public Relations—information and new releases prepared by the company. (*Chapter 11*)

Publicly Traded Company—any company that offers the public the opportunity to invest in it by purchasing its stock that is bought and sold on publicly traded stock exchanges. (*Chapter 11*)

Quarterly Forecast—see Forecast.

Rat Race—not having financial literacy, spending more money than earning, abusing credit cards, and living from paycheck to paycheck. (*Chapter 12*)

Rate—the dollar amount paid by a customer to receive a product or service provided by a business.

Typically, average room rates and average guest checks are used to calculate total room or restaurant revenues. Rates also provide the hourly rate of pay for wage forecasting and scheduling. (*Chapters 1, 8, 9, and 10*)

Rate Structure—a list of the different room rates offered by a hotel. (*Chapter 7*)

Ratios—formulas that are used to calculate appropriate expense levels in relation to different revenue levels. (*Chapters 8 and 10*)

Regular Rate—the room rate that is available to all of the different reservation systems and channels selling rooms at a hotel, including travel agencies, airlines, car rental companies, and the Internet, and generally the first room rate quoted at central reservation centers (800 numbers). Also referred to as *rack rate*. (*Chapter 7*)

Reserve—an account established to collect money to be used at a later date. Same as an escrow account. (*Chapter 9*)

Retention—the amount of incremental revenue dollars that become incremental profit dollars. It is expressed as a percentage and is the same as Flow-through. (*Chapters 1, 6, and 8*)

Revenue—the monetary amount that customers pay to receive a product or service. It can be in the form of cash, checks, credit cards, or electronic transfer. (*Chapter 1*)

Revenue Center—an operating department that produces revenues by providing products and services directly to customers. It includes revenues, expenses, and profits. (*Chapter 4*)

Revenue Management—the process of selling the right product to the right customer at the right time for the right price, thereby maximizing revenue from a company's products and services. (*Chapter 7*)

RevPAR (Revenue per Available Room)—an important measure of a hotel's ability to generate room revenue by measuring both average room rate and occupancy percentage. (*Chapters 1, 7, and 8*)

Risk—the probability of an investment increasing or decreasing in value and at what rate it increases or decreases. (*Chapter 12*)

Secondary Competition—a group of hotels that offer competition, but provide different rates, services, and amenities and therefore are not considered direct or primary competition. (*Chapter 8*)

Securities and Exchange Commission—the government agency with the responsibility of regulating the public stock exchanges (New York Stock Exchange, NASDAQ, and several other exchanges). (*Chapter 11*)

Selling Strategy—the actions and decisions of the senior management of a hotel in opening and closing room rates, arrival dates, and length of stay to maximize total hotel room revenues. (*Chapter 7*)

Shoulder Night—the number of group rooms sold per night before the peak night (Front Side) or after the peak night (Back Side). (*Chapter 7*)

Slippage—the difference between expected or blocked group rooms for each night in a group room block and the actual number of rooms sold for each night in a group room block. (*Chapter 7*)

Source and Use of Funds Statement—a part of the statement of cash flow that shows how cash is created (source) and disbursed (used) among the different accounts on the balance sheet. (*Chapter 5*)

Staff Department—a hotel department that provides assistance and support to the hotel operating departments. They have internal customers. (*Chapter 3*)

STAR Market Report—a monthly report published by Smith Travel Research that provides a hotel with rate, occupancy, and RevPAR information for a specific hotel and its competitive set. (*Chapter 8*)

Statement of Cash Flows—measures the liquidity and identifies the flow of cash in a company. (*Chapters 1 and 5*)

Support Costs—the same as expense centers and are costs that are deducted from total department profits. (*Chapter 4*)

Titles—the top portion of a financial statement that tells the name of the company, type of report, and time period covered. (*Chapter 4*)

Total Department Profits—the summation of the individual department profits of a hotel. Provides the amount of profit resulting from the operating departments of a hotel. (*Chapter 4*)

Trend—a general inclination or tendency. (*Chapter 2*)

Variables—the different components involved in an account and can be revenue accounts or expense accounts. Two variables mean that two components can be managed and analyzed. Variation analysis shows the impact that each component has on the total of each account. (*Chapter 8*)

Variable Expenses—expenses that increase or decrease directly with the volume and level of business. Housekeepers, bellmen, and servers are examples of variable wage positions. (*Chapters 6 and 10*)

Variation—something slightly different from another of the same type. In financial analysis, variation is the difference between a planned number and an actual number. (*Chapter 6*)

Variation Analysis—involves identifying the difference between actual operating performance and established standards. These standards can be last year's actual performance, the previous month's actual performance, the budget for this year, or the most current forecast. (*Chapter 8*)

Vertical Headings—the names of the departments, categories, and accounts that are on the side or center of a P&L that identify the type and amount of financial information recorded on the P&L. (*Chapter 4*)

Volume—the number of units sold, served, received, or bought by customers during a specific time frame. Typically, rooms sold or occupied and customer counts are the volume variables used to calculate total room or restaurant revenues. It also provides man-hours required for wage forecasting and scheduling. (*Chapters 1 and 10*)

Weekly Forecast—see Forecast.

Working Capital—the amount of money utilized in the daily operations of a business, including using the assets and liabilities as well as cash in producing a product or service. (*Chapters 1 and 5*)

Yield Systems or Yield Management—the computer reservation tracking system that combines current reservation booking information with historical reservation booking information. It is used to implement selling strategies that will maximize total hotel room revenue. (*Chapter 7*)

INDEX